Magic and Medieval Society

Magic and Medieval Society presents a thematic approach to the topic of magic and sorcery in western Europe between the eleventh and the fifteenth centuries. It aims to provide readers with the conceptual and documentary tools to reach informed conclusions as to the existence, nature, importance and uses of magic in medieval society.

Contrary to some previous approaches, the authors argue that magic is inextricably connected to other areas of cultural practice and was found across medieval society. Therefore, the book is arranged thematically, covering topics such as the use of magic at medieval courts, at universities and within the medieval Church itself.

Each chapter and theme is supported by additional documents, diagrams and images to allow readers to examine the evidence side-by-side with the discussions in the chapters and to come to informed conclusions on the issues.

This book puts forward the argument that the witch craze was not a medieval phenomenon but rather the product of the Renaissance and the Reformation, and demonstrates how the components for the early-modern prosecution of witches were put into place.

This new Seminar Study is supported by a comprehensive Documents section, Chronology, Who's Who and illustrations. It offers a concise and thought-provoking introduction for students of medieval history.

Anne Lawrence-Mathers is Associate Professor of Medieval History at the University of Reading, and the Director of the Graduate Centre for Medieval Studies. She is the author of *Manuscripts in Northumbria* (2002) and *The True History of Merlin the Magician* (2012) as well as many articles on medieval magical texts, women and manuscripts.

Carolina Escobar-Vargas is Lecturer in Medieval History at the University of Reading. She completed a PhD thesis on 'The Image and Reality of the Magician Figure in Twelfth-Century England' in 2011 and has delivered several conference papers on related topics.

Introduction to the series

History is the narrative constructed by historians from traces left by the past. Historical enquiry is often driven by contemporary issues and, in consequence, historical narratives are constantly reconsidered, reconstructed and reshaped. The fact that different historians have different perspectives on issues means that there is often controversy and no universally agreed version of past events. Seminar Studies was designed to bridge the gap between current research and debate, and the broad, popular general surveys that often date rapidly.

The volumes in the series are written by historians who are not only familiar with the latest research and current debates concerning their topic, but who have themselves contributed to our understanding of the subject. The books are intended to provide the reader with a clear introduction to a major topic in history. They provide both a narrative of events and a critical analysis of contemporary interpretations. They include the kinds of tools generally omitted from specialist monographs: a chronology of events, a glossary of terms and brief biographies of 'who's who'. They also include bibliographical essays in order to guide students to the literature on various aspects of the subject. Students and teachers alike will find that the selection of documents will stimulate the discussion and offer insight into the raw materials used by historians in their attempt to understand the past.

Clive Emsley and Gordon Martel
Series Editors

Magic and Medieval Society

Anne Lawrence-Mathers and
Carolina Escobar-Vargas

LONDON AND NEW YORK

First published 2014
by Routledge
2 Park Square, Milton Park, Abingdon, Oxon OX14 4RN

and by Routledge
711 Third Avenue, New York, NY 10017

Routledge is an imprint of the Taylor & Francis Group, an informa business

© 2014 Anne Lawrence-Mathers and Carolina Escobar-Vargas

The right of Anne Lawrence-Mathers and Carolina Escobar-Vargas to be identified as authors of this work has been asserted by them in accordance with sections 77 and 78 of the Copyright, Designs and Patents Act 1988.

All rights reserved. No part of this book may be reprinted or reproduced or utilised in any form or by any electronic, mechanical, or other means, now known or hereafter invented, including photocopying and recording, or in any information storage or retrieval system, without permission in writing from the publishers.

Trademark notice: Product or corporate names may be trademarks or registered trademarks, and are used only for identification and explanation without intent to infringe.

British Library Cataloguing in Publication Data
A catalogue record for this book is available from the British Library

Library of Congress Cataloging in Publication Data
Lawrence-Mathers, Anne, 1953–
  Magic and medieval society / Anne Lawrence-Mathers, Carolina Escobar-Vargas. – 1 [edition].
    pages cm. – (Seminar studies in history)
  Includes bibliographical references.
  1. Magic–Europe, Western–History–To 1500. 2. Europe, Western–Civilization–To 1500. I. Title.
  BF1593.L39 2014
  133.4′30940902–dc23
                                                                                    2013043370

ISBN: 978-0-415-73928-3 (hbk)
ISBN: 978-1-408-27050-9 (pbk)
ISBN: 978-1-315-77747-4 (ebk)

Typeset in 10/13.5pt ITC Berkeley
by Graphicraft Limited, Hong Kong

Printed and bound by CPI Group (UK) Ltd, Croydon, CR0 4YY

Contents

Acknowledgements	viii
Chronology	ix
Who's who	xiii
Glossary	xx
List of plates	xxiii

	INTRODUCTION	1
1	MAGIC AND POLITICS	4
2	MAGIC IN THE CHURCH	13
	Monks and charms	13
	Palmistry and divination	17
	Monastic astrology?	19
	Peter Lombard, Gratian and the development of law and theology in relation to magic	21
	The Pope who was a necromancer: the Black Legend of Gerbert of Aurillac	23
3	THE UNIVERSITIES	27
	Magic and the twelfth-century Renaissance	27
	Classifications of magic	30
	Astrology and the astrolabe	33
	Astral and image magic: the bases of ritual magic	35
	The *Ars Notoria*	37
	The *Sworn Book of Honorius*	38
	Alchemy	40
	Dealing with the growth of magical literature	41

4	**MAGIC AND SECULAR SOCIETY**	44
	Gerald of Wales on miracles, wonders and magic in Wales and Ireland	45
	Penitentials, confessors' manuals and early lawcodes	48
	Natural magic and its uses	52
	Lapidaries	54
	Herbals	56
	Bestiaries	57
	Conclusion	59
5	**MEDICAL MAGIC**	60
	The problem of charms	61
	Natural magic and medical magic	63
	Astrology and medicine	66
	The Zodiac Man	69
	Medicine, magic and popular practice	70
6	**CONCLUSION: THE RISE OF MAGICAL CRIME**	75
	William of Auvergne	76
	Ritual magic and Aquinas's demonology	78
	Fourteenth-century show trials	80
	Heresy and witchcraft	82
	The onset of the witch craze	87

DOCUMENTS 89

1	Sibylline prophecies	90
2	Joachim of Fiore and Richard I	90
3	Report of astrological fears and predictions in 1186	92
4	Roger Bacon, Introduction to the *Great Work*, 1266	93
5	John of Salisbury, *Policraticus*	93
6	Michael Scot and the Emperor Frederick II	95
7	Twelfth-century Anglo-Norman horoscopes	97
8	Prognostication by thunder	98
9	Excerpts from the *Dream-book of the Prophet Daniel*	99
10	Peter Lombard, *Sentences*	100
11	Gratian, *Decretum (Decretals)*	101
12	Magical circles, demons and necromancy	102
13	William of Malmesbury on Gerbert of Aurillac	104
14	Hugh of St Victor, *Didascalicon*	106
15	Adelard of Bath, Treatise on the astrolabe	107
16	*Ars Notoria*: General instructions, and texts relating to astronomy	109

17	The Emerald Table	111
18	Magical books in universities	112
19	Penitentials	113
20	Lapidary	113
21	Herbals	115
22	The Bestiary	117
23	On animals	118
24	Sphere of Apuleius	119
25	Zodiac Man	120
26	*Speculum astronomiae*	121
27	Guibert de Nogent, *Monodies (Melancholy Memoirs)*	122
28	Albertus Magnus on precious stones	122
29	On natural magic	124
30	St Thomas Aquinas on demons	125
31	*Super Illius Specula*	127
32	Bernard Gui, *Manual for Inquisitors*	128
33	Stephen Tempier, List of condemned opinions and works, 1277	129

BIBLIOGRAPHY 131

INDEX 140

Acknowledgements

The authors wish to thank their colleagues and students in the Graduate Centre for Medieval Studies at the University of Reading for challenging and helpful discussions. They are also very grateful to the British Library for permission to publish photographs of MSS Sloane 172, fol. 37 and Sloane 2030, fols 125v and 126r. Finally, they thank Patricia Stewart for her generosity in supplying the Latin text for the Bestiary extracts.

The translations in the Documents section are the work of the authors of this book, who take responsibility for all errors. References are provided to the published or manuscript sources upon which the translations are based.

Whilst every effort has been made to trace copyright holders, this has not been possible in all cases. Any omissions brought to our attention will be remedied in future editions.

Chronology

    a. ante
    c. circa
    C century

70	Dioscorides, *De materia medica*
77	Pliny the Elder, *Natural History*
c.C2–C4	Pseudo-Apuleius Platonicus, *Herbarius*
Early C3	Solinus, *Polyhistor*
c.C4	Earliest versions of the *Sphere of Apuleius*
a.430	St Augustine, *The City of God*
C6	Latin bestiary
C6	*De herbis femininis*
c.C6	*Curae herbarum*
c.615–30s	Isidore of Seville, *Etymologies*
C8	*Penitential of Theodore*
789	Charlemagne's general admonition, including a ban on all sorcerers, magicians and enchanters
C9	*Canon Episcopi*, first recorded by Regino of Prüm in the early C10
a. c.856	Rabanus Maurus, *Treatise on beasts*
C10–C11	Early treatises on the astrolabe associated with Gerbert of Aurillac, Llobet de Barcelona and Hermann le Boiteux
c.930	Laws of King Athelstan
963–75	Record of Bishop Aethelwold of Winchester's acquisition of an estate confiscated from a woman convicted of attempted murder by image magic.
a.930	Bald, *Leechbook*
Late C10–early C11	*Lacnunga*
c.1080s	Constantine the African, *Liber Pantegni*

1085	Hugh of Flavigny, *Chronicle*
c.1090	Marbod of Rennes, *Liber lapidum*, dealing with 60 stones
Late C11	Bayeux Tapestry
C12	Pseudo-John of Seville, *Isagoge in astrologiam*
C12	Circulation of prophecies by the Sibylla Tiburtina
C12	Translation of Theel, *Liber sigillorum*
C12	Translations of Sahl ibn Bishir, *Liber Temporum*
C12(?)	*Ars Notoria*
c.1100	Walcher of Malvern, Lunar Tables
1110	Petrus Alfonsi, *Dialogues against the Jews*
c.1110	Petrus Alfonsi, *Disciplina clericalis*
1119–31	*Gesta Herewardi*
1120s	Petrus Alfonsi, *Epistola ad peripateticos franciae*
1120s	Hugh of St Victor, *Didascalicon*
c.1120	Adelard of Bath's translation of Abu Mashar, *Isagoge Minor*
c.1125/6–34	William of Malmesbury, *Gesta Regum Anglorum*
1130s	Geoffrey of Monmouth, *Prophetiae Merlini*
c.1130–40	John of Seville's translation of Alcabitius, *Liber introductorius*
1133	Eclipse discussed in John of Worcester, *Chronicle*
1132–52	Hugh of Fouilloy, *The Aviary*
1135	Orderic Vitalis in possession of a copy of the *Prophetiae Merlini*
1136	Plato of Tivoli's translation of Ptolemy, *Centiloquium*
1136–38	Geoffrey of Monmouth, *History of the Kings of Britain*
1138	Plato of Tivoli's translation of Ptolemy, *Quadripartitum*
c.1140	Gratian, *Decretum*
1141	Raymond of Marseilles, *Liber judiciorum*
1147–48	Hildegard of Bingen, *Scivias* approved by the pope
Mid-C12	Anglo-Norman horoscopes in BL, MS Royal App. 85
c.1150	Geoffrey of Monmouth, *Vita Merlini*
1155–57	Peter Lombard, *Sentences*
1159	John of Salisbury, *Policraticus*
c.1160	Eadwine Psalter (with earliest known Latin Chiromancy)
c.1181/2	Walter Map, *De nugis curialium*
1186	Recorded Great Conjunction of the planets in Libra
1186–87	Gerald of Wales, *Topography of Ireland*

1189	Gerald of Wales, *Expugnatio Hibernica*
c.1189–1204	Peter of Cornwall, *Pantheologus*
1190	Joachim of Fiore meets Richard I of England
1190	Maimonides, *Guide for the Perplexed*
c.1191	Gerald of Wales, *Journey through Wales*
c.1192	Roger of Howden, *Deeds of King Richard*
c.1194	Gerald of Wales, *Description of Wales*
Early C13	Pastoral manual of Thomas of Chobham
C13	*Tractatus de herbis*
C13	Compilation of treatises on the astrolabe attributed to Messahala
C13	*On fifteen stars, fifteen stones, fifteen herbs and fifteen images* or *Quadripartitum Hermetis*, translation from a C8 version by Messahala (Mashâ'allâh)
C13	*Book of Angels, Rings, Characters and Images of the Planets* (copied in a 15C manuscript)
Early C13	Robert de Boron, *Merlin*
Early C13	Woman accused of sorcery in the court of King's Bench during the reign of King John
First half C13	*Sworn Book of Honorius*
c.1214	Gervase of Tilbury, *Otia Imperialia*
1215	IV Lateran Council
c.1223	Cesarius of Heisterbach, *Dialogue of miracles*
c.1230s	Bartholomew the Englishman, *On the Properties of Things*
1233	Gregory IX, *Vox in Rama*
c.1228–30	William of Auvergne, *De legibus et sectis*
c.1231–36	William of Auvergne, *De universo*
1246	Guido Bonatti predicts a conspiracy against Frederick II
c.1246–59	Vincent of Beauvais, *Speculum historiale*
2nd half of C13	*Liber Raziel*
1250s	Alexander IV addresses questions on whether or not inquisitors should deal with magic
c.1253	*Lapidary of Alphonso X*
c.1254	Gilles de Thebaldis and Pierre de Reggio translation of Hali Abenragel, *De judiciis astrorum*
c.1256–58	Translation into Castilian of the *Picatrix*
a.1259	Latin translation of al-Kindi, *De radiis stellarum*
c.1260–70	Albertus Magnus, *Speculum Astronomiae*

1265	Thomas Aquinas, *Summa Theologica*
c.1267	Roger Bacon, *Opus Tertium*
c.1270s	Guido Bonatti, *Liber introductorius ad judicia stellarum*
1289	Adam Stratton accused of using magic to improve his position at the English court
1297–98	John of Freiburg's Pastoral Manual
c.1301	Pseudo-Arnold of Villanova, *De sigillis*
1301–03	Walter Langton, Bishop of Coventry, accused of sorcery and necromancy
13 June 1303	Accusations of sorcery levied against Boniface VIII at the French court
11 October 1303	Pope Boniface VIII's death
1307	Beginning of the process against the Knights Templar
c.1308–21	Dante's condemnation of Michael Scot in the *Divine Comedy*
1309–11	Posthumous case against Pope Boniface VIII
1314	Accusation of sorcery levied against Enguerrand de Marigny at the court of Louis X
1316	Mahaut of Artois accused of using love magic against Philip V of France
1317	Hugues Geraud, Bishop of Cahors, accused and convicted of having hired professional magicians to perform harmful magic against Pope John XXII
1320	Matteo and Galeazzo Visconti charged with a plot to kill Pope John XXII by means of poison and ritual and image-magic
1320	Letter of John XXII instructing inquisitors in southern France to turn their attention to criminal magic
1326	Issue of papal bull *Super illius specula* by Pope John XXII
1327	Francesco d'Ascoli is the first university master to be burnt alive by the inquisition
c.1327	Bernard Gui, *Manual for Inquisitors*
Late C14–early C15	Large scale witch trials in the Rhine Land, Bavaria and parts of Switzerland
1420s	Bernardino of Siena's sermon 'On the Scourges of God'
1431	Accusations against Joan of Arc, including charges accusing her of being in possession of a mandrake root
1441	Eleanor Cobham, Duchess of Gloucester, accused of using magicians against Henry VI, including the alleged professional sorceress Margery Jourdemayne
c.1486	Heinrich Kramer and Jacob Sprenger, *Malleus Maleficarum*

Who's who

Adelard of Bath (c.1080–c.1150): English scholar and natural philosopher. Adelard of Bath had a keen interest in Arabic scholarship. This drove him to travel widely, first to the south of Italy and then to the Holy Land. He is the author of two treatises on natural philosophy, a small tract on birds and a treatise on the astrolabe. He is also responsible for several translations of Arabic works on astrology/astronomy into Latin, including the astronomical tables of al-Khwarizmi and the *Isagoge minor* by Albumasar.

Albertus Magnus (c.1200–80): theologian, philosopher and scholar of great renown, earning him the appellation 'the great' during his lifetime. A member of the Dominican order, he was key in the Aristotelian revival of the thirteenth century. He was also a keen student of natural philosophy, producing several works on minerals, animals and plants, astronomy and cosmology. He was instrumental in the development of the idea of natural magic by crediting the theory of occult properties in nature.

Albumasar (Abû Ma'shar) (787–886): Persian astrologer and philosopher, pupil of Alkindi. Author of the influential *Introductorius Major* and the *Isagoge Minor*, both works translated into Latin from Arabic in the twelfth century.

Alkindi (al-Kindî) (d. a.866): philosopher and astrologer who lived in Baghdad; credited with the initial assimilation of Neoplatonic and Aristotelian ideas into the Islamic world. He was responsible for early translations of Aristotle and Plotinus, and himself wrote: *De mutatione temporum*, a treatise on astrometeorology which was translated into Latin in the twelfth century; and *De radiis stellarum*, an influential work on theoretical magic, translated into Latin during the thirteenth century.

Apuleius (c.125–c.170): Roman writer, famous for his *Apologia*, a text in which he defended himself against the accusation of having used magical means to marry a certain Pudentilla. Apuleius was also responsible for the composition of the *Golden Ass*. During the Middle Ages, he was credited with compiling a herbal, which is now believed to be a collection of texts dating from the sixth century.

Aristotle (384–322 BCE): Athenian philosopher and student of Plato. His *libri naturales* proved extremely influential from their first translation into Latin in the thirteenth century. His ideas were central for both Islamic and Christian philosophy. However, not all of his works were equally well accepted, with some of his texts being condemned by the Church and the University of Paris in 1270 and 1277.

Augustine of Hippo (354–430): saint, Bishop of Hippo, and Doctor of the Church. A voluminous writer on theology, heresy and the Christian view of history. His book, *The City of God,* was one of the most influential texts of the medieval period, and included fundamental discussions of demons and of pagan ideas on spirits.

Bernard Gui (c.1261–1331): member of the Dominican order, appointed inquisitor in Toulouse in 1307, and responsible for dealing with several hundred cases of heresy. After nearly twenty years of personal experience, he wrote his *Practica Inquisitionis Heretice Pravitatis* as a manual for other inquisitors conducting trials for 'heretical depravity'.

Boniface VIII (c.1234–1303): born Benedetto Caetani, he became pope after the abdication of his predecessor Celestine V in 1294. His pontificate was a controversial one, dominated by his struggle with Philip IV of France over the king's taxation of the clergy. He died shortly after a confrontation with Philip's agents in Anagni, and was subjected to a posthumous trial, during which agents and allies of the French king accused him of heresy, idolatry and necromancy.

Cesarius of Heisterbach (c.1180–c.1240): prior of the Cistercian monastery of Heisterbach in Western Germany and author of the *Dialogus miraculorum*, an influential and popular collection of texts originally intended for the instruction of novices at his monastery.

Constantine the African (c.1020–c.1090): born in northern Africa, he became a teacher of medicine in Salerno and a monk at the Italian Benedictine monastery of Monte Cassino. He brought into Italy a collection of medical works, some of them Arabic translations of books by Hippocrates and Galen which were unknown in western Europe. There were also works by more recent Arab physicians and philosophers. He made this material available in Latin versions, and played a fundamental role in the development of medieval medicine.

Dioscorides (c.40–c.90): Greek writer responsible for the composition of *De materia medica,* a treatise dealing with the medicinal properties of plants.

His work was very influential in the compilation of later medieval herbals and lapidaries.

Galen (c.129–c.200) Greek physician responsible for the composition of several medical and philosophical texts. His medical texts were translated into Arabic by the ninth century, thus becoming the basis of both Islamic and later Christian medicine.

Geoffrey of Monmouth (d.1154/5): English writer and historian, whose career is largely obscure. He wrote the very popular and influential *History of the Kings of Britain,* which told the legendary history of the Britons from their mythical origins in Troy until the Anglo-Saxon era. He was also responsible for composing two books about Merlin, the *Prophetiae Merlini* and the *Vita Merlini*.

Gerald of Wales (c.1146–1220/3): author and ecclesiastic, responsible for the composition of several works recounting the natural and political histories, as he saw them, of Ireland and Wales. He knew Wales well, and travelled in the entourages of King John and of Baldwin, Archbishop of Canterbury. His works record details of the 'marvels' of Ireland and Wales.

Gerbert of Aurillac (c.946–99/1003): elected Pope Sylvester II in 999, he was a renowned scholar with a particular interest in the study of the *quadrivium*. He spent some time studying in Christian Spain as a young man, before becoming a Master, and eventually Bishop of Reims. He became pope under the sponsorship of the emperor Otto III. After his death, he was the object of accusations and anecdotes presenting him as a magician, astrologer and necromancer.

Gervase of Tilbury (b.1150s, d. c.1222): educated in Italy and France, he entered the service of Henry II and William II, king of Sicily before finally settling in Arles under the sponsorship of the emperor Otto IV. He was an experienced courtier and politician, and an expert on canon law. It was to Otto IV that he dedicated his *Otia Imperialia*, a work he had been engaged with for about thirty years before its completion c.1215. This book provides an encyclopaedic coverage of the marvels and powers of the natural world.

Gratian (d. a.1159): Italian scholar and monk, who taught law in Bologna and was responsible for the composition of the *Decreti*. This compilation of c.4000 texts on canon law touched all areas of church regulation and was profoundly influential, becoming one of the standard textbooks of canon law at the universities. It deals with issues of magic under two headings: the case of a priest who practises magic; and the case of magic used to hinder fertility and conception. The materials assembled were frequently consulted and reused.

Guido Bonatti (d. c.1296): astronomer and astrologer, he made himself famous for his defence of the art of astrology. Like Michael Scot before him, he was in the service of the Emperor Frederick II. He is credited with the composition of the *Liber astronomicae*, c.1277.

Hali Abenragel (Ali Ibn Abî l-Ridjâl) (d. c.1037): Arab astrologer, author of the *De judiciis astrorum*, a work first translated into Castilian as *El libro conplido en los iudizios de las estrellas* by Yehuda ben Moshé, under the sponsorship of King Alfonso X. His views on judicial astrology were very influential.

Hermes Trismegistus: mythical figure, possibly representing the union between the Greek God Hermes and the Egyptian god Thoth, and dating back to the Hellenistic period. Hermes Trismegistus was credited with the authorship of the extensive hermetic corpus, within which the *Emerald Table* sets out fundamental ideas for alchemy. He was mentioned as a prophet by Augustine, which helped the acceptance of texts attributed to him.

Hippocrates (c.460–c.370 BC): the 'father' of medicine, he is believed to be the first to have proposed that illness derives from an imbalance of the body's humours. He influenced Galen and later Arab and Christian scholars.

Hugh of St Victor (c.1096–1141): theologian and philosopher active in Paris during the first half of the twelfth century. He left a large and influential corpus of works dealing with theology and the liberal arts. In his *Didascalicon*, he produces an exposition of knowledge, its function, subjects and divisions, including magic and its parts.

Isidore of Seville (c.560–636): Bishop of Seville, best known for his influential *Etymologies*, an encyclopaedia of classical knowledge that was to prove very popular in the medieval period, thus ensuring its survival in the Latin world. He did not compile a systematic consideration of magic, but gave fundamental definitions of specific topics, such as Divination.

Joachim of Fiore (c.1132–1202): Cistercian monk and scholar, his contemporaries believed he was in possession of 'the prophetic spirit', meaning that his prophecies circulated widely, especially in Italy, during the medieval period. Even during his lifetime, political leaders and their advisers sought out his counsel. However, some of his doctrines were condemned in the Lateran Council of 1215, with a further condemnation in 1256 by Pope Alexander IV.

John of Salisbury (late 1110s–1180): scholar, cleric and Bishop of Chartres. He studied in Paris in the 1130s and spent time in the service of two Archbishops of Canterbury. One was Thomas Beckett, to whom he addressed one of his most renowned works, the *Policraticus*, a moralising discussion of what he understood to be the vices of twelfth-century courts.

John XXII (1249–1334): born Jacques Duèze in Cahors, he studied theology and law at Montpellier and Paris and then taught both canon and civil law at Toulouse and Cahors. In the controversies involving Boniface VIII he supported the motions to suppress the Templars, but defended Boniface against the attacks coming from the French court. Shortly after his election to the papacy in 1316 he allegedly discovered various plots to murder him through the use of magic, and in 1322 he took the important step of ordering inquisitors to include magic within the scope of their enquiries.

Marbod of Rennes (c.1035–1123): teacher at the cathedral of Angers, and Bishop of Rennes from 1096. An accomplished Latin poet, he wrote primarily religious and didactic works; his verse *Lapidary* was his most popular composition.

Merlin: mythical poet and seer, of unproven historicity. He is believed to be based upon the prophet and seer, Myrddin, who appears in a group of early Welsh sources. Geoffrey of Monmouth's *History of the Kings of Britain* was the first to use the name Merlin, and to locate this new figure within the context of the Anglo-Saxon invasions of Britain. In this pseudo-historical work, however, Merlin's role in relation to King Arthur was limited to aiding the latter's conception. One of the most widely read parts of the whole work was Merlin's long sequence of political prophecies, inspired by a 'prophetic spirit'.

Messahala (Mâshâ'allâh) (fl. c.762–815): Persian-Jewish astrologer working for the court of the Abbasid caliph al-Mansur. Author of the *Epistola de rebus eclipsium et conjunctionibus planetarum* among several other treatises, some of which were translated into Latin during the twelfth century.

Maimonides (Moses ben Maimon) (1135–1204): Spanish Jewish philosopher, astronomer, and physician, active in Morocco and Egypt, he was in the service of the Sultan Saladin. He wrote influential works on Jewish philosophy, law and religion including the *Guide for the Perplexed*, a work that syncretises Aristotelian philosophy with Jewish theology. He produced ten known medical works, updating those of Hippocrates and Galen; these included a very extensive list of medicinal substances.

Michael Scot (d. c.1235): translator, philosopher and astrologer, he spent some time in Toledo c.1210–20, where he translated scientific and astrological texts from Arabic into Latin, and produced various works commentating on Aristotle. He entered the service of Frederick II in the 1220s as a physician and astrologer. He composed works on natural philosophy, the most influential of which was his *Liber introductorius*, an introduction to the study of astrology which deals also with cosmology and the nature of the universe.

Peter Lombard (c.1100–160): Italian theologian, author of the encyclopaedic collection known as the *Sentences*, which became the standard textbook of theology in medieval universities. Peter Lombard studied at Bologna, Reims and then Paris, where he was a student of Abelard, and became Archbishop of Paris for a brief period c.1158.

Peter of Abano (c.1250–1315): Italian philosopher, physician and astrologer, he taught at the University of Padua, where he was renowned for his interest in medicine, Aristotelian philosophy and astrology. He was tried by the Inquisition on charges of heresy, atheism and of practising magic and died in prison before the conclusion of his trial.

Petrus Alfonsi (fl. 1106–26): Jewish physician, scholar and translator of scientific works, born in northern Spain, he converted to Christianity on 29 June 1106, under the sponsorship of King Alfonso I of Aragon. He is the author of works on morality and religion. He was in England sometime in the first quarter of the twelfth century, where he may have acted as a physician for Henry I. He also collaborated with scholars like Walcher of Malvern and Adelard of Bath in the translation of Arabic works of astrology into Latin.

Philip IV of France (1285–1314): famously involved in the controversy with Boniface VIII over taxing the Church. His officials used the various legal means at their disposal, including levying accusations of heresy, idolatry and magic, to discredit several of his political enemies, including Boniface VIII and the Knights Templar.

Pliny the Elder (23–79): Roman writer, author of the *Naturalis historia*, a vast work on natural philosophy which served as one of the bases for medieval treatises on the natural world. Material from Pliny's collection was much reused in herbals and lapidaries.

Ptolemy (c.90–c.168): astronomer, astrologer and mathematician, credited with the composition of the *Almagest* and the *Tetrabiblos*, both works which became highly influential in the medieval West after their translation into Latin during the twelfth century.

Roger Bacon (c.1219–92): Franciscan friar, scientist and philosopher active in Oxford and Paris. He wrote extensively, and his *Opus maius*, an influential work dealing with mathematics, optics and astronomy, shows the range of his knowledge. His views on alchemy, prophecy and astrology, in particular, went rather beyond the mainstream.

Solinus (C3–4): author of the *Collectanea rerum memorabilium*, a description of the natural world which drew heavily on Pliny's *Natural History* but placed the information into geographical and historical context.

Stephen Tempier (d.1279): canon of Notre Dame, Paris, teacher of theology, bishop of Paris from 1268. Contested the more radical philosophies based upon Aristotle, and attempted to maintain orthodoxy in the teaching of philosophy and theology at Paris. In 1277 he issued several condemnations of heretical arguments, supported by the papacy. The most celebrated of these is his list of 219 errors, including a long list of views on angels and on spirits. To this was added a general condemnation of works on ritual magic, as well as a named text on geomancy. However, his views were eclipsed by those of Aquinas.

Thomas Aquinas (1225–74): Italian theologian and philosopher, Aquinas is one of the greatest figures of the medieval school of philosophy known as Scholasticism. A Dominican, he was a student of Albertus Magnus and in 1252 became professor of theology in Paris. He was keen on reconciling Aristotle with Christian doctrine, a feat he accomplished by using Aristotelian natural philosophy to inform theology.

Walcher of Malvern (d.1135): doctor, philosopher and astronomer of probable Lotharingian origin, he joined the Benedictine abbey of Great Malvern, becoming its second prior. He collaborated with Petrus Alfonsi in the translation of astronomical tables from Arabic into Latin. His observations on two eclipses in 1091 and 1092 demonstrate his expertise in astronomy and the use of the astrolabe. He is the author of Lunar Tables and *De dracone*, both concerned with the phases and movements of the moon.

William of Auvergne (c.1180–1249): theologian and philosopher, he was named Bishop of Paris in 1228, an office which he occupied until his death. He was one of the first Latin writers systematically to engage with the theological and philosophical problems posed by the increasing number of works on natural philosophy from Arabic and Greek origins. William's careful examination drove him to propose the existence of occult properties in nature which, if correctly channelled, could be of aid to the erudite. However, he was also quick to recognise the theological and spiritual dangers created by some views on this issue.

William of Malmesbury (c.1090–c.1142): Benedictine historian, he spent most of his life in the community he joined as a boy in Malmesbury. He is the author of the influential *Gesta Regum Anglorum*, an account of English history from the time of Bede in 735 until his own death in 1142. This work includes not only accounts of numerous marvels, but also stories concerning experiments in natural philosophy as well as the alleged astrological and necromantic activities of Gerbert of Aurillac.

Zahel (Sahl ibn Bishir) (c.786–c.845): Jewish astrologer, astronomer and mathematician, he is thought to have been the first to translate Ptolemy's *Almagest* into Arabic (from the Greek). He is credited with the composition of the *Liber temporum* and the *Liber introductorium ad astrologiam*, both influential works on practical astrology.

Glossary

Adjuration: an appeal or command, placing compulsion upon another by calling upon the name of God or of a supernatural entity.

Aeromancy: divination by means of the air.

Alchemy: a branch of philosophical study, built on the combination of Greek philosophy with Arab and older forms of science. A key aim was to transform both matter and human beings into purer forms, freed from the flux and corruption of the sublunary world.

Astral magic: form of magic aiming to harness the occult powers of the celestial bodies.

Astrolabe: portable instrument used for astronomical measurements and calculations, which allows for the mapping of the sky at any given moment, thus aiding in the production of horoscopes, as well as time measurement and navigation.

Astrology/astronomy: in the medieval period these terms were used interchangeably to describe the art of observing the celestial bodies, and of using such observations for calculating and predicting natural phenomena and events affecting human lives.

Augury: practice of divining the future from the behaviour and entrails of birds and animals.

Charms: a term covering a wide range of usually informal practices, mostly combining verbal formulae and physical objects in order to bring about a desired effect (usually protective or curative).

Chiromancy/palmistry: divination by means of the lines of the hands.

Divination: predicting the future by any variety of supernatural means.

Egyptian days: the days in each month believed to be unlucky or dangerous to health. The lists were taken from Roman calendars into medieval ones.

Elections: astrological calculations relating to the identification of favourable moments for starting an enterprise. May simply involve studying the planetary positions at a chosen time, or may relate these to aspects of the enquirer's natal chart.

Geomancy: divination by means of the earth. By the high Middle Ages the term also applied to a complex method, drawn from Arabic sources, of generating sets of dots, each arranged in one of 16 patterns, and interpreting them by astrological techniques.

Horoscope: a reading of the configuration of the planetary bodies at a certain moment, including their relation to each other in the celestial and zodiacal plan.

Hydromancy: divination by means of water.

Inquisition: ecclesiastical tribunal set up for the suppression of heresy in the thirteenth century under the papacy of Innocent III. The Inquisition existed in most European countries faithful to Rome, but inquisitorial tribunals were prevented from operating in the British Isles.

Interrogations: in astrology, interrogations provided answers to precise questions, particularly whether a specified thing would or would not happen or succeed. They used examinations of planetary positions at the time the question was asked.

Judicial astrology: refers to the practice of making judgments by casting horoscopes, including elections and interrogations. This was the subject of much discussion, due to possible clashes with the doctrine of free will.

Liberal Arts: the basis of Classical and medieval education, made up of the *Trivium* (grammar, rhetoric and logic) and the *Quadrivium* (arithmetic, geometry, music and astronomy).

Lot-casting: see Sortilegia.

Lunaries: a generic term for texts which provided the basis for predictions by relating various phenomena (such as dreams) to the day of the lunar month on which they occurred or were planned to take place.

Malefici: practitioners of evil magic, perceived as both spiritually and physically harmful, including love magic, divinations and incantations.

Medical humours: according to Hippocratic theory these were the four main fluids of the human body, i.e. blood, phlegm, yellow bile and black bile. They were associated with the four temperaments, the sanguine, phlegmatic, choleric and melancholic; and also with the qualities of heat, cold, moistness and wetness.

Nativities: in astrology, nativities were primarily horoscopes cast for the day and time of birth of an individual.

Natural philosophy: the pre-modern term for the systematic study of the natural world and the phenomena connected with it.

Necromancy: initially, divination by means of the dead; later the term was applied to any form of illicit transaction involving the (knowing or unknowing) invocation of demons.

Onomancy: name interpretation or divination from names.

Physiognomy: divination by means of the physical features of an individual.

Prognostics: a term covering a wide range of methods of foretelling the future, by interpreting dreams, natural phenomena, and verbal or numerical data. In scholarship on medieval magic, the term is usually applied to the texts setting out the instructions for making such forecasts.

Pyromancy: divination by means of fire.

Quadrivium: Four of the seven classical Liberal Arts; this term was applied to the 'scientific' arts of Geometry, Mathematics, Music and Astronomy/Astrology.

Revolutions: in astrology, revolutions related to the return of the sun to the point of the zodiac it occupied at a chosen starting point (for instance, the day of a wedding).

Ritual magic: forms of magic involving ritual practices, usually based on complex textual instructions, and often involving liturgical elements. Frowned upon by the Church as a perversion of Christian worship, and because of suspected abuse of the sacraments, such as the consecrated host, as well as because of the possibility that the summoning or worship of demons was involved.

Sibyls: divinely-inspired prophetesses of the ancient world, some of whose prophecies were accepted by medieval Christians as genuine.

Sortilegia: a complex term, whose meaning shifted across the medieval period. In early texts, it refers most frequently to casting of lots, especially by means of random selection of a biblical text, which was then interpreted for guidance. This was known as the *sortes sanctorum*, or lots of the saints, and until the eleventh century was widely accepted. By the thirteenth century theologians classified *sortilegia* with negative and harmful forms of magic, accusing practitioners of superstition and misuse of religious texts for purposes of fortune-telling. It thus took on the additional meaning of 'sorcery'.

List of plates

The following plates appear between pages 74 and 75.

Plate 1   The Caladrius bird, as depicted in a Durham book of c.1200, now London, BL, MS Royal 12 C xix

Plate 2   Demon tempting a woman; one of the figures of the damned, from the central portal of the south transept of Chartres Cathedral, 1205–1240

Plate 3   Alchemists at work, as depicted in a fourteenth-century French alchemical manuscript

Plate 4   Anglo-Norman horoscopes, now London, BL MS Royal App 85 (fol. 2)

Plate 5   Harvesting a Mandrake, from a copy of *Tacuinum Sanitatis,* now Vienna, Nationalbib. MS Nova 2644 (fol. 40r)

Plate 6   Moorish astrolabe from Cordoba, c.1054

Plate 7   Image for astronomy and astrology, in a fourteenth-century English manuscript of the *Ars Notoria,* now London, BL MS Sloane 1712 (fol. 37r)

Plate 8   Illustrations for a treatise on palmistry, from a thirteenth-century English collection of theological, scientific and prognostic texts, now London, BL Sloane 2030, fols. 125v-126r

Introduction

The aim of this book is to provide readers with the tools, both conceptual and documentary, to reach informed conclusions as to the existence, nature, importance and uses of magic in medieval society. In order to make this possible, we focus on western Europe rather than the whole continent, and on the period from the eleventh century to the fifteenth. The far northern and eastern zones of Europe followed rather different historical trajectories during this time, and were drawn into the dominant cultural, political and legal structures at varying dates and in different ways; thus their relationship to the history of magic requires separate consideration. Equally, the assimilation of new knowledge about the natural world, the earth, and the cosmos within which it was placed, is crucial to the story we tell, and was a process which gathered force in the eleventh century and continued to the end of the Middle Ages. Our survey therefore begins with the first stages of this great movement of cultural change, when early 'intellectual explorers' from Christian Europe crossed not only the seas and mountains but also the linguistic and religious barriers which separated them from the classical and Arabic works and forms of knowledge available in the Byzantine and Arab Empires. It ends in the late fifteenth century, because by that time all the necessary components which were to be drawn upon in the 'Witch Craze' of the early-modern period were present, and yet both the stereotype of the witch and the procedures needed for conducting witch trials were in their very early stages. Indeed, it is the contention of this book that the witch craze was not a medieval phenomenon but rather the product of the Renaissance and the Reformation.

At the theoretical level we make an equally key argument, and that is that, contrary to some previous approaches, it is not possible to separate magic out from other areas of cultural practice. Rather, what we hope to show is that not only was the definition of the various possible forms of magic a matter of important contention across the period considered, but also that the practices of magic could be encountered across all classes and areas of medieval society. Indeed it was this very fact which made the achievement of a clear definition, which could be uniformly applied, appear so urgent to those whose duty it was to maintain and defend the spiritual health of medieval society. There was universal agreement that harmful magic was destructive to the individual and to society, and so needed to be dealt with; but this could not be undertaken until a clear and legally enforceable definition had been reached and promulgated – and this took time, when knowledge was expanding so rapidly. One thing on which all authorities agreed was that, if magic drew upon forces which did not come from God or from the powers which He had granted directly to His Creation, it must be drawing upon the devil and his demons. This was obviously extremely dangerous, and made magic as threatening as heresy. Nevertheless, this does not mean that the medieval Church automatically set itself to eradicate all forms and sources of new knowledge as possibly demonic. Rather, as in any society (including our own) new knowledge, the technologies it generates and the physical applications it opens up, required scrutiny and control. Practitioners of new forms of learned, scientific magic in the twelfth and thirteenth centuries made claims as boundary-breaking in their own time as those of modern genetic scientists are now. Emanations from other planets (including the sun and the moon) were believed to have fundamental effects upon life on earth, and experts in the new, learned magic claimed to be able to harness them, in order to bring about specific results for selected individuals as well as to open up knowledge of the events which the planets were going to influence in the future. The same model was applied to concepts of health and the combatting of disease, as well as to methods of charting the surface of the earth and finding ways to bring influence to bear upon geographically distant parts of it. It is thus impossible to treat magic as a separate pursuit, of interest only to learned scholars on the one hand, or to uneducated peasants who lacked clear understanding of their own religion on the other. For this reason we do not attempt to 'tell the story' of magic as a single area of activity across the period from the eleventh to the fifteenth century, and this book is not arranged chronologically.

What we have done is to organise the book thematically, and in terms of concrete areas of social practice. We thus start with the milieu of medieval courts, and the rulers and advisers who dominated them. Magic was taken very seriously at this social level, although it was of necessity treated with great discretion. This was not only because of the increasing disapproval put on record by various theologians and social commentators; it was also because one of the most attractive applications of political magic was in providing 'secret services' for the powerful. Thus various types of magician were employed to perform functions which ranged from the relatively straightforward casting of **horoscope**s and forecasting of weather and wealth to highly secret attempts to bring about political assassinations by magical means. We argue that magic at court was something much larger, and more

Horoscope: a reading of the configuration of the planetary bodies at a certain moment, including their relation to each other in the celestial and zodiacal plan.

serious, than a form of elite entertainment, whether actual or as a theme in literature written for aristocratic audiences. Similarly, magic was very real within the medieval Church itself, especially once it is taken into account that the Church included within its structures the cathedral schools and emerging universities within which many of the scholars who became experts in magic received their education. Perhaps the most 'democratic' types of magic were those which tackled illness, since members of all social classes wished to avail themselves of the protections and cures which various forms of magic could offer. A whole chapter is devoted to this, because it raises perhaps some of the most complex questions of definition and distinction between magic, religion and science.

The final argument of the book is that the growing technical powers of magic, together with the increasing numbers of powerful, learned and ambitious people involved in its practice and patronage, inevitably increased both its visibility and its apparent danger. Although magic was never, in the medieval period, a threat on anything like the scale it was claimed to be in the early-modern period, nevertheless theorists and legislators, both ecclesiastical and secular, became increasingly concerned. Twelfth-century compilers of fundamental reference works on law and theology compiled and annotated fundamental materials on magic, which were further expanded in the thirteenth century. Moreover, as the acceptable boundaries of the new **natural philosophy** were mapped and codified in the thirteenth century, together with the university syllabuses through which all this knowledge was formally delivered to students, so the question of whether certain books should be banned arose more urgently. By the late thirteenth century lists of forbidden books were drawn up and promulgated, and they included works on magic; possession of any of them was from that point something carrying a formal punishment. The tracing of these strands, and examination of just how the components for the early-modern prosecution of witches were put into place, is dealt with in the final chapter of this book.

Natural philosophy: the pre-modern term for the systematic study of the natural world and the phenomena connected with it.

Each chapter and theme is supported by a set of documents, each chosen and newly translated for this book. Many have not previously been available in modern English versions; and the full set is intended to make it possible for users of this book to examine the evidence side-by-side with the discussions in the chapters, and to come to informed conclusions on the issues set out above. Diagrams are included, since a considerable proportion of medieval magical practices had a visual component. Further evidence is provided by the illustrations, which reproduce medieval images of magical beings as well as providing photographs of equipment such as **astrolabes** and of surviving medieval horoscopes. Both textual and visual sources have been chosen to represent as wide a range as possible of the elements which made up medieval magic; what remains is for readers to assess the evidence and to consider the arguments set out in the book in its light.

Astrolabe: portable instrument used for astronomical measurements and calculations, which allows for the mapping of the sky at any given moment, thus aiding in the production of horoscopes, as well as time measurement and navigation.

1

Magic and politics

As for all politicians and military leaders, advance information on the actions of enemies and rivals was of crucial importance for medieval rulers; and this was an area where magic of various sorts offered major advantages for practitioners and their patrons. Similarly, although the Church had for centuries offered guidance on both the Calendar and the likely pattern of weather for each year, magicians could offer much more detailed forecasts, and could tailor them to a specific region. Finally, for those willing to engage in something so dangerous, certain forms of magic offered contact with supernatural forces capable of providing help in battle or even of bringing down enemies at a distance. It is thus hardly surprising that both chroniclers and political theorists showed increasing concern about the power and influence of magicians at court, even though these forms of magic were strictly forbidden – often by the laws enforced in the names of the very same rulers. Nevertheless, a surprising amount of evidence survives about both actual practitioners of these forms of magic and the growing fear of powerful magicians.

The main problem with this evidence is establishing how it should be interpreted; and a case in point is the record of how William the Conqueror supposedly employed a French-speaking witch in his campaign to conquer the Isle of Ely. This story is told in the *Deeds of Hereward* (the famous outlaw, also known as 'the Wake'). The Latin text, *Gesta Herewardi*, appears to have been written in the early twelfth century, though its prologue states that it was based on an account in Old English, written soon after the events by a priest called Leofric, who was a member of Hereward's own household (Martin, 1978: 7–12; and Fairweather, 2005). The oldest surviving copy is in a thirteenth-century manuscript dealing with the history and property of Peterborough, and known as the Register of Robert of Swaffham (Peterborough D & C, Ms 1). The witch appears in Chapters 23 to 25 of this biographical work, in the section where William the Conqueror's campaign against the Isle of Ely is being heroically resisted by Hereward and his followers. It is one of William's loyal supporters, Ivo de Taillebois, who recommends the employment of a mysterious old woman, known for her ingenuity and 'art', who will be able to strike the defenders with panic and terror, and who will need to be well paid for this service. Her employment is clearly both confidential and disreputable, since she is brought hastily and in secret, and is placed in the household of a widow loyal to William. Here, however, she is discovered by Hereward himself (disguised as a potter). Hereward listens to the women's conversation, and follows them into a nearby field at midnight, where they make offerings at a spring and speak to its 'guardian'. He is thus able to prepare his fighters against the arts of the witch.

What happens is that, when the Norman army has prepared siege works and fortifications in the swamps and marshes that made Ely an island at this time, the witch is placed on the top of a tower, so that she can see Ely and its people. She then speaks for a long time, haranguing the defenders, repeating incantations against them, and finally baring her bottom at them (a unique element in this story). However, Hereward's soldiers successfully set fire to the wooden structures of the Normans, and in the panic the witch is killed by a fall whilst the Norman army is once again defeated. William the Conqueror's conclusion is that this defeat was a deserved punishment for the employment of an 'abominable woman' who used 'damnable arts'.

This story contains many of the elements found in such accounts, including the reference to eye witnesses (in this case the priest, Leofric) and the emphasis on the wickedness of both practitioners and their employers. It is, however, highly unusual both in featuring a woman as having such rare and expensive skills and in its account of her derisive gesture in baring her bottom at the king's enemies. How widespread, then, were such incidents? The level of interest in highly placed and powerful practitioners of magic is demonstrated by the speed with which information about the newly discovered British magician, Merlin, spread across Europe in the twelfth century. Merlin's feats of magic and prophecy were first revealed by Geoffrey of Monmouth in the 1130s, and by 1135 the Norman chronicler, Orderic Vitalis, had a copy of the 'Prophecies of Merlin' (Geoffrey of Monmouth, ed. Reeve and Wright, 2007; Lawrence-Mathers, 2012: 15–30). By 1138 the story had spread to Mont-St-Michel, and by 1140 Merlin and his prophecies were famous at the royal court in Paris. It was not long before they reached Italy and Germany. Unlike William the Conqueror's witch, Merlin was recorded as successful in all his magical enterprises, which included transporting the stones of Stonehenge from Ireland to England, bringing about the birth of King Arthur, and prophesying the whole future history of the kings of Britain. This was clearly magic on a very different scale. However, before looking at accounts of powerful, male magicians it is important to note that other women were recorded as both prophets and experts in forms of magic which were taken seriously in centres of power. The most famous female prophet was Hildegard of Bingen, known as the 'Sibyl of the Rhine'. She was born into an aristocratic family in what is now Germany, and vowed to the religious life by her parents at the age of eight (in 1106). It seems that Hildegard had experienced visions since her childhood, though she only began to record them as an adult. Her first book of visions, the *Scivias*, was approved by the pope in 1147–48, and covered not just revelations of things to come but also descriptions of the whole universe and of the kingdom of God (Hildegard of Bingen, trans. Hart and Bishop, 1990). Receipt of such revelations made Hildegard famous, and led both political and ecclesiastical leaders to consult her. Only a small part of Hildegard's correspondence survives, but it is enough to show how seriously leading European figures took her insights and advice. Further books followed, which were in turn scrutinised for guidance on current disputes and political issues. However, as befitted an abbess, Hildegard's contact with European leaders was mostly by letter and messenger; she is not recorded as having accepted employment at court.

The figure to whom Hildegard was compared, the sibyl herself, was rather different. This prophetess from the classical world was of pagan origin, and experts in classical writings were aware that there were once several sibyls, based in different regions of the ancient world [*Doc 1*]. St Augustine, one of the great founders of the Christian Church, had accepted that at least one sibyl had had genuine prophetic revelations about the coming of Christ, which he discussed in one of his most influential works, *The City of God*. Isidore of Seville added to this in the early seventh century by providing a list of the sibyls known to the ancient world in his encyclopaedic, and highly influential, work, the *Etymologies* (Isidore, *Etymologies*, trans. Barney et al., 2006). Scholars and churchmen in the early Middle Ages knew little more than this about the **sibyls**, apart from Virgil's account of how Aeneas encountered a sibyl in the Underworld, and how she prophesied about his future descendants, the Romans. However, the sibyl came to prominence in the twelfth century with the circulation of a great set of prophecies known as the words of the Tiburtine Sibyl or *Sibylla Tiburtina* (Holdenried, 2006). According to this revelation, a Last Emperor would fight great battles against the enemies of true religion, whilst the career of the Antichrist would precede the final Day of Judgement (as predicted in the Bible). There was no real suggestion that the sibyl herself, in any of her forms, was still alive; but her prophecies were of clear relevance for supporters of the Crusades and for the career of the Emperor Frederick II. After the latter had triumphantly recaptured Jerusalem, he was frequently compared by European chroniclers with the Last Emperor. The perceived similarity was so strong that many believed, encouraged by the ongoing prophecies of the Cistercian monk and scholar Joachim of Fiore that they were actually living in the Last Days.

> **Sibyls:** divinely-inspired prophetesses of the ancient world, some of whose prophecies were accepted by medieval Christians as genuine.

Joachim's own fame was greatest in Italy, where his prophecies were eagerly circulated and consulted, and where the prophet himself could be invited to meet political leaders and their advisers. Joachim's studies had led him to the conclusion that humanity was about to enter the third and final stage of history, the Age of the Holy Spirit. This cataclysmic event was expected in 1260, by which time Joachim himself was dead. Many of his followers lost their belief in his prophecies when 1260 showed no clear signs of the arrival of the Antichrist, but others remained loyal for a considerable time afterwards. However, this disillusionment was still to come when, in 1190, King Richard I of England asked Joachim to come to Sicily and to interpret the visions in the Apocalypse (or Book of Revelation). Roger of Howden's *Deeds of King Richard* and his *Chronicle* both tell how Joachim was escorted into Richard's presence, while the king was holding court [*Doc. 2*]. Taking Revelation 12: 1–6 as his text, the prophet declared that God would give Richard victory over his enemies, but that humanity would very soon have to face the Antichrist, who was now fifteen years old and living in Rome. However, the account goes on to suggest that this prophecy was received with some scepticism, because it contradicted traditional interpretations of the Bible (Roger of Howden, ed. Stubbs, 1868–71: vol. 3, 77–9).

Such scepticism would perhaps have gratified worried churchmen like John of Salisbury, an English theologian and scholar who later became Bishop of Chartres. His *Policraticus* was addressed to both rulers and their courtiers, in the hope of encouraging good behaviour and good government. The growing power of magic and magicians, in John's view, was sufficiently dangerous that it was necessary to devote a whole section of the work to this subject. According to John, twelfth-century magic was still perceived as based upon classical precedents and sources, whilst also merging into up-to-date science of the sort being introduced into western Europe from Greek and Arabic sources. Even the priest who taught John himself as a boy is described as encouraging his young pupils to engage in crystal gazing and 'magical rites', to John's horror [*Doc. 5*]. Nor was he alone. John recounts that as he grew older he met many more practitioners of various forms of magic and **divination**. Their identities are not revealed, apart from the fact that one of them repented and became a monk at Cluny. But already at this relatively early stage in the development of medieval magic it appears that the knowledge and skills required for the practice of magic tended to mean that practitioners needed a Church education, even though their patrons were likely to be secular.

Divination: predicting the future by any variety of supernatural means.

Further confirmation of this comes from another book written by a highly educated Churchman for the instruction of secular rulers and their courtiers. This is the *Otia Imperialia* (*Recreation for an Emperor*) a book which provided a complete overview of world history, geography and natural or supernatural resources, tailored for busy world-rulers (Gervase of Tilbury, ed. Banks and Binns, 2002). Its author was Gervase of Tilbury, an aristocrat and expert on Church law, who served in the courts of Henry II of England, King William II of Sicily, and Emperor Otto IV. He travelled extensively and knew the world of international politics very well. The fact that he dedicated a major section of his book to the marvels to be found in various regions of the earth itself demonstrates the demand for information on these subjects; and it is striking that he included not only supernatural creatures but also human magicians. One such, a learned scholar and scientist from England, is described as having visited the court of King Roger II of Sicily (who had died in 1154). He was given permission by the king to hunt out the tomb of the classical poet, Virgil, in Naples – a feat in which he succeeded thanks to his 'art'. As a result, Virgil's bones were taken to a secure place in a castle by the sea, whilst the 'master' was allowed to carry away a book of incantations and diagrams found buried with the poet. These revealed, amongst other things, what Gervase calls the 'notary art' and will be discussed in more detail in Chapter 3, since they were studied, we are told, by churchmen. What is relevant for this chapter is the interest shown by the king of Sicily in the magical 'art' and 'science' of which this anonymous Englishman was a master. In exchange for access to this expertise, the king was prepared to allow the scholar to ask for major patronage. Understandably, if frustratingly, Gervase the courtier was far too discreet to reveal just what the king wanted his visiting magician to promise!

However, fictional representations of magicians can provide at least exaggerated versions of the services which court magicians could offer, and the level of demand for stories about Merlin is evidence of the strength of interest in magicians and their powers. It was a French poet known as Robert de Boron who was the first to create a full-length narrative poem about Merlin, in the early thirteenth century (Robert de Boron, ed. Micha, 1980). Only later versions of it now survive; but the powers and the historical role attributed to this fictional version of Merlin are truly impressive. Merlin, as in twelfth-century versions of his story, has superhuman powers thanks to the fact that his father was a demon. What is new in the thirteenth century is that Merlin is taken out of his original, pseudo-historical setting in the dark ages, and is placed for the first time in the court of King Arthur. He is presented as Arthur's chief counsellor, as creator of the famous Round Table, and as a source of knowledge about forthcoming events – thanks to his prophetic powers. Merlin's powers in fact are so great that even supervising and guarding King Arthur does not take up all of his time. Instead, further suggestions that magicians made mysterious and fleeting visits to court are provided, since Merlin promises always to come to the king when he is needed – as long as the king promises always to take his advice. For a time

Merlin appears almost infallible, because his prophetic powers enable him to know when Arthur's kingdom truly needs him, and when he can take time to intervene decisively in the struggles of other countries. His magical power is so great that he can also reach distant lands in incredibly short times, and can direct the fate of kings and their battles, all with an eye on the longer-term outcome of these international affairs. Merlin thus appears as entirely benign; and yet the level of his power, and its demonic source, combine to make human courtiers both resentful and afraid. Within the world of courtly romance it is thus fitting that Merlin is finally rendered powerless, and condemned to unending imprisonment, by Viviane the enchantress, his pupil and unwilling lover.

No human being could achieve Merlin's level of power, and none claimed to. However, there was one category of magical practitioners who could achieve levels of fame and reputation almost equivalent to those of Merlin. These practitioners were the astrologers, who were at the cutting edge of new scientific, cosmological and magical discoveries in the twelfth and thirteenth centuries, and who consequently had to be very careful not to break any laws. The burning questions were whether astrology could, and should, predict future developments in human affairs. That masters of the art could calculate the positions of the planets on any chosen date, past, present or future, was not in doubt (once they were in possession of accurate planetary tables). But what did these planetary positions signify?

The level of difficulty of this 'art', and the time taken to assimilate it into western medieval culture, are demonstrated by the fact that it was not until the thirteenth century that court astrologers were accepted as being able to make genuine and detailed forecasts. Perhaps most famous of all were Michael Scot and Guido Bonatti. The former rose to prominence as a theologian and commentator on Aristotle, before working at the court of the Emperor Frederick II [Doc. 6]. He took care to argue for the religious orthodoxy of astrology whilst also emphasising the knowledge which it made available. The stars and the planets, he wrote, exerted hidden, but entirely natural, forces upon the earth and its inhabitants; and astrology was no more and no less than the detailed analysis of these forces. By contrast, the forbidden art of *magia* or actual 'magic' entailed deliberate invocation of the power of demons. He went still further, and argued that, while the stars could not cause earthly events, they could provide signs and clues for those who knew how to interpret them. In more private correspondence he also boasted of how the emperor had consulted him on both medical and military matters, both of which had serious political significance (Thorndike, 1929: 307–37). It is therefore not surprising that by the fourteenth century Scot was believed to have been a practitioner of forbidden, predictive astrology, and was condemned as such by the great poet, Dante. Scot seems to have died in the

1230s, but Bonatti was still at work in the 1290s. Bonatti's whole career seems to have taken place amongst the competing states of Italy, where he worked for leaders of the anti-papal side in the ongoing wars. Like Scot, Bonatti also wrote about astrology and its powers – and was rather less theologically cautious about this. He claimed to have predicted a conspiracy against Frederick II in 1246, and to have warned the emperor in time (Bonatti, trans. Dykes, 2007: Tr 7, part 1, chap. 5). While working for Guido of Montefeltro, Lord of Urbino, he also played an important part in the defence of the town of Forli. In fact the *Annals of Forli* lauded him for having saved the town from the army of Pope Martin IV through his astrological knowledge, which was detailed enough to allow him to direct the movements of the defenders hour by hour.

Skills of an order to allow their possessors to give political and military counsel to emperors and kings were naturally rare, as well as dangerous for their possessors. Writing the history of court magicians is made all the more problematic by the protective secrecy employed by both the 'masters' and their employers. Nevertheless, surviving texts and manuscripts provide further evidence as to the ways in which magical and astrological skills could be deployed at court. Perhaps most sensational is a rather scrappy piece of parchment, now part of British Library Ms Royal App. 85. Folio 2 of this almost unique survivor contains a set of twelfth-century horoscopes, copied out by two different writers in handwriting characteristic of England or northern France around the middle of the twelfth century [*Doc. 7*]. The origin of the horoscopes is now lost, along with any information on how such dangerous works actually survived. They deal with a set of questions about apparently contemporary political events, such as: whether an army from Normandy will arrive; whether a king will succeed in gaining an oath from his barons; and the timing of the death of the Count of Anjou. Each takes the form of a standard astrological diagram, divided up into twelve sections representing the twelve astrological houses. The boundaries of the twelve signs of the zodiac are noted, showing how they intersect with the houses. Each of the seven astrologically significant planets is also marked, within the relevant house and sign. In a few cases the 'decision' or reading is also entered; for instance, that the Norman army will not come. This was politically explosive – and also required arithmetical and astronomical skills which were very rare. For those very reasons there has been debate as to who, in the mid-twelfth-century Anglo-Norman world, could have cast such horoscopes (North, 1986, 1987). Of the two possible candidates the most popular choice has been a scientist and astrologer called Adelard of Bath, who had travelled all the way to Sicily and then Antioch in order to acquire his knowledge, before coming back to England and to probable employment by the Angevin court. Such men were perhaps dangerous – but they were also in possession of highly desirable knowledge. The fact that their association with courts and rulers is hinted at by sources and yet is extremely difficult to trace or define is perhaps unsurprising (if frustrating for historians).

Much less apparently dangerous, and yet still frowned upon by moralists and churchmen, were the providers of magical entertainments at political gatherings and court festivities. That such activities might be undertaken by prominent figures, and that they straddled the fields of art, science, magic and cultural diplomacy is strikingly illustrated by the recorded role of Leonardo da Vinci in providing such 'experiments' for the court of the Medici in Rome. It is Vasari who records how Leonardo tamed an unusually large lizard, before attaching fake wings and horns to it, and terrifying members of the court with his 'dragon' (Vasari, trans. De Vere, 1912–14: 89–105). Another entertainment involved creating a special waxy paste which could be shaped into the forms of small creatures and then inflated. Still another involved playing a practical joke, since specially prepared ox guts were attached to a bellows and then blown up to such an extent that unwary spectators were forced into the corners of the room. Some historians have found Leonardo's interest in such activities rather surprising; but they are highly practical and quite gentle when compared with the courtly entertainments offered in fourteenth- and fifteenth-century texts. Perhaps representative of these is a short work called 'The Book of Rings', which includes instructions for preparing a 'Ring of Mars', made of bronze and bearing the inscribed sign and angel-name appropriate for Mars (sadly omitted from the text). The owner of this ring will be able to make castles, soldiers and mock battles appear and disappear at will, to terrifying effect (Lidaka, 1998: 46–9).

Still more frightening were the exploits with which magicians and necromancers in the employment of powerful courtiers were charged in the late Middle Ages. In 1317 Pope John XXII found convincing evidence that no less a figure than Hugues Geraud, then Bishop of Cahors, had himself used sorcery and poison against the pope (Peters, 1978: 129–31). As a learned churchman, the Bishop of Cahors had access to books of magic and to the requisite skills; but secular members of the elite could pay for such expertise. In 1320 the ruler of Milan, Galeazzo Visconti, was convincingly accused of having forced a learned cleric to create a magical image with which to bring about the lingering death of John XXII. Slightly earlier, in 1314, Enguerrand de Marigny, a member of the French court, was accused of treason, stealing royal revenues and employing a sorcerer and his wife to work magic against King Louis X using wax images. Magicians were apparently numerous at the French court at this time, since Mahaut of Artois was accused in 1316 of employing a sorcerer to use love magic on King Philip V. Her aim was to ensure that the king continued to love his wife, Mahaut's daughter, rather than to kill the king – but this was still a serious crime (Peters, 1978: 121). Similar activities were uncovered somewhat later at the English royal court, when Eleanor Cobham, Duchess of Gloucester, was accused in 1441 of using magicians in a plot against the young Henry VI. Eleanor had apparently hired at least two male clerics and a professional sorceress, Margery Jourdemayne, to make and use wax images. Evidence produced at the trial suggested that Margery, who lived near Westminster, had been active as a provider of magical services associated with 'love' and fertility for female members of the royal court since the early 1430s. Margery seems to have escaped serious punishment for these activities. However, a plot against the king was an extremely serious matter, and Margery was burnt to death for this crime whilst Roger Bolingbroke, the duchess's astrologer-priest, was hung, drawn and quartered for treason after having been put on public display along with his magical apparatus (Griffiths, 1968–69; and Freeman, 2004).

Ritual magic: forms of magic involving ritual practices, usually based on complex textual instructions, and often involving liturgical elements. Frowned upon by the Church as a perversion of Christian worship, and because of suspected abuse of the sacraments, such as the consecrated host, as well as because of the possibility that the summoning or worship of demons was involved.

Magic at court is thus a complex and shifting issue, for a long time visible more in fears and accusations than in actual evidence. However by the thirteenth century texts of **ritual magic** were being circulated among the growing number of ambitious, educated clerics, and even supporters of magical science, like Roger Bacon, were expressing severe disapproval of the more frivolous and illusory types of magic. Still more seriously, by the end of that century practitioners were apparently numerous, at least in the vicinity of courts and centres of power, and capable of offering a full range of dangerous forms of magic to the wealthy and ambitious.

2

Magic in the Church

MONKS AND CHARMS

For the medieval Church there was a clear and fundamental distinction between true religion and magic, since the second involved conscious collaboration with demons and was thus necessarily opposed to devotion to God. However, it has become clear that there was in practice a complex border zone where the two interacted, resulting in forms of religious belief and practice which later appeared as superstitious or at least partly magical. What is perhaps more surprising is that such hybrid blends of magic and religion were both recorded and practised by members of the clergy themselves, who seem to have found no fault with them. For instance, Anglo-Saxon monks and what are now seen as superstitious '**charms**' have been linked together ever since Oswald Cockayne's production of three edited volumes entitled *Leechdoms, Wortcunning and Starcraft of Early England* in the Victorian period (Cockayne, 1864, 1865, 1866). The archaism of Cockayne's title is striking in itself, but does suggest the range of the materials he collected, which cover medical texts and herbals and works on basic astronomy and astrology. The collection is fascinating, but also deeply problematic; just how accurate is it to place all this material together, when it covers such a wide range of interests and applications? Moreover, if all of it derives from monastic and ecclesiastical sources, can any of it truly be seen as magical? The same problem applies to all the material discussed in this chapter. If magic was defined primarily as having to do with demons and with hostility to true religion, then a modern historian needs to be very careful about judging any text approved of by a religious institution as magical. Projection of modern attitudes onto the medieval past will not help in understanding the ideas of that past. This chapter will attempt to resolve these issues by focusing upon evidence, in the form not only of the surviving texts but also of the nature of the books into which they were copied by monastic scribes.

Charms: a term covering a wide range of usually informal practices, mostly combining verbal formulae and physical objects in order to bring about a desired effect (usually protective or curative).

Prognostics: a term covering a wide range of methods of foretelling the future, by interpreting dreams, natural phenomena, and verbal or numerical data. In scholarship on medieval magic, the term is usually applied to the texts setting out the instructions for making such forecasts.

Egyptian days: the days in each month believed to be unlucky or dangerous to health. The lists were taken from Roman calendars into medieval ones.

Inquisition: ecclesiastical tribunal set up for the suppression of heresy in the thirteenth century under the papacy of Innocent III. The Inquisition existed in most European countries faithful to Rome, but inquisitorial tribunals were prevented from operating in the British Isles.

Lunaries: a generic term for texts which provided the basis for predictions by relating various phenomena (such as dreams) to the day of the lunar month on which they occurred or were planned to take place.

The first category of text to be looked at is that known as the '**prognostics**', for the reason that they made available to their readers various means of predicting future events. Most popular in this category (at least in surviving manuscripts) seem to have been prognostics, which provided forecasts of weather and harvests for the coming year, usually based upon the day of the week on which 1 January fell (Liuzza, 2001, 2011; Chardonnens, 2007: 491–500). Related but more specialist were predictions as to coming suffering or good fortune, based upon whether each of the Twelve Days of the Christmas Festival saw wind or sunshine. Also popular were so-called brontologies, or forecasts based upon the day and the time on which a thunderstorm occurred [Doc. 8]. All these were widely distributed across monastic institutions in early medieval Europe, though those from Anglo-Saxon England have been the most studied. Most widespread of all were the lists of unlucky days, known as '**Egyptian Days**', of which there were usually considered to be two in each calendar month (although January seems to have been a particularly inauspicious month). These were so much a part of the accepted views of the early medieval Church that they are frequently found entered into calendars prefacing prayer books and liturgical books for use in monastic and cathedral churches. Medical treatments, such as blood-letting and purging, were dangerous on many of these days, and this was a serious matter for monks, since regular medical treatments were prescribed in the Benedictine Rule itself. Eating certain foods, and engaging in specific activities, were also contra-indicated on these days. This may seem harmless, yet by the thirteenth century the Church itself was taking an increasingly negative view, linked to its growing attempt to stamp out heresy and superstition. It was during this time that the Holy Office, later known as the **Inquisition**, was set up, and guides for inquisitors, such as those active in southern France, linked observation of the Egyptian Days with seriously erroneous practices such as performing charms over plant materials and even misusing the sacraments (see Chapter 6).

Thus far, whatever may be thought of the scientific concepts involved, these prognostics have more the nature of medical, meteorological and agricultural texts than overtly magical ones. Their incorporation into monastic volumes containing prayers for use in specific circumstances; texts on the calculation of the liturgical year; works of instruction for monks; and summaries of geographical and cosmological knowledge is thus scarcely surprising. More troubling, and more difficult to categorise, are the **lunaries**, or lists of days of the lunar month, with varying information on issues such as whether it is safe to let blood; the fate awaiting a child born on each day; the fate awaiting someone who falls sick on each day; and the reliability of dreams experienced on each day. To modern readers these look very much like fortune-telling, an activity which is assumed to have little to do with true religion. However, this view fails to understand a fundamental principle of medieval science (or natural philosophy, as it was then called); namely that the world, as God's creation, could be understood through God's word as revealed in the Bible and interpreted by prophets and theologians. Thus the world was securely placed at the centre of the universe, and the stars and planets were accepted as placed by God to bring light and to mark times, seasons and the patterns structuring human life. Time and the movements of the heavens were not only inter-related but also full of significance; and who better to interpret this significance than a learned member of a religious community? The same argument can apply also to the works on dream-interpretation, and the lists of the meanings to be attributed to objects when they appear in dreams. Their link to biblical example is demonstrated by the fact that many of them are given titles suggesting that they derived from the revelations of the prophet Daniel, who was famous for his accurate interpretation of the dreams sent by God to King Nebuchadnezzar, as recounted in the biblical Book of Daniel [Doc. 9].

More difficult to link to liturgical practice or to theological instruction are the texts offering means of foretelling future events by carrying out alphabetical or numerical calculations. These are usually described by modern writers as forms of divination, which is hard to deny, even though divination was repeatedly condemned by Church councils. One of the first to condemn divination was St Augustine himself, both because of its problematic relationship to the key doctrine of free will and because it made humans especially vulnerable to deception and harm at the hands of demons (see, for instance, *De Doctrina Christiana* (*On Christian Doctrine*) Book 2, Chapter 23, 'Why We Repudiate Arts of Divination'). Interpretation of natural phenomena could be argued not to be divination in this forbidden sense, while dream-interpretation could be claimed as an entirely licit form of attention to messages sent by God. However, other rituals and devices found from the tenth century down to the fifteenth are much more overtly divinatory, and thus more surprising in a monastic context. One which was popular in the early Middle Ages, and strongly associated with medical applications, was the so-called 'Sphere of Apuleius' or 'Sphere of Life and Death'. For this reason it will be considered in Chapter 5, on 'Medical magic' rather than as a form of 'monastic magic'. However, the applications of **palmistry** (or **chiromancy**) and name interpretation (**onomancy**), both of which occurred in monastic volumes, went well beyond the medical, and will be discussed in the next section of this chapter.

That monks and priests, as well as lay people, were believed to engage in forbidden forms of divination is demonstrated by the repeated condemnations found in the early medieval Penitentials. These collections

Chiromancy/palmistry: divination by means of the lines of the hands.

Onomancy: name interpretation or divination from names.

seem first to have been compiled in Ireland and Wales before being taken up in Anglo-Saxon England and the Carolingian Empire. Versions were also produced in Spain and, later, in eastern Europe as the Church in these regions also grappled with problematic behaviour on the part of its members. The challenge of the Penitentials in relation to the history of magic is that they pay almost no systematic attention to it as a problem. This is interesting in itself, since it suggests that magical practices were neither addressed in a systematic way at this time nor thought of as a major problem; but it leaves the question of whether divination and dream-interpretation were considered essentially magical very difficult to answer. What emerges from the Penitentials instead is a growing list of forbidden practices, potentially having to do with supernatural forces or beliefs but variously classified. A well-known example is the Anglo-Saxon punishment of seven years of penance for women who put their daughters into ovens or onto roofs to cure fevers (*Penitential of Theodore*, 1869–78: 190; Frantzen, 1983). This was clearly taken very seriously, because manslaughter only received a penance of three years, but just why it was so wrong is not explained. In its original form it is placed in a wide-ranging group of crimes listed as forms of Idol-Worship, but it is not so serious simply for that reason. Pagan deities are, as was common, equated with demons, but women who actually chant 'diabolical incantations or divinations' are punished only by one year of penance. It is tempting to link it with love magic, since most Penitentials regard that as a female practice, and yet punishments for women who drink semen and blood in an attempt to 'increase love' are listed with matters relating to marriage and sexual conduct, in a separate section. Finally, using both potions and 'art' to cause death is listed – but under 'Murder' and without necessary magical connotations [*Doc. 19*].

What a survey of the Penitentials, and associated royal legislation, does suggest is that texts from continental Europe appear to pay more attention to magic than those from Britain. The Emperor Charlemagne was worried enough about magic that, when he issued a *General Admonition* in 789, intended to reform religion throughout his territories, he included a ban on all sorcerers, magicians and enchanters (or enchantresses). The penalty for unrepentant practitioners of magic was death. This ban was repeated and elaborated in the following centuries, whilst all who performed love magic, divinations and incantations came to be condemned as **malefici**, or practitioners of evil magic. Moreover, by the end of the ninth century it was accepted that all such magic could only work through the involvement of demons. Magic was thus separated from paganism and given a definition, at least of its source of power, which was to last well into the early-modern period.

Malefici: practitioners of evil magic, perceived as both spiritually and physically harmful, including love magic, divinations and incantations.

PALMISTRY AND DIVINATION

This makes it all the more surprising that learned monks continued to be interested in works of divination throughout the medieval period. That this was indeed the case is demonstrated, for instance, by a Psalter made by one Eadwine for Canterbury Cathedral in the middle of the twelfth century (*The Eadwine Psalter*, ed. Gibson *et al.*, 1992: esp. 165–8). Eadwine's Psalter is clearly the product of considerable learning as it offers three Latin versions of the Book of Psalms, with Old English and Anglo-Norman translations, and full glosses and notes. Its producer had a full-page portrait of himself, depicted as a monk and inscribed 'Eadwine, prince of scribes', included in the book. That it was an important possession of the priory is suggested by the fact that it contains an impressive map of the cathedral's buildings and water supply. Uniquely in a Psalter, the route along which water is piped to the monastic buildings, including the guest accommodation and the infirmary, is set out in considerable detail. This suggests an interest in health, water and bathing comparable to that with which Geoffrey of Monmouth credits the secular magician and prophet, Merlin, in his slightly earlier *History of the Kings of Britain*. The association is made still stronger by the fact that the Psalter also contains two divinatory texts which were extremely unusual both at this time and in this context.

The first is a chiromancy, or exposition of palmistry, and the second is an onomancy, or method for deriving answers from the interpretation of names and other verbal information. That these texts were not seen as illicit is suggested by the facts that they were placed immediately after commentaries on the Lord's Prayer and the Creed, and that they were copied out by the same scribes as the religious texts. The treatise on palmistry is the earliest known such work in Latin to survive, although it is related to earlier texts in Arabic. Its copyist was apparently unfamiliar with the procedures involved, since the description of the main lines to be found on the hand is not always clear. This is understandable, since the only contemporary discussion of chiromancy comes from as far away as Toledo. The text itself is related to slightly later Latin treatises on the same subject, and provides familiar insights into subjects such as the likelihood of death in foreign lands or of future promotion, but its actual sources are unknown. That palmistry was accepted at both the royal and the archiepiscopal courts is shown by John of Salisbury's statement that Thomas Becket, while Chancellor for Henry II and still Archdeacon of Canterbury, had consulted a palmist before undertaking a military campaign (*Policraticus*: Book 2, chap. 27). If Becket had become a patron of this palmist then the early appearance of his 'trade secrets' in a Canterbury manuscript, presented as part of the cutting-edge skills available to the cathedral priory c.1160, is more easy to understand.

The text on the interpretation of names is equally precocious in western Europe at this time, and is surprising in that it also has strong associations with Arabic sources (Burnett, 1992). It is thus likely that it was made available by the same specialist, because access to such sources was extremely rare. The procedure here is related to those found in medical works, since numerical values are to be calculated for names and significant words, following tables provided by the text. Further tables allow a conclusion as to whether the querent will be successful or unsuccessful, depending upon where 'their' number appears. In fuller and later versions this text is associated with the Greek philosopher Aristotle and the 'secrets' he supposedly made available to Alexander the Great. Its value for makers of policy in both secular and ecclesiastical affairs was potentially great, and it thus appears that Canterbury had acquired the services of a highly regarded 'artificer' in the mid twelfth century. It is true that these texts are strongly practical as presented here; but otherwise we seem to be in a milieu very similar to those of the courts of great secular lords, as discussed in Chapter 1. Indeed, bishops were often both closely connected to great aristocratic families and highly educated, and thus exercised considerable patronage and influence over scholarship in their dioceses. Successive bishops of Lincoln, including both Alexander 'the Magnificent' and Robert were patrons of architects, poets, historians and scholars, and Geoffrey of Monmouth dedicated works to both. Geoffrey's *Life of Merlin*, written in classicising Latin poetry, offered the learned Bishop of Lincoln and his court learned disquisitions on: how springs acquire their health-giving properties; the movements of the planets; and how to interpret the flight of birds, amongst other relevant material (Geoffrey of Monmouth, ed. and trans. Clarke, 1973).

Further proof of the level of demand for texts bringing together physical science, medicine and divination is the growing popularity of the 'Books of Fate'. These drew upon a wide range of classical and Arabic sources to produce complex and self-consciously learned compilations, often with elaborate diagrams, which were in demand in monasteries and cathedral schools in twelfth-century Europe. What they do is to simplify the process of divination by offering ready-made answers to specified questions. The user is given lists of questions, set out in groups relating to categories such as health and fortune, and then supplied with instructions on how to use dice, coins, rotating wheels and so forth to produce a final number or symbol. When this is located in the relevant table of answers, the consultation is complete. In case this appears rather simple, the texts and the knowledge they contain are credited to famous scholars and philosophers, such as Pythagoras and Socrates. Tabulated forms of divination from the stars and from birds are included in these 'Books of Fate', linking them both to classical works on divination and astrology and to the new scientific texts being translated from Arabic at this time. They continued to be popular, among wealthy members of the laity as well as with the clergy, into the late Middle Ages. A particularly impressive example is the one produced by the chronicler, Matthew Paris of St Albans (Matthew Paris, *Prognostica*, ed. Brandin, 1932). This dates from the middle of the thirteenth century, and was apparently made for his own monastery. It is now Ms Ashmole 304 in the Bodleian Library, Oxford.

MONASTIC ASTROLOGY?

Surviving manuscripts make it clear that Latin versions of Arabic works on astronomy, astrology, divination and the wonders of the earth were enthusiastically acquired by monasteries and cathedrals across Europe in the twelfth and thirteenth centuries. The newest and most exciting area of knowledge was astrology, which will be discussed in detail in Chapter 3, on learned magic in the universities. However, the distinction between astrology and astronomy was not easy to define in this period, and a practical knowledge of astronomy was important for monks and priests as well as for professional scholars. This was partly because all educated clerics were expected to understand the calculations involved in finding the date of Easter for any given year – a procedure which required knowledge of the equinoxes and leap years as well as of the lunar calendar. For monks, the Benedictine Rule also specified that they should time their daily and nightly services in relation to specified events such as daybreak and nightfall. Given that the length of daylight varied considerably across the year (as it still does) and that fully accurate clocks were not available, every monastery needed an expert to make observations of the rising and setting of key stars, and to correlate these with tables of astral positions at different points of the night through the year (McCluskey, 1990).

This was also important since it was widely accepted, on the model of the star which had guided the wise men to Bethlehem and to the cradle of the infant Christ, that God offered signs to humanity through the medium of the heavenly bodies. Amongst key events which were frequently interpreted as likely to have such significance were lunar and solar eclipses. Still more important, clearly, were darkenings of the sun and of the skies which fell frighteningly outside the regular pattern of eclipses. However, for such events to be identified, it was necessary for the dates of regular eclipses to be known – and this was knowledge available to very few until the late Middle Ages. It was again in the twelfth century that Arabic treatises on the planetary and solar positions required for eclipses, and on the calculation of their occurrence, became available in Latin, after preliminary studies by ambitious scholars in the eleventh century. An exemplary practitioner of this very complex set of skills was the Lotharingian scholar, Walcher, who was appointed prior of Malvern in the late eleventh century. He was a student of the Christian calendar and the complex calculations required to establish the date of Easter each year, but went beyond this to a direct engagement with Arabic astronomy and astrology. While travelling in Italy in 1091 he had observed a lunar eclipse, and was startled to learn when he returned to England that it had been visible there at a different hour of the night. This led him to make an especially careful observation of a lunar eclipse in 1092, using the revolutionary technology of the astrolabe, a device which was itself borrowed from Arabic scientific advances. It was from this observation, and his knowledge of the path of the moon, that he calculated a new set of tables providing more accurate times for the occurrence of new moons for the years 1036 to 1111 (Burnett, 1995: 51–3). It may seem odd that he bothered to calculate these for nearly sixty years into the past; but he chose a set of years whose characteristics, he believed, would repeat cyclically into the future, and which could thus easily be updated. It was the new availability of knowledge such as this which was beginning to revolutionise the observations and deductions of chroniclers from the early twelfth century onwards.

However, such texts still needed expert readers to make use of them, and these were only trained up in large numbers when the universities began to expand. Chronicles written by learned monks in the first half of the twelfth century show enthusiasm for this science, coupled with a real difficulty in following its detailed calculations. For instance, the chronicle compiled by John, a monk of Worcester, drew upon Walcher's very scarce astrological and astronomical knowledge. In discussing a solar eclipse which took place in 1133, John quoted from Walcher's treatise, itself based on the teaching of Petrus Alfonsi. This Spanish scholar, who had converted to Christianity from Judaism, and was expert in Arabic astronomy, seems to have given instruction to Walcher, and very probably visited England during the reign of Henry I. Walcher's treatise explained the positions of both the sun and the moon needed for a solar eclipse, together with the rules which governed their paths across the sky. However, John himself was not sufficiently confident to calculate for certain whether the event of 1133 was indeed an eclipse, especially as he had received reports that it was only total in some parts of England. What he did instead was to quote Walcher of Malvern's version of the Arabic work on the path of the moon and its points of intersection with that of the sun. Readers able to make the requisite calculations could then judge for themselves before proceeding to make deductions as to the significance of the darkening of the sun in 1133 (John of Worcester: vol. 3, ed. and trans. P. McGurk, 1998: 210–11; Lawrence-Mathers, 2013).

A similar combination of religious interest and scientific uncertainty is found when other chroniclers discuss both strange behaviour by the moon and the appearances of comets. What is surprising to a modern reader is the lack of confidence shown by monastic historians as to whether a particular, fast-moving, 'star' was or was not a comet. Classical and theological sources were unanimous in the opinion that the appearance of a comet was a very significant event. They also provided the information that comets had 'tails' or, in some versions, were 'hairy'. But what exactly did this mean? Interpretations could be very different, as is clear if the Bayeux tapestry's depiction of Halley's Comet is compared with other medieval images of comets. If a fast-moving star was simply surrounded by a glowing light, was it or was it not a comet? It is scarcely surprising that the chronicles also record that rulers and Church leaders summoned experts to give their opinions on such matters and, if possible, to agree on the meaning of astral and planetary phenomena. Still more difficult was the border line at which the acceptable, and urgent, interpretation of heavenly signs became unacceptable indulgence in predictive astrology. The latter problem continued to be argued, and to grow, throughout the rest of the medieval period. But for the moment it is important to consider how the theologians and lawyers of Christian Europe sought to define, analyse and make known the problematic boundary between acceptable natural philosophy and unacceptable magic.

PETER LOMBARD, GRATIAN AND THE DEVELOPMENT OF LAW AND THEOLOGY IN RELATION TO MAGIC

Like the Fathers of the Church before them, medieval Christian theologians emphatically condemned magical practices as sinful, seeing in them a perilous activity that was clearly dangerous for the integrity of the human soul. However, their work tended to be scattered in different books and collections, making it hard to consult. A still more serious problem developed in the eleventh century, as the body of theological texts grew rapidly and in an unstructured way. By the mid twelfth century, when this process was gaining further impetus, it was becoming urgent for authoritative statements on doctrine, and the penalties for infringement, to be made available. A more systematic legal ban on magical practices was produced, not as an issue in its own right, but as part of this larger movement. In addition, 'practical theology' or the branch of theology which was applied to daily life, was increasingly split off to become a formal body of Church law (known as canon law) which in turn made prosecutions more straightforward. Following St

Augustine in particular, theologians and canon lawyers continued to emphasise the sinfulness of magic, and increasingly defined it as demonically inspired crime. This was not yet the time of active persecution and there was still much that was not defined; however, the foundations of the legal arguments used in the late-medieval persecution of magic had been laid.

In theology itself, the crucial work was that of Peter Lombard, author of the encyclopaedic collection known as the *Sentences* or *Sententia* (1155–57) [*Doc. 10*] (Rosemann, 2007). As part of his exposition on the creation and nature of corporeal and spiritual things in the second book of this work, he discusses the growing question of demons and the powers they can exercise over aspects of God's creation. He argues that it is part of the nature of demons to perceive truths about earthly things which are hidden to mortal men. Thus, they can deceptively appear to be able to predict the future, and with their lies they can manipulate men wicked or foolish enough to consult them. This is the sinister reality which underlies the deceptive glamour of magic. The illusory and deceitful nature of the magical arts, so strongly defined by St Augustine in the formative period of Christianity, is thus reinforced in this fundamental theological collection. According to Peter Lombard, it can only be illicit transactions between men and demons which lie behind the apparent effectiveness of magical arts – and this is also the reason for the force of his condemnation.

The discussion of magic as demonically inspired crime is also present in the book that became the standard textbook of Church law, used for training canon lawyers in the schools of Paris and Bologna from the second half of the twelfth century onwards. This is the *Decretum*, first issued c.1140, of Gratian, another great encyclopaedia, set out in several parts [*Doc. 11*]. As with the earlier Penitentials, magic is not a major subject of concern in this work, and yet enough is given to lay down the key terms and texts which would determine its handling by the legal authorities of the Church for centuries to come. Perhaps most important is the fact that magic appears in two different aspects, discussed first as an issue within the very serious crime of heresy and secondly under problems relating to marriage. Its first appearance, where it is explicitly considered as heretical, is within the discussion of the hypothetical case of a cleric who practised magic and divination. In case the idea of a cleric indulging in magic is surprising, it should be remembered that the skills involved in summoning and consulting demons, and finding answers to formal questions about future events, required the kind of higher education which only the Church could provide. This case is part of the twenty-sixth *causa* of the thirty-six set out here, and within it Gratian establishes that divination, even when apparently religious in inspiration, is in fact sinful since, as for Peter Lombard and St Augustine, it is held only to be able to work through the powers of demons. He then proceeds to reproduce much of Isidore of Seville's seventh-century listing and definition of the magical arts, as well as categorising practitioners of magic in a manner very similar to that set out by John of Salisbury. The analysis leads to the sombre conclusion that all magicians, illusionists and practitioners of divination should be excommunicated. The second, and final, appearance of magic is as part of the discussion of male impotence as a reason for ending a marriage. This is in *causa* thirty-three, and here it is established that demonic magic can actually affect the minds and bodies of men sufficiently to make them unable to consummate their marriages, although penitence, exorcism, prayer and charity can all counter its negative effects (Rider, 2006: 58–64). Magic is clearly a matter to be taken very seriously; and the means to do so were now systematically provided and clearly located.

THE POPE WHO WAS A NECROMANCER: THE BLACK LEGEND OF GERBERT OF AURILLAC

During the central Middle Ages, stories asserting the active involvement of members of the Church in illicit necromantic practices were not uncommon. As mentioned earlier, John of Salisbury offers an account of his own experiences as a child under the care of a necromantic priest in his *Policraticus* [Doc. 5]. Similarly, in his *Dialogus miraculorum* (*Discussion of Miracles*) Cesarius (c.1180–c.1240), prior of the Cistercian monastery of Heisterbach in Western Germany, offers an interesting anecdote in which a clergyman named Philip is said to be often hired by knights and sometimes even by priests to summon demons into his presence. He accomplishes this remarkable feat through the use of a protective circle, which allows him to communicate with the demons in alleged safety [Doc. 12]. These accounts by John and Cesarius provide examples of lower clergymen dabbling with the necromantic arts, but other similar accounts discuss the practice of **necromancy** within the highest ranks of the Church. By the twelfth century Gerbert of Aurillac (born c.946, Pope Sylvester II 999–1003) was renowned not only as a pope and an intellectual with an unusual expertise in mathematics, but also as a supposed practitioner of necromancy and magic. This 'Black Legend' appeared in the middle of the eleventh century and developed throughout the twelfth and thirteenth centuries. The first written reference to Gerbert's suspect behaviour appeared some 80 years after his death, in Hugh of Flavigny's *Chronicon Virdunense . . .* (*Chronicle of Verdun*) (c.1085). Here the 'strangeness of his habits' is stressed, and Gerbert is associated with the term *praestigia*, which had strong connotations of the forbidden arts.

Necromancy: initially, divination by means of the dead; later the term was applied to any form of illicit transaction involving the (knowing or unknowing) invocation of demons.

Several other features were gradually incorporated into the legend, with three motifs reappearing constantly: Gerbert's use of necromancy to advance his career; his fatal deception by a demon; and the posthumous dismemberment of his body. But it was not until the twelfth-century English Benedictine historian William of Malmesbury reworked the story in his *Gesta Regum Anglorum* (*Deeds of the Kings of England*) that a full account was put together [*Doc. 13*]. While earlier versions of the legend simply accepted Gerbert's necromancy as given, providing no explanation of how he acquired this knowledge, William supplied answers to such questions. He was the first writer to link Gerbert's necromancy explicitly with his high learning. According to William, Gerbert travelled to Spain to acquire exotic forbidden knowledge from a Saracen master, who taught him all the arts, both licit and illicit. This is interesting, not only because it establishes a clear link between magical knowledge and the Iberian Peninsula, but also because it accorded with Gerbert's biography as recorded by his pupil, Richer de Saint Remy. Richer wrote that Gerbert left the monastery of Saint Geraud in Aurillac as a young scholar, to expand his education in the arts of the ***quadrivium*** (see Chapter 3) at the monastery of Santa Maria de Ripoll, near Barcelona, where he stayed for two years (Richer de Saint-Remi, ed. and trans. Lake, 2011: 62–6). By the twelfth century it was believed that, while in Spain, Gerbert became acquainted with the latest Arab mathematical developments; and that he then introduced the abacus and the astrolabe into northern Europe (as well as creating mechanical water clocks, amongst other marvels). William of Malmesbury additionally claims that Gerbert learnt astrology, **augury** and necromancy from his Saracen master, and used this expertise to escape after stealing his master's prized volume on the magical arts and seducing his daughter. While fleeing, he first resorted to his astrological knowledge to read the movements of his pursuer in the night sky and thus evade him. Upon reaching the seashore, however, Gerbert found himself at an impasse and summoned a demon to aid him. In a tradition echoing the story of Theophilus and his pact with the devil, Gerbert entered into a pact with 'his' demon in order to assure his safe return to France. Once safe, he continued making use of this pact and devised a talking head which enabled him to prophesy the future. As in other versions of the legend, Gerbert used this talking head to advance his political career within the Church, was deceived by the demon and had his body posthumously dismembered as evidence of his deathbed repentance (William of Malmesbury, ed. and trans. R. A. B. Mynors *et al.*, 1998: 278–95).

There are several important elements in William's account of Gerbert. The first is his emphasis on Gerbert's mathematical expertise, which is linked to the period of time he spent learning the arts of the *quadrivium* in Spain. This explains both where and how Gerbert became a necromancer. Furthermore,

Quadrivium: Four of the seven classical Liberal Arts; this term was applied to the 'scientific' arts of Geometry, Mathematics, Music and Astronomy/Astrology.

Augury: practice of divining the future from the behaviour and entrails of birds and animals.

he adds both astrology and augury to the list of Gerbert's dangerous arts. The question is why William includes this expanded account in his text. Like John of Salisbury in his *Policraticus*, William is reflecting the problems posed to traditional Christian scholarship by new and sophisticated sciences of Arab provenance. He was writing as the international scholars previously discussed were translating astronomical tables, and other astrological materials. One of these scholars, Petrus Alfonsi, may have acted as a physician for Henry I; and the twelfth-century horoscopes discussed in Chapter 1 suggest that there were astrologers very close to the English court.

That William was acquainted with developments in astrology is evident in his description of Gerbert's knowledge. William claims that Gerbert surpassed 'Ptolemy in knowledge of the astrolabe, Alhandreus in that of the relative positions of the stars, and Julius Firmicus in judicial astrology' (William of Malmesbury, ed. and trans. R. A. B. Mynors, *et al.*, 1998: 280). Julius Firmicus Maternus's late-classical work had long been available to scholars, although it did not make it possible to draw up horoscopes to forecast future events (**judicial astrology**). However, William's reference to the newly available works of Ptolemy and Alhandreus indicates that he was familiar with developments in France, the Empire and Spain. Thus, William seems to be worried by the same developments as John of Salisbury. By associating these practices with a necromantic pope, William emphasises the slippery slope awaiting anyone who engages with these practices. But he does not condemn the astrologer per se, and thus shows the ambiguous attitudes towards such practices which characterised twelfth-century writers. William does not explicitly debate the issue, but by applying the expertise of a twelfth-century astrologer to his description of Gerbert the necromancer, he adds to the voices expressing concern about links between the new Arabic astrological knowledge and illicit magical practices. As for Gerbert's Black Legend, other twelfth-century writers, including Walter Map in his *De nugis curialium* (*Courtiers' Trifles*), added to the tale (Walter Map, 1983: 351–63). However, it was William's version of the story that was incorporated into Vincent of Beauvais's *Speculum historiale* (*Mirror of History*). This popular thirteenth-century world-history, written with royal patronage, survives in more than 100 medieval manuscripts and was very influential in the medieval period (Boudet, 2006: 270–1).

As this chapter has shown, the problem of whether monks and clerics knowingly practised magic is not one which can be easily answered. This is partly because the definition of magic as practices involving recourse to the power of demons, whilst apparently clear, actually left much to be decided. The intentions of the practitioner, and his or her trustworthiness, were major factors. However, they could not be decisive, since it was established that demons were skilled in deluding humans, and they could conceal their

Judicial astrology: refers to the practice of making judgments by casting horoscopes, including elections and interrogations. This was the subject of much discussion, due to possible clashes with the doctrine of free will.

intervention in various forms of divination and enquiry into future events. Even deciding what was 'natural', in order to separate this category at least from the results of demonic activity, was not simple at a time when the exact forms and powers of the natural were still the subjects of much exploration and argument. Sophisticated authors and observers of their own society did not fall into the trap of simply equating all new knowledge of the natural world with suspect magic; yet they were also aware that professional astrologers and diviners were offering their skills and services to highly placed members of secular and clerical society. When even a pope could be led into the hands of a demon by a combination of ambition and unbridled enquiry into exotic knowledge, the world of learning (the territory of the clergy) was a dangerous place indeed. What this chapter has shown is that, even within the Church itself, staying with traditional practices relating to the interaction of the human individual and the surrounding environment could become problematic. As knowledge of the natural world, its structures and its forms grew at an unprecedented rate, and as theology and law became much more precise in their classifications and judgments, so such traditions as the performance of ritual charms and observation of Egyptian Days came to be condemned as superstitious and smacking of heretical magic. What then could be the fate of the new, 'Saracen' ideas and practices, even if they fitted within the traditional, Roman, framework of the *quadrivium*, or advanced fields of scholarly study?

3

The universities

MAGIC AND THE TWELFTH-CENTURY RENAISSANCE

The previous two chapters have shown that magic, in various forms, fulfilled major functions in the centres of political and religious power in medieval Europe. This chapter looks specifically at learned magic, and at its growth within the context of the great expansion of formal and higher education from the twelfth century onwards. This expansion is closely connected to the growth of literacy, record-keeping and bureaucracy that accompanied the rise of centralised states in Europe during the same period, and which was even further advanced within the Church. Also important was the rapid rise in the size and number of towns, itself accompanied by an impressive expansion in banking, trade and the provision of professional services. Society was changing rapidly, in ways which opened up new careers for those with the means and education to enter them. At such a time, skills and knowledge which made it possible to seek to know the future – or even to control it – were both in high demand and becoming more sophisticated in the scientific and theological disciplines upon which they drew. Moreover, since attempting to harness and use supernatural powers, whether angelic or demonic in nature, required preparation of a highly specific and learned sort, it is easy to see why studying forms of learned magic was attractive to university students (and masters). By the second half of the thirteenth century various magical ideas and texts were included in the list of forbidden studies issued by the Paris authorities in an attempt to keep the academic body free from the infections of heresy and demonic temptation [*Doc. 33*] (Peters, 1978: 88–91).

At a practical level, it is easy to see why knowledge of the times when storms and tempests were likely to arrive was of considerable interest to those engaged in military activities, international trade and agriculture. Developments in astrology and mathematics made it possible for specialists to issue forecasts tailored to specific dates and regions, for those who could afford such services. For diplomats engaged in negotiations, or bankers considering requests for loans, analyses of the personalities and dependability of those with whom they were dealing were of obvious value, if they could be trusted. The growing field of what was known as **physiognomy**, and was claimed to have been first established by Aristotle, offered interpretations of individuals which could answer such questions. These were based upon physical characteristics, complexion and facial features. Such knowledge was highly attractive, as is shown by the rapid spread of popularisations and translations in the later Middle Ages (Pseudo-Aristotle, *Secretum secretorum* (*Secret of Secrets*), ed. Manzalaoui, 1977).

> **Physiognomy:** divination by means of the physical features of an individual.

This was also a time when rising populations, new technology and new wealth were making it possible for Europeans to expand their own frontiers and to come into closer contact with the wider world. Most notorious of such movements is the Crusades, which included not only the well-known expeditions and territorial conquests in the Middle East but also the subjugation of large regions to the north and east of the European heartland. The map of the known world became both larger and much more detailed, and there was considerable interest in the natural phenomena which it contained. Encyclopaedias of such knowledge, in the form of bestiaries, lapidaries and herbals, grew both in numbers and in contents, and gave considerable space to the 'wonders' which the world contained, and to the things which could be achieved by those who could obtain the relevant substances and who knew how to use them.

In all these fields, large amounts of new knowledge became available during what is known as the Renaissance of the twelfth century; and this knowledge continued to be added to, and to be refined and deepened, until the end of the Middle Ages. Indeed, it laid the foundations for key areas of the better-known Renaissance of the early-modern period. But the sudden opening up of large fields of knowledge is challenging, and this is especially the case when the knowledge in question offers (or threatens) to make possible things which were previously impossible. None of this new knowledge challenged the fundamental concept that the world was created by God exactly as described in the Bible. However since much of it, such as the newly translated works of the great philosopher Aristotle, was of non-Christian origin, considerable adjustments were required. Some of it, whether explicitly magical or not, was so challenging that it took considerable study before its implications could be agreed and evaluated. For all of these processes, the great expansion of cathedral schools and universities, which took place within the institutional and intellectual structures of the Church, was crucial. The universities developed formal programmes of study in areas approved by society and the Church, and only those who succeeded in passing the examinations in the requisite subjects could acquire the coveted licences to teach or to practise in certain key professional fields.

The subjects of study in the universities were carefully defined, and were under scrutiny from intellectuals and from senior members of the Church hierarchy, both locally based and in the papal court. Similarly careful agreement and scrutiny went into the definition of what made up each programme of study, and what were the core, compulsory texts which students should study. The intellectual world of the medieval universities was founded upon authoritative texts, which made both their selection for the syllabus and their interpretation for students matters of considerable importance. The fundamental model for the organisation and acquisition of knowledge was that of the late Roman Empire. Central to this model was the division of formal knowledge into the Seven Liberal Arts. These were: Grammar, Rhetoric, Dialectic, Mathematics, Geometry, Music and Astronomy/Astrology. However, not all of these were equally valued in medieval, Christian Europe, and the body of knowledge available for some was very much smaller than for others. In a society where study of the Bible was the most highly valued intellectual activity, and where Latin was the universal language of formal religion and scholarship, the first three of the Liberal Arts had a predominant position. These were the subjects which provided the training for, and induction into, the highly valued field of Theology.

However, it was accepted that study of God's creation was also of value, if undertaken within the parameters established by theologians. Such study was not an entirely separate field, but could support the great effort to deepen understanding of the works of God. This 'natural philosophy' was an area which saw enormous expansion as the works of Aristotle on the natural world became available, together with many more recent studies in fields such as optics and astrology by Arab philosophers and scientists. Geometry and mathematics were crucial for the understanding and assimilation of these, and the study of the four 'scientific' subjects, known as the *quadrivium*, grew rapidly (Wagner, 1986). This expansion was not planned, and was partly dictated by the chance of which books became available at any one time, which led to the growth of tension between the new works and their supporters on the one hand and the established model of valuable knowledge on the other. For the purposes of this book, it is important to note that in medieval Europe, just as in the classical world and the Arab Empire, magic did not constitute an organised or unified field of knowledge. Moreover, the medieval terms translatable as 'magic' carried negative associations, which meant that to designate any text or subject as magical was to identify it as illicit. Thus the place of learned magic in the rapidly expanding world of medieval scholarship is a complex subject. It is of some comfort to know that this was also the case in the medieval period, and that a series of leading scholars, especially those with some responsibility for higher education, attempted to provide guides on this tricky issue. The difficulty of the problem can be judged from the fact that almost all their attempted solutions differed from one another, and none gained overall acceptance. By the end of the thirteenth century a more empirical solution, that of scrutinising the learned works in circulation, and identifying those which were undesirable or dangerous, was adopted. However, this is still not entirely helpful for the history of magic, since clear distinctions between that which was magical and that which was heretical were not needed in a list of banned propositions and texts. It is therefore important to give some description of the attempts made to classify and define magic.

CLASSIFICATIONS OF MAGIC

Formal discussions of magic in the medieval West depended heavily upon that universal resource, the seventh-century survey of available knowledge compiled by Isidore of Seville. His detailed typology of magic, based partly upon classical developments, was used by twelfth-century authors such as Gratian and John of Salisbury, as has been seen. His *Etymologies* presented an authoritative list of magical practices and their constituent parts, treated as forms of forbidden knowledge, but divided amongst various categories. Twelfth-century authors expanded on descriptions and classifications of magic within wider outlines of human knowledge, based upon the framework of the Liberal Arts. The inclusion of descriptions of astronomy/astrology is thus predictable, for it had been traditionally regarded as part of the *quadrivium*. What is surprising is that numerous authors openly associated the art of astronomy/astrology with readings of the future – and that they did not necessarily condemn this. Still more surprising is that some such attempts to classify knowledge included largely forbidden forms of magical art, like necromancy. This does not mean that they approved of it, for they certainly did not; but what is striking is that they regarded it as real, and as an area of learned (if dangerous and destructive) enquiry.

Astrology/astronomy: in the medieval period these terms were used interchangeably to describe the art of observing the celestial bodies, and of using such observations for calculating and predicting natural phenomena and events affecting human lives.

The art of **astrology/astronomy** was thus accorded an important place within descriptions of the Liberal Arts even though there was difficulty in classifying some of its more dubious forms. A twelfth-century preface to Adelard of Bath's astrological translations seeks to relate them to a general discussion of the Liberal Arts. It comes to the highly unorthodox conclusion that the study of astronomy/astrology, or *astronodia*, as it refers to it, must constitute the 'goal of all knowledge' (Burnett, 1987: 136–8). According to this preface, *astronodia* incorporated both *astrologia* and *astronomia*. However, according to this treatise, also known as the *Ergaphalau* (sometimes attributed to Adelard of Bath), the art of *astronomia* in itself allows for readings of the past, the present and the future, through the charting of the stars (Burnett, 1987, 143–4). Moreover, *astronomia* can be divided into two branches: one which provides the practitioner with prophetic knowledge of things that cannot be altered; and another which permits the manipulation of future events through foreknowledge. Both claims to prophetic knowledge and assertions of the power to alter future events are representative of what led to serious criticisms of astrology by contemporary writers like John of Salisbury.

An expert on astrology in various forms was Petrus Alfonsi, a converted Jew of Spanish origin, who may have visited the court of Henry I and was certainly active in France in the first decades of the twelfth century. He wrote on the Liberal Arts, as they were studied in northern Europe, from the point of view of an interested observer. What is surprising is that, as well as demonstrating his belief in the importance of the science of the stars, he included references to the 'art' of necromancy within his wider view of the Liberal Arts. In his *Disciplina clericalis* (*Instructive Stories for Clerks*), a moralising text, he claims the existence of six fixed disciplines: dialectic, arithmetic, geometry, medicine, music and astronomy, all of which belonged to the traditional programme of study (Petrus Alfonsi, ed. and trans. E. Hermes and P. Quarrie, 1977). The inclusion of astronomy within this group of six fixed arts is not surprising; Alfonsi had argued its importance in his *Epistola ad peripateticos Franciae* (*Letter to the Students of France*), encouraging them to take up the study of astrology/astronomy above all other arts (Tolan, 1993: 163–80). He acknowledged the arguments of Christian scholars such as John of Salisbury, who claimed that it contravened Christian doctrine. However, for Alfonsi such attitudes were frivolous and inept; for him, astronomy/astrology was a vital element in the study and understanding of natural philosophy. When discussing the identity of the seventh and last liberal art in his *Disciplina*, he is also controversial. According to him there is disagreement among the philosophers on what this art should be: for the philosophers who admit the possibility of foretelling the future, the seventh art is necromancy; for those who do not believe in this, it is philosophy; and for those who do not care for philosophy then it is grammar (Petrus Alfonsi, ed. and trans. E. Hermes, 1977: 114–15). This unconventional portrayal of the arts, due perhaps to Alfonsi's alien culture, is striking for its bold inclusion of necromancy among the traditional Liberal Arts, thus aligning it with ideas of respectable learning and specialisation. That such a claim should be addressed to students perhaps illustrates the sort of material against which John of Salisbury was arguing.

This raises the issue of what Petrus Alfonsi understood by necromancy, and valuable evidence for this is given in a passage of his *Dialogi contra Iudei* (*Dialogues Against the Jews*) (Petrus Alfonsi, trans. I. M. Resnick, 2006).

Through a dialogue between his past Jewish self – Moses – and his present Christian self – Petrus, the *Dialogi* portray Alfonsi's arguments on what he perceives as the superiority of Christianity in comparison to contemporary Judaism and Islam. When discussing the existence of evil and the devil, Moses asks Petrus for proof of the existence of devils such as Haroth and Maroth. As a part of his reply, Petrus offers a description of the art of necromancy. According to him, necromancy is divided into nine parts, four of which are related to the four natural elements – water, earth, air and fire – and what operates in them naturally. The remaining five, however, deal with what can be affected by the invocation of evil spirits or devils (Petrus Alfonsi, trans. I.M. Resnick, 2006: 221). Thus for Alfonsi, the art of necromancy included not only the study of the natural world itself, but also the supernatural powers which could be forced or persuaded to operate upon it. In other words, both a large part of 'science' or natural philosophy and actual trafficking with demons.

An equally telling attempt to analyse and classify magic appears from a rather opposite point of view in Hugh of St Victor's *Didascalicon* (*On the Study of Reading*), written in the late 1120s [*Doc. 14*] (Hugh of St Victor, trans. J. Taylor, 1991). Contrary to the opinions of scholars like Petrus Alfonsi and the anonymous author of the *Ergaphalau*, Hugh of St Victor offers a rather grim picture of the magical arts, while still placing them within the context of high learning. For him, magic cannot be counted as a 'philosophical system' because it is based upon a false creed; its practice can lead people away from God and persuade them to fall into idolatry. Equally seriously, it undermines virtuous behaviour and leads the minds of those who pursue it into every type of crime and wickedness. Its practice is therefore to be strongly discouraged. Hugh of St Victor identified five types of magic: divination, astrology, **sortilegia**, *maleficia* and *praestigia*. Following classical writers as well as Isidore, he asserts that divination, or *mantike*, can be divided further into five constituent parts: **geomancy**, or divination by means of the earth; hydromancy, or divination by means of water; aeromancy, divination by air; pyromancy, divination by fire; and necromancy, or divination by means of the dead. This latter art takes place through the sacrifice of human blood, which attracts the thirst of demons and causes them great pleasure. Futile *mathematica*, or astrology, has three divisions, the first of which is *aruspicina*, the interpretation of internal organs in animals, portents and lightning. The interpretation of the movements and flight of birds is part of *auguria*; whilst the art of casting horoscopes, looking for people's destinies in the stars, is part of *horoscopia*. *Sortilegia*, or the **casting of lots**, is practised by those who use guess work or intuition to discover the future. Acts of harmful magic, or *maleficia*, have the capacity to accomplish dreadful results by means of demonic incantations or magical ligatures. Finally,

---

Sortilegia: a complex term, whose meaning shifted across the medieval period. In early texts, it refers most frequently to casting of lots, especially by means of random selection of a biblical text, which was then interpreted for guidance. This was known as the *sortes sanctorum*, or lots of the saints, and until the eleventh century was widely accepted. By the thirteenth century theologians classified *sortilegia* with negative and harmful forms of magic, accusing practitioners of superstition and misuse of religious texts for purposes of fortune-telling. It thus took on the additional meaning of 'sorcery'.

Geomancy: divination by means of the earth. By the high Middle Ages the term also applied to a complex method, drawn from Arabic sources, of generating sets of dots, each arranged in one of 16 patterns, and interpreting them by astrological techniques.

Lot-casting: see Sortilegia.

conjuring tricks and illusions, or *praestigia*, involve demonic deception when a demon plays games with the human senses via fantasies and hallucinations which give the appearance of transforming one thing into another. The dangers of such practices are very clear.

ASTROLOGY AND THE ASTROLABE

Among the most popular scientific innovations of the high Middle Ages was the astrolabe. Of varying sizes and portable, it allowed the astronomer/astrologer to calculate with relative ease the positions of the stars for various latitudes at a required time, thus rendering complicated and highly inaccurate astrological tables redundant. It made the casting of horoscopes a much easier task and was very popular amongst scholars during the twelfth century, when a range of treatises on the astrolabe were both translated and composed by Latin scholars [*Doc. 15*] (North, 1989: 211–20). These works were important, because the astrolabe is a complex instrument, and cannot be effectively used without instruction. The earliest original Latin treatises on the astrolabe can be associated with scholars active in the tenth and eleventh centuries, and with Gerbert of Aurillac, Llobet de Barcelona and Hermann le Boiteux in particular. These early treatises described how to build an astrolabe, or how to use it; but in general they were confusing texts and difficult to use. With the new wave of translations from Arabic in the twelfth century this problem was partly solved, and the contributions of scholars such as Adelard of Bath and Raymond de Marseille added further knowledge. A compilation of various treatises, falsely attributed to the eighth-century Jewish astrologer Mashallah, was very popular in university circles from the thirteenth century onwards (Boudet, 2006: 51).

The use of the astrolabe allowed for a wider practice of astrology in the central Middle Ages. It was now possible to chart planetary movements more easily, and astrologers were no longer limited to interpretations based solely on the movements of the sun or the moon. Nevertheless, having an astrolabe was not enough, as astrologers also needed to know the rules for astrological judgments if they wanted to cast a horoscope. Throughout the twelfth and thirteenth centuries a great number of astronomical and astrological treatises were translated into Latin, partly solving this problem. The most important, such as the *Quadripartitum* (*Four Books*) and the *Centiloquium* (*Hundred Sayings*) attributed to Ptolemy, the *Isagoge minor* (*Short Introduction*) by Abu Mashar and several treatises by Mashallah, explained the theory behind different astronomical operations (Wedel, 1920). Other texts concentrated on the rules and principles behind judicial astrology, covering issues like **elections** and **interrogations**. A popular example of this is the *Liber temporum*

Elections: astrological calculations relating to the identification of favourable moments for starting an enterprise. May simply involve studying the planetary positions at a chosen time, or may relate these to aspects of the enquirer's natal chart.

Interrogations: in astrology, interrogations provided answers to precise questions, particularly whether a specified thing would or would not happen or succeed. They used examinations of planetary positions at the time the question was asked.

(*Book of Times*) by Sahl ibn Bishir, a Jewish astrologer from the first half of the ninth century, which survives in an impressive total of 43 medieval manuscripts (Boudet, 2006: 54).

The most renowned astronomical treatise, which became the preferred manual on the subject in medieval universities, was the *Liber introductorius* (*Introduction*) by Alcabitius, a tenth-century Arab astrologer active in the court of the emir Sayf ad-Dawla. The *Liber introductorius* was translated by the celebrated translator, John of Seville, in the 1130s and is divided into five parts. The first and most basic deals with the division of the zodiac into twelve signs, the element (fire, air, water or earth) to which they relate, their gender, and their diurnal or nocturnal aspect. The work goes on to explain their temporal value, which depends upon the passage of the sun through each one of them during the year. He also discusses the nature of the seven planets (which included the sun and moon). More advanced topics are: the significance of the planets when in different positions in the zodiac; their dignities and houses (that is, the signs in which they have special power); and the degrees or angles of their astronomical relationship to one another (Boudet, 2006: 57–64). All of these are important issues in astrological interpretation. It is for the calculation of planetary movements, and of their positions in the different astrological houses throughout the year, that it is necessary to consult an astrolabe, if not complex sets of tables.

By the thirteenth century, both historical records and surviving treatises show that there were learned individuals in western Europe capable of drawing up complex astrological charts, and using them as the basis for offering predictions and interpretations on a range of questions. The *Isagoge in astrologiam* (*Introduction to Astrology*), by Pseudo John of Seville explains the casting of **nativities**, **revolutions**, elections and interrogations. Nativities are primarily horoscopes cast for the time of birth of an individual, while revolutions relate to the return of the sun to the point of the zodiac it occupied on an initial given moment (for instance, the day of a wedding). Elections relate to the identification of favourable moments for starting an enterprise; and interrogations provide answers to precise questions. Further information on elections and interrogations comes especially in the *De judiciis astrorum* (*On the Judgements of the Stars*) by Hali Abenragel and in the *Liber introductorius ad judicia stellarum* (*Introduction to the Judgements of the Stars*) by Guido Bonatti. Astrologers able to offer such skills could achieve considerable fame and reputation, as Bonatti's own career demonstrates (see Chapter 1). Such techniques were the preserve of a small intellectual elite, but evidence of their work survives, for instance, in the Anglo-Norman political horoscopes discussed in Chapter 1 [*Doc.* 7]. We also have illustrative examples, such as the horoscope for a child born in 1141 found in the *Liber judiciorum* by Raymond of Marseilles. That astrological predictions were taken seriously is

---

Nativities: in astrology, nativities were primarily horoscopes cast for the day and time of birth of an individual.

Revolutions: in astrology, revolutions related to the return of the sun to the point of the zodiac it occupied at a chosen starting point (for instance, the day of a wedding).

shown by the anxiety caused in 1186 by the concentration of all the planets in Libra, as recorded by chroniclers across Europe. Not many of the worrying predictions were realised, although the Chronicle of Roger of Howden demonstrates the level of concern in England [*Doc. 3*].

ASTRAL AND IMAGE MAGIC: THE BASES OF RITUAL MAGIC

Despite the negative views of some commentators, most astrologers emphasised that they were not magicians, since their predictions were based purely upon interpreting the movements of the planets. The powers which brought about the predicted effects were those vested by God in the cosmic entities which He had created. There was no real doubt that the planetary bodies emanated rays which affected at least the material aspects of earthly life, including the human body. This scientific belief underlay what is commonly known as **astral magic**, in which operators ventured to harness and exploit the powers of the stars. The basic theory of astral magic appears in the influential treatise *De radiis stellarum* (*On the Rays of the Stars*) by the ninth-century Arab astrologer al-Kindi (Adamson, 2007: 181–205; Weill-Parot, 2002: 155–74). Translated into Latin sometime before 1259, this work has been called the 'most important treatise of theoretical magic in the history of the medieval West' (Boudet, 2006: 130). The 'stellar rays' emitted by celestial bodies are claimed to play a central role in maintaining the harmonious working of the cosmos itself. Within this, all sublunary motion, whether in individual bodies or broader natural processes, is driven and acted upon by stellar rays. Their exact make-up, force and ultimate effects depend upon the disposition of the heavens – but could also be affected by humans equipped with the necessary knowledge. This was the theoretical foundation for image magic. Powers and forces operating in the layers of air between the earth and the moon (and beyond) were believed to be intrinsically connected to earthly forms which shared part of their nature. Thus sounds, images, gestures, smoke and vapours could be created, capable of producing their own rays, which could draw upon, and subtly affect, the power vested in the original, celestial form. The manipulation of such rays through an appropriate form, or 'image', constituted a powerful magical operation, further mediated through the spoken word. This theory may appear extreme; but it was incorporated into mainstream scholastic philosophy by Albertus Magnus. His *Speculum astronomiae* (*Mirror of Astronomy*) provided legitimacy for the theory underpinning image magic (Zambelli, 1992). The acceptance that the power behind image magic was based upon the workings of the universe was crucial, since it provided evidence that the performance of

Astral magic: form of magic aiming to harness the occult powers of the celestial bodies.

incantations, suffumigations and ritual gestures was not intended to summon demons or to harness their powers.

A practical application of al-Kindi's theory is provided in the *De sigillis* (*On Seals*) (c.1301), a text attributed until recently to the Catalan astrologer and physician, Arnald of Villanova (c.1240–1311). This work instructs on the production of magical talismans (Skemer, 2006: 132; Ziegler, 1998: 245–50). It includes detailed instructions, which must be followed at the correct astrological times, and lists appropriate materials, invocations and prayers. Thus, for producing a seal linked to the power of Libra, for example, the practitioner starts by taking pure gold. This is melted and cast, to produce a round seal. The operator should utter a specified prayer and recite a particular psalm. This must be done at the appropriate astrological time; in this case, while the sun is entering Libra, and after the moon has been in Capricorn or Aquarius. On one side of the seal a human figure holding scales must be engraved, also at the correct astrological moment. The edges and the other side of the seal must also be engraved. If correctly prepared, according to Pseudo-Arnald, this seal has enormous power. It will protect against demonic attack or sudden death. It will make its wearer gentle, compassionate, wise, decent and full of good advice. It can provide material gains, in the form of profits in business affairs. It has medical benefits, protecting against illnesses of the blood and against kidney pains. Finally, it has the power to repel acts of harmful magic and to protect the household from bewitchments. For complete effectiveness, appropriate piety must be shown, so that whoever wears it will sail safely upon the sea, provided that frequent prayers for God's mercy are uttered; when asking for God's forgiveness of one's sins, then it must be worn with reverence and fear of God (Weill-Parot, 2002: 480–2; Maxwell-Stuart, 2005: 100–3).

Another, and much less high-minded, example of image magic can be found in the *Liber lune* (*Book of the Moon*), a text of Arabic origin attributed to Hermes Trismegistus. This work describes magical effects such as the binding of someone's tongue, the twisting of their limbs, or even the destruction of an entire region. The desired effect is to be produced through engraving images relating to the lunar mansions, and doing so under specified circumstances. Thus, precise instructions are given as to the time of the day, the material to be employed, and the recitation of names related to particular astrological spirits or times. Given the presence of these ritualistic elements, it is possible to argue that a text such as this belongs to the category of ritual magic, that is, magic intended to harness the powers of spirits (whether angelic or demonic). However, the *Liber lune* is found in manuscripts which also include works on natural philosophy, medicine, astrology, **alchemy** and magical theory. These include the work by al-Kindi discussed in the previous paragraph and the *Speculum astronomiae* by Albertus Magnus (Klaassen, in

Alchemy: a branch of philosophical study, built on the combination of Greek philosophy with Arab and older forms of science. A key aim was to transform both matter and human beings into purer forms, freed from the flux and corruption of the sublunary world.

Fanger, 1998: 11–13). Thus medieval readers of the treatise seem to have grouped it with texts of astrology and science rather than with overt works of ritual magic.

THE *ARS NOTORIA*

The *Ars Notoria*, a text on ritual magic which survives in at least fifty manuscripts, was particularly popular among university students, although the large number of surviving copies suggests that it was more widely read than many magical works. Written under the alleged authority of Solomon, it has its origins in twelfth-century monastic contexts and promises the acquisition of advanced academic learning through the ritual use of prayers and figures (or diagrams). It is these which give the work its name, since they are called *notae*. Users were promised that their memory, eloquence, understanding and perseverance would be strengthened, and that they would gain complete knowledge of the **Liberal Arts** [*Doc. 16*] (Fanger, 1998: 216). For university students this effectively meant their entire degree syllabus, and more. This would be accomplished through the intercession of angels and the Holy Spirit, following the performance of a complex series of rites involving purifications, confessions, orations and invocations, together with meditation upon the relevant images or *notae*.

Liberal Arts: the basis of Classical and medieval education, made up of the *Trivium* (grammar, rhetoric and logic) and the *Quadrivium* (arithmetic, geometry, music and astronomy).

Each image related to a different art within the university syllabus, and the complete set was organised in three sections, accompanied by text (Fanger, 1998: 219–22). The first section begins with what are called Generals – that is, the faculties needed to embark on the specialised knowledge of the Liberal Arts themselves. These Generals are memory, eloquence, understanding and perseverance. Next come the Specials, or introductions to the seven Liberal Arts together with prayers to ensure knowledge of each. The second section describes the rituals which accompany the prayers of the Specials, as well as additional comments. The prayers are arranged in order, starting with the *trivium* and progressing to the *quadrivium*, then culminating with philosophy and theology. Precise instructions are given at the beginning of each prayer as to the *nota* needed to secure the effectiveness of the ritual. The third section, titled 'Ars Nova' (*The New Art*) in the text, includes ten prayers which are meant to rectify any problems the practitioner may have had with the rituals in parts I and II. Despite its evident ritualistic elements, there is no evidence of immediate attempts to proscribe the *Ars Notoria*. Surviving manuscript copies indicate that it was included in monastic libraries (e.g. Oxford, Bodleian Library, Bodley 951), and it was not categorised with necromantic texts. This is perhaps because its only danger was to the practitioner's own soul. However, its use of *verba ignota*, or names and terms in a mixture of

Greek, Hebrew, Chaldean and Arabic, led to problems. These were identified by some later commentators as the names of demons, and ultimately led to the work's condemnation.

THE *SWORN BOOK OF HONORIUS*

Related to the *Ars Notoria*, but presenting itself overtly as a work of ritual magic, is the *Sworn Book* or *Sacred Book* (*Liber iuratus sive sacer*). The name of the supposed author comes from the opening section of the work, as it is given in the oldest surviving copies, two fourteenth-century manuscripts in the British Library (Mss Sloane 313 and Sloane 3854). This states that the author of the book is Honorius, son of Euclid, and a scholar of Thebes – a claim which is not to be taken seriously, since the text is clearly medieval. At least an early version of it may have been circulating amongst students in Paris in the thirteenth century, since the Bishop of Paris, the theologian William of Auvergne, condemned a *Sacred Book* as a work of magic; though whether this was the same text that was copied a century later cannot now be certain (Mathiesen, in Fanger, 1998: 143–62). The learned bishop certainly saw the work he mentioned as highly dangerous, and condemned it together with texts containing idolatrous images or *notae*, as well as associating it with forms of learned magic which claimed to be the work of the biblical King Solomon (Thorndike, 1929: vol. 2, 279–80). Nevertheless, the *Sworn Book* itself demonstrates just as much hostility to the Church establishment as theologians like William of Auvergne were expressing towards ritual magic. This contest will be discussed in more detail in a later chapter; for the moment, the most important point is that magicians and senior churchmen were expressing open hostility towards one another, whilst each side was also well informed about the activities of the other.

Does the *Sworn Book* contain magic of a type which would disturb Church leaders? The answer is very definitely that it does, whilst at the same time protesting that magicians are actually more virtuous than orthodox churchmen, due to the exigencies of their 'art'. Still more worrying for all those in positions of power and responsibility would be the fact that it provides evidence of a growing, secret, organisation of magicians, sworn to spread and to protect their art. This evidence comes in the Prologue, and follows an account of how the *Sworn Book* itself was created to preserve magic from attempted destruction by the pope, the cardinals and the bishops. Scandalously, the argument made is that the leaders of the church have been deceived by demons, as part of a plot on the part of the devil to destroy something which could be of great benefit to humanity (magic). As the author points out, ritual magic involved a human supposedly being able to bind and command a spirit; and for this to be possible, the human would have to be in a state of purity. How could such an art, and its masters, be evil? Just how high the stakes were is shown by the accusation which the Church levied against magicians, which is also reported in the *Sworn Book*. This was that magicians, knowingly or unknowingly, offered worship to demons, and thus to the devil himself. Even worse, their illusions led others into error, and thus to damnation. The *Sworn Book* claims that it was the deluded severity of this attack which forced magicians to go into hiding, with the *Sworn Book* itself as the key to their art and the badge of their membership of the new, sworn brotherhood of practitioners (women are explicitly excluded, and are never to be allowed to see the book). The book itself is so precious that no practitioner should give copies to more than three others, and no copy can ever be destroyed. If a dying master has no successor then he must literally take his copy to the grave.

A list of chapters contained in the complete *Sworn Book* follows the Prologue. There are ninety-two in the list, although the last two are explicitly stated to be kept back, since they provide instructions on how to raise the dead and how to create animals from the earth. These were indeed the worst and most forbidden forms of magic; but in fact they are not the only missing chapters in the text as it survives. The full list of chapters promises knowledge of the great names of God; power over angels and spirits; knowledge of all creation (including the planets, the stars, purgatory and hell itself); knowledge of past, present and future; power over the weather; power over health and sickness; command of great wealth; the ability to deceive other humans in a range of ways. It will be noticed that the list descends rather sharply from the spiritually elevated to the overtly material, and even to the corrupt, since power over others is of all types. After such promises, it is either a disappointment or a relief to find that the surviving text of the main part of the book offers just two, very complex, complete rituals. These are very effective samples of the magician's art, since both combine ritual practices such as drawing magical shapes, creating seals and images and reciting secret names and invocations, with the performance of daily masses and the recitation of prayers and hymns. The longest would require a full twenty-eight days to perform, and promises that the successful practitioner would achieve an actual vision of God in glory, surrounded by the nine orders of angels and all the blessed spirits (Mathiesen, in Fanger, 1998: 150–5). This may seem dangerous only to the magician himself; but its theological implications were enormous. Moreover, the other ritual promises command over spirits, some explicitly destructive, and the acquisition of enormous powers. The temptation of such knowledge is very clear, especially at a time when it fitted closely both with religion and with the ever-expanding study of the earth and the cosmos.

ALCHEMY

Alchemy was one of the last of the magical arts to arrive in medieval Europe, and remained one of the least known. This was partly because it made even heavier demands on its followers than did ritual magic. Would-be alchemists had to deal both with often baffling texts and heavy expenditure on laboratories, assistants and equipment (Sherwood Taylor, 1976: 15–23, 82–92). In theory this was amongst the most exciting of all the new areas of learning, since it offered nothing less than the ability to transform one form of matter into another, and even to change one's own physical and spiritual state [*Doc. 17*]. This claim rested upon a whole theoretical model of matter, nature, and the forces which could produce new material appearances. It was crucial that no claim was made to change matter itself, since that would involve the power of miracles, something reserved only for God. But with that reservation, it was possible for alchemists to argue successfully that their 'experiments' did not trespass into forbidden territory. The potential power opened up by this 'art' made it attractive to many in the newly emerging universities, even though it never gained a formal place in the curriculum.

Evidence of the late arrival of alchemy is that the first known Latin translation of an alchemical text was made in the middle of the twelfth century, and by the early thirteenth century only a handful had been added. This was tiny in relation both to the work going into astrological studies at the same time and to the range of alchemical works available in Arabic by c.1200. Part of the explanation is probably that, unlike astrology, alchemy was not a necessary part of medieval medicine; thus it never enjoyed the same level of popularity and demand. On the other hand, it remained the most erudite of all the forms of learned magic. Its theological aspects were both challenging and complex, since they demanded knowledge of issues such as the nature of matter and, by extension, the nature of the Creation. Writers of alchemical treatises from the thirteenth century on also claimed that the practice of alchemy involved a highly demanding form of physical and spiritual discipline. In this view alchemists were not only experimenters seeking to understand the most challenging aspects of natural philosophy but also the possessors of unique insights into the mysteries of creation. It is hardly surprising that such claims evoked a mixed reaction, and that the treatises were issued under the names of safely dead philosophers and theologians. This helped increase interest in the treatises in their own time – but it has had the effect of making it almost impossible to be definite on the authorship of many alchemical works, and has added to the complexity of an already difficult subject.

One of the things which make the history of medieval alchemy so obscure is that it did not have a place within the Liberal Arts. This, together with its philosophical complexity and its separation from medical study as well as from theology, meant that although alchemical works continued to appear through the thirteenth and fourteenth centuries there is very little evidence of formal teaching of alchemy. Indeed, its successful practice was usually attributed to individual possession of a secret, which could only be transmitted from one adept to another. Without this secret, the available alchemical works were notoriously hard to understand, and positively dangerous to put into practice, given their use of strong acids, poisons, furnaces, and other such life-threatening and expensive materials (Sherwood Taylor, 1976: 93–100). The evidence of the treatises also suggests that alchemical 'experiments' were not written simply as practical instructions but rather as a sort of theoretical explanation and justification of the 'Art'. Modern writers and scientists who have attempted to clarify the procedures supposedly described have largely concluded that it is impossible. Historians are thus left with a branch of learning which is claimed both as a forerunner of chemistry and as a form of highly esoteric magic, whose textual and practical records are extremely obscure and mostly pseudonymous. Nevertheless, the level of learned interest in alchemy and the number of scholars who made informed reference to it were both high from the end of the twelfth century on.

Several of the most famous and respected of the great theologians and teachers of the thirteenth century were among the scholars who worked on areas at least linked to alchemy and who showed some knowledge of it. For instance the internationally famous theologian and natural philosopher, Albertus Magnus, wrote on the subject of metals and minerals and accepted that matter could change from one external form to another under certain conditions [*Doc. 28*] (Albertus Magnus, trans. D. Wyckoff, 1967). However, he did consider that such transformations were extremely difficult for even learned humans to bring about. This did not prevent a very large number of alchemical texts being falsely attributed to him. Something similar seems to have happened to his English contemporary, Roger Bacon, who, like Albertus, studied internationally and was highly influential (though also controversial) (Singer, 1932).

DEALING WITH THE GROWTH OF MAGICAL LITERATURE

It is clear that following instructions such as those discussed in this chapter was a demanding and expensive process, and that choice of the best branch of magic for a specific purpose would be important. In his *Guide for the Perplexed* the Spanish Jew, Moses Maimonides (1135–1204) divided magical procedures into three categories. These related to plants, animals and minerals;

time and dates; and people (Moses Maimonides, trans. M. Friedlander, 1904). The last category in particular used recognisable ritual elements. According to Maimonides, some magical operations need all three types of procedure to work simultaneously. Thus, when collecting particular substances, such as a given number of leaves from a given plant, or a particular animal part, attention must be given to the time of day. Moreover, the sun, or a particular sign of the Zodiac, should be in a specified position. More controversial was the additional recitation of certain words, or performance of particular gestures, since these fell into categories condemned by St Augustine, but these also are dealt with by Maimonides. Simple effects might need only one of these three types of procedure, and could be acceptable to all. However, for all operations it is necessary to observe the position of the stars, because each plant, animal and mineral is connected to a particular star.

This appears to be closely linked to al-Kindi's theory of stellar rays; however, Maimonides describes such theories as 'stupidities' and 'madnesses', and clearly associates them with superstitious and idolatrous belief. His own explanation of how ritualistic procedures worked is that they were offerings of worship by the practitioner to the appropriate star. The planet or star in turn grants what is asked because of the pleasure it takes in the operation performed. Maimonides, who wrote this text for an intellectual audience, and aimed to explain certain particularly puzzling Biblical terms, presents an orthodox and negative attitude towards magical practices. His testimony is important because it shows understanding of the basic principles underlying the workings of image magic, but unlike other writers, who took a neutral or positive position towards it, he emphatically condemns it. Maimonides sees in astral magic a form of idolatry and consequent theological deviation. His position, whilst showing more detailed knowledge of forms of magic based upon Arab astrology, is in fact not dissimilar to that of slightly earlier writers, like John of Salisbury. What is clear is that, throughout the twelfth century, debate as to the acceptability of the ever-growing range of new forms of scientific magic, and their relationship to existing theories and classifications, continued to grow.

Throughout the thirteenth century, the spread of texts containing elaborations of magical rituals and diagrams, with ever-longer lists of exotic names, led writers like William of Auvergne to condemn learned magic. Many texts themselves were indeed destroyed, but their contents are suggested by the fact that learned theologians found it necessary to assert that there was no divinity in the 'angles of Solomon's pentagon' and that the 'rings and seals of Solomon' were 'a form of idolatry involving execrable consecrations and detestable invocations and images' (Thorndike, 1929: vol. 2, 279). In his *Opus Tertium* (*Third Work*), Roger Bacon produced a list of all the books that needed to be prohibited by law, amongst which he cited the *Ars Notoria*

(Thorndike, 1929: vol. 2, 279). Albertus Magnus alludes to that work in passing in his *Speculum Astronomiae*, referring to the detestable use of images in engraved astrological objects. The most systematic opposition comes unsurprisingly from Thomas Aquinas's *Summa Theologica* (*Survey of Theology*), in his section on superstitious observances. He comes to the conclusion that the *Ars Notoria* must be condemned for its use of figures and unknown words. Strikingly, his detailed condemnation of the text shows how well informed he was on the matter, proving that theologians examined the works which concerned them (Thomas Aquinas, trans. T. F. O'Meara and M. J. Duffy, 2006: vol. 40, 71–5).

What scholars and theologians in the new university centres nevertheless continued to share was a strong interest in the rediscovered scientific works of Aristotle and the Arabic commentaries on them. The great project of the thirteenth-century, university-trained, scholars was to produce a new 'theory of everything'. They aimed to integrate the exciting but potentially dangerous non-Christian learning with deeper study of God's creation of the universe, based on the accounts in the Bible. This was a subject which attracted some of the most ambitious students amongst the expanding universities of medieval Europe. It formed part of the study of theology, the most elevated subject on the medieval curriculum, and this had the paradoxical effect of leading men aiming at high-flying careers into studying potentially dangerous texts. Thus, despite the concerted and informed efforts of scholars, Church authorities and state powers, the struggle to define and to police the boundaries of acceptable and unacceptable knowledge could never be finally resolved.

4

Magic and secular society

So far, the chapters of this book have presented magic as an influential, and politically important, element in medieval society – and also as one which required specialised knowledge and unusual skills. Learned churchmen and university graduates had access to the necessary knowledge, and to the expensive equipment which was needed to practise as an astrologer, alchemist or summoner of spirits. Equally, lawyers and theorists who attempted to define magic, and to police the boundaries between acceptable and unacceptable uses of its powers, required specialist knowledge to do so. At the minimum, fluency in Latin and access to a well-stocked library were needed by the practitioners of the types of learned and ritual magic which played their parts in political centres, monasteries, cathedrals and universities. It was also helpful to have knowledge of the law, or a powerful protector, to avoid falling into legal difficulties. However, none of this means that magic was of no use or interest to those who were not learned. Privileged knowledge of coming natural disasters, wars or royal alliances was of clear economic significance for merchants and businessmen, who could plan their own journeys and investments accordingly. On a more obviously illegal level, the means to weaken or even destroy rivals might also be worth a considerable amount of money. All these could be bought, by those who had sufficient wealth and were prepared to take the risk of breaking both Church and royal law, since they could hire specialist magicians to perform these services for them. But does this mean that magic was available only to the privileged and the rich?

The main problem facing any attempt to look at the forms of magic available to the poor is a lack of surviving evidence. Christianity frowned upon the inclusion of possessions in burials, and so the sorts of charms and amulets found by archaeologists in some early medieval graves almost never appear when later cemeteries are excavated (Gilchrist, 2008). Moreover, the poor could rarely afford objects made of the types of materials which survive well when buried, or which were adorned with images or inscriptions. Their magical objects and talismans, if they had any, would be more likely to consist of scraps of textiles, plant materials, stones and animal bones; in other words, things which would be hard to distinguish from rubbish, if they survived at all. The study of the magic of the poor is thus of necessity based upon either the laws passed by those who sought to discipline and control them, or the writings of preachers and chroniclers who recorded the strange or troubling behaviour which they observed. None of these sources were produced by those sympathetic to the people and customs they wrote about. More than that, these authors often consulted learned works of reference in order to make sure that they used the correct terminology, and showed that they themselves held the correct views. Their works are thus often difficult to interpret, since it can be hard to tell just how observation and theory are being blended. For these reasons this chapter will look at the forms of magic employed in what might be called 'everyday life', but will attempt to distinguish between the experiences of the rich and those of the poor.

GERALD OF WALES ON MIRACLES, WONDERS AND MAGIC IN WALES AND IRELAND

An example of the problem is provided by the ambitious and highly educated writer now known as Gerald of Wales. He was a member of the powerful, Anglo-Welsh, aristocratic dynasty known as the Geraldines, and spent much of his life attempting to establish and to occupy the post of Archbishop of Wales. In this ambition he failed, but he nevertheless enjoyed the patronage of the Angevin royal dynasty as well as of powerful members of the Church in England and Wales. He was appointed Court Chaplain by King Henry II of England, and accompanied the future King John on his expedition to Ireland in 1185. His knowledge of Wales was so highly esteemed that he was chosen by Baldwin, Archbishop of Canterbury, to accompany him on tour through south and north Wales, preaching to raise support for the crusades. After these experiences, Gerald took the unusual decision to write about his expertise and observations on Ireland and Wales, their inhabitants, their history, and their condition in the late twelfth century. These books offer valuable details of the customs and beliefs of the people whom Gerald encountered, including what appear to be their beliefs about the supernatural; but all these details are filtered through the lens of Gerald's biblical and classical scholarship.

In the case of Wales, Gerald emphasises the importance of local prophets and inspired poets, who sometimes uttered apparent nonsense and sometimes provided genuine insight into the future. He gives a general account of the traditional 'awenyddion' in his *Description of Wales*. They were clearly consulted by individuals experiencing problems, and in response to questions would immediately go into a trance, and pour out words 'as if possessed by devils'. It was incumbent on the questioner to listen carefully, and to extract an answer from their stream of words since, when brought out of the trance, the poet-prophet would remember nothing. Gerald gives what appears to be a carefully neutral description of this practice, but then has to analyse it and place it within the explanatory categories provided by his own intellectual milieu (Gerald of Wales, trans. Thorpe, 1978: 246–51).

He considers the possibility that the inspiration comes from demons, who may actually possess the individuals and speak through them; but he appears reluctant to accept this conclusion. More positively, he points out that the awenyddion appear to experience dream-visions, accompanied by physical sensations of sweetness and of written texts being actually placed in their mouths. These details are, as Gerald notes, comparable to the accounts given by biblical prophets; and moreover the awenyddion themselves are clearly orthodox Christians, who invoke God and the Trinity before going into their trance. In the latter respect they are superior to the Trojan and Roman prophets whom Gerald goes on to discuss. This is clearly a serious issue, since Gerald pursues it for five pages, in a book only 54 pages long overall. He acknowledges the danger that these local prophets may be the playthings of demons, or may knowingly be indulging in sorcery, but overall he appears sympathetic, pointing out that God grants true prophecies even to pagans, and that many who have received divine visions have shown symptoms of frenzy and madness comparable to the behaviour of the awenyddion. Thus for Gerald this group can be protected from accusations of dabbling in forbidden magic and divination. Sadly, however, whilst the terms of Gerald's discussion were of great significance in his own time, they are unhelpful for modern readers who wish to understand the beliefs of the awenyddion and those who consulted them.

Equally multi-layered is Gerald's account (in his *Journey Through Wales*) of a famous, contemporary prophet, called Meilyr. He not only foretold the future with impressive accuracy but also had knowledge of hidden and supernatural things. Like the awenyddion he appeared to be affected by madness – but in his case this was due to an experience which was at once sexual, supernatural and traumatic. What happened was that, one Palm Sunday, Meilyr encountered an attractive girl in a deserted spot and proceeded to make love to her. To his horror he suddenly saw that what he was holding so tightly was not a girl but a monstrous creature, covered in rough hair. He went out of his mind, and remained so for several years, until healed by the clerics of St David's. Even after this cure he retained the capacity to see, name and talk to invisible spirits, through whom he was also able to prophesy. These spirits are almost certainly demons, as far as Gerald is concerned, and Meilyr's prophecies are unsurprisingly varied in their degree of truth. One of the spirits is clearly demonic, since it is an incubus which has seduced 'a certain young woman' and which reveals secrets to several of her neighbours. Meilyr not only knows the incubus by name but also prophesies that its appearance signifies ensuing misfortune, giving concrete details of Henry II's coming campaign. Sadly for Meilyr, his prophecy was correct, but he failed to see that he himself would die of wounds received during a siege (Gerald of Wales, trans. Thorpe: 116–20).

Once again Gerald proceeds to apply a theological analysis to this evidence, and in this case comes to the conclusion that Meilyr's information did indeed come from demons, who betrayed him as they do all their dupes. Clearly, Meilyr is no sorcerer, since he is never described as using any ritual means to summon demons or communicate with them; and he is described as completely illiterate, although interested in handling books. The importance of this case, in Gerald's account, is that Meilyr gave clear proof that demons are all around, even if they are invisible to ordinary human senses. Still more worryingly, they draw sinful humans into interacting with them, and will even impart genuine knowledge in order to entice the unwary. The means by which they can make themselves perceptible to humans are also discussed in learned terms, but Gerald shows no interest in the ideas or terminology drawn upon, for instance, by the Welsh villagers whom the incubus-demon variously seduced.

Even if exact details of medieval Welsh practices of prophecy and oracular utterance cannot be extracted from Gerald's accounts, two things emerge strongly. The first is that there was a considerable and widespread demand for supernatural guidance in Welsh society. The traditional means of satisfying it was provided by the awenyddion, who appear to have been widely accessible. Gerald's account suggests that they were willing to respond to anyone who questioned them and was prepared to listen carefully to their answer. The second is that the Church in Wales seems to have been generally tolerant of these traditional practitioners and isolated individuals like Meilyr. The latter was taken into the care of healers in St David's, and even accepted into several local monasteries as a source of information on the moral and spiritual 'health' of members of the religious community. In contrast to this, Gerald of Wales (and, presumably, his Anglo-French audience) took these prophetic practices seriously, but found their relationship to theological teaching on magic, divination and sorcery rather problematic.

In Gerald's earlier book, on Ireland, the approach was different, as Ireland is depicted more simply as a land of natural marvels and wonders, rather than of human use of, or abuse by, the supernatural (Gerald of Wales, trans. Forester, ed. Wright, 2000: esp. 33–62). The natural marvels include types of fishes and frogs which are not found in any other territory, as well as the beneficent climate and the absence of poisons. Miracles are separately considered, as is the apparently intermediate category of wonders (that is, things which at least appear to be contrary to nature). The list of wonders is long, and includes both islands which are lethal to one sex or the other and islands where no-one can die, together with an even longer list of wonder-working wells. In none of these, however, is human agency directly involved. The inhabitants of Ireland are scrutinised only in Part three of the book, and it is noticeable that, although Gerald goes out of his way to criticise their customs and their version of Christianity, he does not accuse them of practising magic. Whilst this is far from proving that the population of twelfth-century Ireland had no interest in magic or the supernatural, it does at least suggest that Gerald stayed close to the information and evidence which he collected, and that he was not inclined to project magical beliefs onto the societies he described for the entertainment of his Anglo-Norman audience.

PENITENTIALS, CONFESSORS' MANUALS AND EARLY LAWCODES

Another possible source of information on the magical beliefs and practices of those who left no records of their own is offered by the manuals issued by the medieval Church to guide priests who were responsible for giving instruction to the laity. In the early Middle Ages these mostly took the form of Penitentials (see also Chapter 2), which were handbooks on the types of sin which a priest might encounter and on the penances which he should impose upon the sinners. Later, these were replaced by longer works, giving fuller guidance to priests dealing with the confessions of lay people. Both offer detailed and apparently circumstantial descriptions of various forbidden forms of fortune-telling, love magic, and healing, in tones which strongly suggest that these were practices which the priest would actually encounter during his career. However, both were in fact based upon older collections of Church law and doctrine, which themselves included extracts going back as early as the fourth century CE and originating anywhere within the old Roman Empire. This obviously means that they have to be handled with extreme care by anyone looking for an actual description of lay beliefs and practices in any medieval society.

An important, and particularly problematic, example is provided by the legal text known as the *Canon Episcopi*, which sets out a specific duty for bishops. This is first recorded in the early tenth century, when Regino of Prüm included it in his collection of Church, or 'canon' law (Kors and Peters, 2001: 60–3). In the twelfth century it was mistakenly believed to be part of the decrees issued by the Council held at Ancyra in 314 CE, and for that reason was enshrined in collections of canon law. The actual origins of the text are now lost, although they appear more likely to be in the Carolingian than the Roman Empire. This is frustrating for the historian of magic, since this text gives a brief, but sensational, account of a magical ritual to which bishops are instructed to give special attention. It opens with a general warning against sorcery, as an 'art invented by the Devil', whose practitioners are to be ejected from their communities forthwith. In a slightly different category are certain women, 'perverted by the Devil', who falsely believe that they take part in night-time flights, mounted upon magical animals. These supposed flights involve 'great multitudes' of women, who perform rituals in honour of a pagan goddess identified in the text as Diana. Belief that such flights can happen is, according to the text, widespread, and so strong as to be a serious threat to true religion. The bishops are to teach the truth of the matter, which is that these women have been deluded by the devil and his servants. Their experiences are entirely illusory, but are none the less threatening for that, since both the women themselves and those who believe in their powers are in thrall to Satan and are infidels, if not actual worshippers of the devil.

The impact of this instruction, given long-lasting force by its inclusion in the key textbook of canon law, is hard to exaggerate. It clearly constitutes a major contribution to late-medieval and early-modern ideas about witches and their practices. But where and when, if at all, did these deluded women actually live? The closest we can probably come is to repeat that the language and original context of the *Canon episcopi* suggest that it was first written in the ninth-century empire of Charlemagne. Its description of what is presented as a widespread pagan threat to Christian belief is unlikely to have been entirely invented; but the language used, and a brief reference to Roman beliefs, make it clear that it already represents a learned interpretation of reported events. Moreover, the whole point of the text, and its inclusion in Church law, is to suggest that this threat exists anywhere and everywhere. After all, it was well known that women, as daughters of Eve, were always prone to fall victim to the seductions of the devil, and thus to bring terrible harm to all of society. No formal learning was required for this form of magic, because the women were simply the willing dupes of demons.

But does this mean that all medieval beliefs in the magical practices and powers of uneducated women were simply the product of clerical misogyny? The answer appears to be no, since the deluded women of semi-pagan parts of the Carolingian Empire have parallels elsewhere. Anglo-Saxon England was a region where Penitentials appeared relatively early, drawing upon the fundamental models provided by the Church in Ireland and Wales. One of the most influential of these works was the *Penitential of Theodore*, a collection probably edited together in the eighth century but claiming to be based upon the teaching of Theodore of Tarsus, a seventh-century Archbishop of Canterbury. It thus brings together Irish textual models, the learning of a theologian from Asia Minor, and supposed Anglo-Saxon sins. An important point about this Penitential is that it pays considerably less attention to magical sins than do the later, Carolingian Penitentials. Nevertheless, its section on marriage and sexual behaviour assumes that those who practise illicit means of obtaining and keeping love will be women, who will perform certain rituals in order to keep the affections of men. Moreover, its section on pagan worship identifies pagan deities with demons, and then attributes the performance of 'diabolical incantations or divinations' to women (although only a light penance of one year is assigned). The same section includes another female practice which has proved very hard to interpret. This is the description of how women place their daughters on roofs or in ovens in order to cure their fevers, mentioned in Chapter 2. Why this was specifically pagan is not explained; but it is punished with the severe penance of seven years, and was thus clearly a serious matter, as well as an entirely female one. That this belief was not exclusive to Anglo-Saxon England is shown by the presence of comparable beliefs in Penitentials not only from the Carolingian Empire but also from Visigothic Spain [*Doc. 19*]. Nor was the belief promoted entirely by the Church, since in Anglo-Saxon lawcodes, from those of King Alfred onwards, it is again women who are said to be most likely to invite magicians (*malefici*) into their homes, and are to be punished for doing so (Whitelock, 1979: 407–37).

The fact that collections of royal law survive from Anglo-Saxon England makes it possible to compare their concerns with those of the Penitentials. In the Laws of King Athelstan, issued in c.930, the term 'witchcraft' is used in relation to both sorcery and secret killing, and seems to relate to the crimes of men rather more than to those of women. The punishment for all these activities is death. Similarly, a record of how Bishop Aethelwold of Winchester came into possession of an estate at Ailsworth, explains that it had previously belonged to a widow and her son, but that they were found guilty of attempted murder by magical means, leading to the death of the mother and the exile of the son. The record dates to 963–75, and provides details which explain how secret killing and witchcraft were connected. What had happened was that a man named Aelfsige had become seriously ill, and suspicion fell upon the widow and her son. When their home was raided, a 'murderous instrument' was found hidden in the woman's chamber, by means of which pins had supposedly been driven into Aelfsige, causing his illness. The result was that the woman was drowned at London Bridge (which scarcely sounds like a legal proceeding), her son fled into exile and their property was confiscated by the king, who then awarded it to Aelfsige (Whitelock 1979: 562–3).

As well as attempted murder, both law codes and medical texts show belief in individuals, often but not always women, who had the power to cause terrible pain and illness by chanting and invoking supernatural forces (Olsan, 2003). The latter are frequently identified with pagan deities, but since these are usually stated to have been demons this is a rather technical distinction. However, concern about a revival of paganism in the eleventh century seems to have inspired further legislation about all 'idolatrous' and 'superstitious' supernatural beliefs. This fear that the majority of people were poorly educated and susceptible to being led astray, or falling into superstitious magical beliefs, persisted throughout the medieval period. In the early thirteenth century new measures were taken by the Church, intended to improve the educational level of the clergy, and to ensure that parish and local clergy maintained contact with their parishioners. Lay people of all classes were to have access to regular confession, and new manuals were issued to help their confessors respond to what they heard. These Pastoral Manuals were clearly in demand and survive in large numbers from the late thirteenth century on, but once again the apparently circumstantial details they offer turn out very often to be derived from older texts such as the Penitentials rather than from individual confessions (Rider, 2011).

Nevertheless, even if these Manuals influenced the perceptions of priests rather than reporting the behaviour of their parishioners, they would have the effect of setting up widespread beliefs about what was going on across Christian Europe – and the picture was worrying. They all show concern about the widespread practice of divination, fortune-telling, interpreting of omens, invoking of minor supernatural beings, and superstitious or magical medical cures. Something new in these collections is that concern about lingering paganism has been replaced by concern about superstitious misuse of powerful words or substances produced by the Church itself. The simple recitation of prayers approved for the laity, such as the Lord's Prayer, whilst gathering medicinal herbs was perfectly acceptable, but observing 'rituals' at the same time, or chanting unfamiliar words or names was not. Similarly, wearing written copies of prayers while undertaking certain tasks was acceptable, but other beliefs about written prayer texts were much more worrying. William of Rennes mentions a belief that written copies of the Gospel texts read out in church on Ascension Day had supernatural powers, strongest if they were copied down while the words were actually being read out in church – and this is to be condemned nearly as strongly as the wearing of written characters and secret names said to bring success and protection to the owner. All these, together with the descriptions of lay healers who placed their hands on the sick and said prayers or chanted strange '**adjurations**' over them, sound believable as descriptions of behaviour which incorporated

Adjuration: an appeal or command, placing compulsion upon another by calling upon the name of God or of a supernatural entity.

elements of magical beliefs and customs on the part of those outside of the clergy and the elite; but none of them can be proved to have happened in actual practice.

Similarly problematic are the stories told by preachers from the thirteenth century onwards. These also make dramatic use of details about 'domestic magic' – which is usually swiftly punished. An example comes from the compilation of miracle stories put together by the Cistercian monk, Cesarius of Heisterbach, which, as seen in Chapter 2, was a popular source of such improving anecdotes. This story is put into the mouth of a monk, who visited a woman (called Hartdyfa de Cochem) who suffered greatly because she was possessed by a devil. The woman's priest told the monk how he had spoken to the devil concerned, and learned that the woman deserved her suffering because she had stolen the consecrated bread from mass, and crumbled it over her vegetable patch, to protect the cabbages from caterpillars. The woman herself confessed to this behaviour, and agreed that she deserved her punishment (Cesarius of Heisterbach, ed. Strange, Cologne, 1851: vol. II, 170–1). Was this a true story? It is impossible to tell; but what is much more certain is that such tales helped to feed the belief in the later Middle Ages that it was 'women who hardly know the rudiments of faith' who were most likely to fall into the clutches of demons through their incorrigible meddling in superstition and magic.

NATURAL MAGIC AND ITS USES

The forms of magic which spread in university circles were, as has been shown, complex and demanding. Achieving mastery would require considerable investment of time and resources, and would be impossible for those without higher education. Activities such as summoning spirits were also believed to be very dangerous, and were certainly not to be engaged in lightly. Finally, knowledge of the secrets of the universe was not necessarily attractive to everyone in medieval society. Thus the appeal of learned and ritual magic was mostly to a restricted group of clerical scholars, who in turn sought patrons who could afford to support their researches. There was however another branch of magic, which emerged amongst learned circles alongside ritual magic, which was much more widely attractive in secular society, and this was natural magic.

Natural magic was first identified as a part of natural philosophy (that is, the study of the natural world) dealing with the natural but occult properties of things. These 'marvellous virtues', described in reference works such as herbals and lapidaries, were accepted as part of God's creation. They offered an alternative understanding of magic; one in which desired supernatural effects could be explained through the powers of the natural world rather than those of spirits or demons [Doc. 29]. Study in this field was greatly expanded by the translation of Arabic works on advanced astrological techniques for harnessing the effects of planetary powers on physical bodies. The detailed analysis and explanation of natural magic as an acceptable category of knowledge, and one distinguishable from ritual magic, came first with the thirteenth-century theologian and Bishop of Paris William of Auvergne. William's knowledge of, and growing concern about, forms of magic will be discussed in more detail later on, but his cautious acceptance of the idea of natural magic was first expressed in his *De fide et legibus* (*On Faith and Laws*), written c.1228–30. The concept appeared again in his *De universo* (*On the Universe*) (c.1231–36), an extensive treatise describing the material and spiritual worlds. An idea related to that of natural magic was also used in the *Speculum astronomiae* (*Mirror of Astronomy/ Astrology*), attributed to Albertus Magnus, another theologian and expert on magic. This text moves discussion forward into the area of how such natural but hidden properties may be exploited by following specified procedures at appropriate times (Kieckhefer, 1997: 8–17).

The presence of occult properties in nature, and especially in stones, had been accepted in the fundamental works of St Augustine. His views were taken up, and made available to the medieval imperial court, in Gervase of Tilbury's *Otia imperialia*. This encyclopaedic survey of the world and its history includes a chapter on the powers of stones. Here, the virtues of gems were classified as *mirabilia*, natural phenomena present in daily life but beyond human comprehension. Examples of *mirabilia* are given in Gervase's stories about Solomon's ability to imprison demons in rings by using seals, signs and spells and about Merlin's use of the powers inherent in the great stones which he assembled at Stonehenge (Boudet, 2006: 133–7). Gervase's definition is thus broader than Augustine's. In the case of precious stones, Gervase proposes that their marvellous powers are given by both intrinsic and extrinsic virtues. The former are identified with their natural properties, while the latter are added by rituals of consecration or exorcism. For him, the words of the rituals enhance and confirm the inner virtues of the various gems, originally given to them by God. It is nevertheless clear that the notion of natural magic could intermingle with concepts and practices associated with demonic or ritual magic. Gervase was not alone in this blurring of boundaries, since ritualistic elements are present, for example, in some lapidaries. It was this which made the idea of natural magic increasingly worrying to theologians, despite its apparent attractions, as they made growing efforts to define and police the boundary between the natural and the supernatural. The issues raised will become apparent in the following sections.

LAPIDARIES

Until at least the twelfth century, Western lapidaries were mainly based on texts of Greek or Latin origin. This tradition was then greatly enriched by material coming from the Arabic world. Early Latin lapidaries depended, directly or indirectly, upon the *Natural History* of Pliny the Elder who, alongside traditional data on the properties and virtues of stones also mentioned simple amulets, astrological stones and talismans. Care was taken in these earlier texts to apply a selective filter to Pliny's material. Some scepticism was also expressed in relation to the material drawn from Solinus's *Polyhistor* (a chronological list of wonders and marvels) and Isidore of Seville's *Etymologies*, both of which made use of Pliny but with varying additions. During the eleventh century a text of Greek or Alexandrine origin, attributed to one Damigeron, supposedly a magician expert in ancient Egyptian lore, became more widely known. This work was probably translated into Latin as early as the fifth century, and seems to have been known in Anglo-Saxon England. It was an actual lapidary, unlike the much broader works of Pliny and Solinus, and unlike the works of the great Greek medical writers, Galen and Dioscorides, who also discussed stones as part of their catalogues of medical materials. It is similar to other lapidaries in that it offers short descriptions of the appearance, qualities and powers (both medical and magical) of the stones it lists (Halleux and Schamp, 1985). Its more magical elements focus upon astrological imagery and engravings. However, it was known in medieval Europe largely through its use in a much more widely distributed work.

This famous medieval lapidary is the *Liber lapidum* or *Book of Stones*, written c.1090 by Marbod of Rennes, chancellor of Angers and Bishop of Rennes. Marbod describes the medical qualities of sixty stones in 732 verses, attributing their marvellous powers to God's endowment. The text, which enjoyed a great success – surviving in c.250 manuscripts – drew largely on Solinus, Isidore and Damigeron. Marbod does not make any reference to the possibility of enhancing the stones' power through engravings. However, his poem does take into account basic astrological principles, mainly concerned with the position of the heavenly bodies. The prologue makes reference to the mysteries of stones, and stresses that knowledge of these is both hidden and sacred. According to Marbod this was reserved for a small group of initiates. An example of the nature of his material is provided by his treatment of the diamond, a particularly suitable stone for the magical arts. 'Foremost of all amongst the glittering race', it makes its bearer indomitable and can drive away night spirits and idle dreams. It is good against 'black poison', and it helps to overcome quarrels and strife. Medically, it cures insanity, but it is also used to repel rough enemies. Marbod advises that the stone should be worn enclosed in silver or gold, preferably as a bracelet.

Similarly useful to magicians is the stone known as chelonite, for once washed and placed under the tongue it gives the power to foretell the future. Heliotrope can also be used for predicting and foretelling future events. Furthermore, it offers lifetime protection to its wearer, the one who carries it cannot be cheated, and if joined together with the herb of the same name, and strengthened through the use of appropriate incantations and sacred words, it has the marvellous virtue of making invisible those who wear it. As a medical stone, it can stop the flux of blood and expel poisons. Supernatural protection is also available through the use of stones like the topaz, which is described as being most useful for guarding against the terrors of the night, as it has the property of frightening and expelling demons, when strung on the hairs plucked from an ass's tail. But no other stone is as powerful as the sinister *diadocos*, which has the property of revealing diverse images of devils, and can summon the shades of the dead. Furthermore, its owner cannot be 'called back', even immediately after death (Marbod, ed. J. M. Riddle, 1977: 34–118).

From the twelfth century onward, translations of further Greek and Arabic texts accelerated the production of books on the properties of stones in the Latin West. The underlying idea of the hidden properties of gems gradually acquired more precise astrological expression. The *Liber sigillorum* (*Book of Seals*) attributed to 'Theel' (the name appears in various forms), a text probably deriving from a late-antique Greek original, offers a prologue claiming that the seals of the title were those produced by the Jews on their exodus from Egypt. The author claimed to know figures and symbols that conferred considerable power when engraved onto stones. In agreement with divine will, these engravings are related to the movement of the astrological signs and the course of the planets. In the case of magical stones, the text mentions that they need to be consecrated, as described for the 'galactides', the last of the stones mentioned. This text is followed in some manuscripts by the *De lapidibus*, (*On Stones*) a work attributed in the manuscripts to a King Azareus and addressed to King Ptolemy. This text advances the idea that the powerful engravings mentioned by Theel are actually to be found in nature and cannot be merely invented by men (Pingree, 1987: 64–6).

Another work which directly linked the power of the stars, stones and herbs via images is *On fifteen stars, fifteen stones, fifteen herbs and fifteen images*, a text also known as the *Quadripartitum Hermetis*. This Latin text, probably derived from a Greek or Arabic original, explicitly offers instructions for the making of powerful talismans. The oldest copy survives in a thirteenth-century manuscript and is divided in four parts. The first deals with fifteen fixed stars, the second with fifteen stones, and the third with fifteen herbs. The final section offers fifteen images and engraved characters, each linking one star, one stone and one herb with an appropriate image. According to the author of this treatise, all four elements are essential to produce the desired effect (Weill-Parot, 2002: 216–18). This work thus closely associates astrology and the production of talismans with the lapidary tradition. In such cases the boundaries between ritual magic, with its worrying associations with spirits and demons, and natural magic were shown to be alarmingly permeable. This became problematic from the thirteenth century onwards, as such material was taken up into the growing number of encyclopaedic reference works. The latter treated the information selected as part of natural philosophy rather than overtly magical, and offered little comment on the production of astrological images. Nevertheless, the very idea of natural magic was increasingly open to question.

Lapidary texts belonging firmly to the Latin tradition do not openly mention a connection to astrological talismans. Even the texts attributed to Theel and Azaerus, at least in their Latin versions, placed the fabrication of talismans outside the reach of the craftsman. In the rare exceptions where a link between engraving onto stones and harnessing astral powers is clear, as in *On fifteen stars* . . . , the connection is only made through the indication of an appropriate astrological moment. However, talismanic texts explicitly derived from the Arabic tradition of astral magic were also available in the medieval West from the thirteenth century. This is especially the case with the material developed in the court of Alfonso X 'El Sabio', King of Castille and León. A contemporary manuscript containing four lapidary texts of unknown provenance is attributed to Alfonso's court [*Doc. 20*]. According to the prologue of its first text, Alfonso's scholars would have found the Arabic material in Toledo. Generally learned and interested in natural philosophy – his court is associated with the compilation and translation of some of the most remarkable magical texts of the Middle Ages, the *Picatrix* and the *Liber Raziel* (*Book of Raziel*) – he is believed to have commissioned the Jewish scholar Yehuda ben Moshé to produce a translation of these lapidaries into Castilian. Scholars have credited Yehuda with the actual compilation of the text, which appears to draw upon various astrological lapidaries, some perhaps of Jewish origin, as well as Dioscorides's *De materia medica* (*On Medical Materials*). The lapidary texts assembled in this collection are unique in the detailed way in which they link the stones mentioned by Dioscorides with astrological principles (Weill-Parot, 2002: 125). They do not, however, use astrological images, but focus instead on how the virtues of named stones may be strengthened by specified astrological configurations.

HERBALS

Like lapidaries, apart from listing the medicinal properties of herbs, medieval herbals dealt with their occult hidden properties. Belonging to an ancient literary tradition, these beautifully illustrated texts survived in an almost unbroken tradition from Late Antiquity to the later Middle Ages. Herbal treatises are divided into chapters, each one dealing with a specific plant. A typical chapter provides the name of the plant, gives a list of synonyms for its name, and then sets out a description of its characteristics, distribution and habitat. It will also include selected theoretical information, together with practical advice on the medical properties of the plant; how each plant should be gathered and prepared; producing and using relevant medicines; and finally of any contra-indications (Collins, 2000: 25). The chapter will usually be accompanied by an illustration of the plant, mostly based upon the images in source manuscripts rather than upon observation of actual plants.

Until the thirteenth century, the number of herbal treatises was limited. There were two main compilations, both originating from Late Antiquity. The medical treatise by Dioscorides, *De materia medica*, dealt with plants as well as with stones. There is evidence that it was known to Isidore of Seville, who probably used it in his *Etymologies* (Collins, 2000: 148). The most important illustrated herbal in the Latin West was the *Herbarius* (*Herbal*), attributed to Apuleius Platonicus, and compiled between the second and fourth centuries CE. The *Herbarius* usually appears together in manuscripts with the *De herbis femininis* (*On Female Herbs*) or the *Curae herbarum* (*Herbal Cures*), both illustrated herbal treatises derived mainly from Dioscorides. *De herbis femininis* was probably compiled in southern Europe before the sixth century; the *Curae herbarum* can also be dated to c. sixth century CE. It was only in the thirteenth century that a new illustrated herbal with a lasting influence was compiled: the anonymous *Tractatus de herbis*. The *Herbarius* of Apuleius Platonicus itself survives in c. 60 manuscripts dating from the sixth to the fifteenth century, showing just how important it was throughout the medieval period. It draws on Pliny's Latin work on medicine, as well as on Dioscorides. The basic text was probably revised in the seventh century, but most copies contain about 130 chapters, dealing with the same number of plants. As with Marbod's descriptions of stones, Apuleius's *Herbarius* specifies the occult or hidden properties of herbs. In the case of mugwort or 'monoclonos', [*Doc. 21*] the text indicates that it is good for pain in the feet and the gut. On journeys, it is useful to protect the traveller from fatigue. Furthermore, it has the properties of protecting the household, putting demons to flight and diverting the gaze of evil men. Preparation involved the drying and powdering of the plant, which was then incorporated into medicinal drinks and poultices.

BESTIARIES

The Bestiary, or Book of Beasts, provided an account of another major portion of the natural world. Once again, its text is based upon learned authorities, and it presents short descriptions of all sorts of animals, both real and imaginary. Following a theological agenda, the object of the Bestiary was to edify and instruct sinful humanity, rather than simply to document and analyse the natural world (Barber, 1992: 7). Each creature is thus presented as a moral entity, conveying a specific message to the human reader. The mystical significance of each derives especially from the authoritative text of the Holy Scriptures, and from commentaries upon them. The basic bestiary material was probably translated into Latin in the sixth century, from the Greek *Physiologus*, and sought to give an explicitly Christian interpretation of the natural world. Like the herbals, its chapters are usually accompanied by illustrations, which can be either basic or luxurious in execution and artistic style. Also like the herbals, the chapters follow a standard structure; here, this starts with a description, followed by the moral and then the deeper meaning.

The Bestiary text had an especially complex process of transmission and tended to be in a continuous state of revision. A luxurious thirteenth-century English copy, now MS Bodley 764, illustrates how the contents of any manuscript could be tailored to the interests and means of individual patrons. Its immediate source was a late twelfth-century copy of the Bestiary, but to this was added wide-ranging material. There are excerpts from a treatise on beasts by Rabanus Maurus, the learned ninth-century Archbishop of Mainz. To these are added tales from Gerald of Wales's *The Topography of Ireland*, Hugh of Fouilloy's *The Aviary* and Peter of Cornwall's *Pantheologus*, all twelfth century. Like other English bestiary manuscripts of the thirteenth century this is fully and expensively illuminated. Whereas the basic *Physiologus* text, which does not vary greatly, is fairly short, English versions such as this one could expand it to four times its length. The first set of additional material was taken (yet again) from Isidore of Seville; but luxury works like the Bodleian Bestiary were, as has been seen, expanded into wide-ranging encyclopedias of the natural world and its geography and resources. In the twelfth century, a structural innovation had appeared which subdivided the expanding material into beasts, birds, snakes and fishes. Like most luxury copies, this Bestiary is arranged in this fashion (George and Yapp, 1991: 1–28).

As in lapidaries and herbals, the Bestiary text also includes descriptions of hidden or occult properties. A striking example is the hyena, which lives in the graves of dead men and feeds on their bodies [*Doc. 22*]. This animal is described as having magical properties: it follows shepherds, can imitate the sound of the human voice, and can get into locked houses at night. If dogs fall under the hyena's shadow while hunting, they lose their voice; and if the hyena looks at an animal three times that animal will be unable to move. It carries a stone in its eye, called 'hyenia', which can foretell the future if placed under the tongue. Its unnatural mating with lions in Ethiopia is the origin of a specific type of monster called the 'crocote'. However, some creatures had semi-magical healing powers. The excrement of the Caladrius, a type of river bird, for instance, can cure weak eyes. For that reason alone the bird should be kept in the courts of kings. Still more valuably, if the bird was brought into the presence of a sick person, it would indicate whether the sufferer would live or die by turning its head towards or away from their sickbed. Rather more surprising is that the wolf also has a benign power. According to Solinus, the wolf has a little patch of hair in its tail that can be used as a love charm, and which was thus in high demand. Wolves were actually aware of this and, facing imminent capture, would tear off this part of their body of their own accord. Since the Bestiary text warns that the hair has no effect if it is taken from a dead wolf, a hunter dealing with an uncooperative wolf would be faced with the need to capture it alive in order to benefit from this property. Equally mysterious is the statement that, if the wolf sees a man before the man sees the wolf, then it can 'catch' the man's voice and thus force the man to take no notice of it [*Doc. 23*].

CONCLUSION

In themselves, the informative reference works described here cannot be classified as books of magic. Nevertheless, the material presented emphasises that in many ways modern historians face the same problems as medieval theologians in identifying magic. St Augustine's famous comment on time – that he knew what it was until he tried to define it – applies in many ways to magic also. As has been shown, the categories of natural marvels, natural magic and demonic magic, although clear and logical in themselves, can be difficult to apply to 'real-life' examples, whether in the natural world or in human behaviour. Both in the ways in which societies attempted to deal with risks and with an unknown future, and in the ever-growing knowledge about the natural world which was transmitted from literate to illiterate individuals and is preserved in the books described here, the categories were difficult to keep separate. This problem is still more acute in the case of medicine, as will be seen in the next chapter. What this chapter has already shown, however, is that interest in magic was not confined to the learned. For everyone from villagers to members of the imperial court, information on magic, and even expert consultants, were available.

5

Medical magic

Of all the areas where magic was closely integrated into medieval society, those of formal and informal medicine offer perhaps the most fascinating and yet most ambiguous material. Throughout the medieval period, drawing upon theories established by classical science and philosophy, it was accepted that nature had powers to cure and to heal. Medieval doctors, like medieval philosophers and magicians, had access to herbals and lapidaries, often possessing (or claiming) classical origins, which listed medicinal powers amongst the properties of the plants and stones which they covered. What is complex for historians, just as it was complex for practitioners in medieval Europe, is the distinction between powers which were 'occult' yet natural, and those which exceeded what could be natural, and thus implied the hidden presence of supernatural agents (in other words, demons). This distinction was first put into formal terminology by St Thomas Aquinas in the thirteenth century, and his formulation brought helpful clarity to an area which had proved extremely hard to police (Aquinas, trans. McAllister, 1939). Even so, the criteria were inevitably capable of different interpretations; and this led to different decisions in apparently similar cases. Given the rising fear of demonic intervention, and of human collaboration with demons, in the late Middle Ages, it is perhaps not surprising that informal and amateur curative practices came under ever closer scrutiny – with harsh results for some practitioners. For professionally trained doctors, decisions as to exactly how far their use of astrology could be taken, and just what methods were acceptable and safe as means of tapping into such sources of healing power as the planets, needed constantly to be made. Indeed, as the skills and technologies available to doctors expanded from the twelfth century onwards, such decisions became both more necessary and more challenging.

THE PROBLEM OF CHARMS

Medical magic in the early Middle Ages has for some time been discussed under the label of 'charms' by many historians. This term is useful in suggesting a category which was in some ways outside of officially accepted practice, and yet not perceived as seriously threatening. However, it is unhelpful in blurring distinctions which were very important during the medieval period itself. More recently it has been accepted that these 'charm' texts, which are usually short, are related to the broader category of 'prognostics', because they occur in manuscripts offering ways of forecasting various future events, as well as in medical collections. The designation 'charms' can also be criticised as misleading, since it suggests that these texts and the practices they describe were consciously transgressive or heterodox, and this is contradicted by the fact that they are preserved in manuscripts from major monasteries and churches.

Many of these 'charms' are preserved in the Old English medical collections known as *Lacnunga* and *Bald's Leechbook* but even in this form it is clear that they draw upon wide-ranging sources, including some of classical origin. They have been much studied as examples of 'magic' within both medical practice and religious institutions. (For the *Leechbook* see Cockayne, vol. II, 1865; for selected charms, vol. I, 1864. See also Jolly, 1996.) However others, covering a range of purposes, are also found in manuscripts containing texts to be performed during church services, or are described in historical works, or (most surprising of all) are found in collections of laws. The extent to which they were actually seen as magical is thus open to question. They deal with protection of individuals or livestock; prevention of theft or recovery of stolen property; and medical protection or cure. Among the latter, it is perhaps not surprising to find words and rituals intended to protect those going through childbirth, or medical problems as dangerous as bleeding or swellings. Others are perhaps not so threatening, yet still very painful or disruptive, such as toothache, eye pain, or insomnia. In most cases, what is striking is that the words and gestures are, both from their manuscript context and from their terminology, expected to be performed by a monk, a priest or at least an individual in holy orders. It is not clear whether these functions would be performed only for members of the ecclesiastical community which owned the manuscript, or whether, as has been suggested in some cases, a priest was expected to offer them as part of his support and protection for a secular community. In either case, the charms require recognisably religious actions, such as making the sign of the cross, together with the recitation of short prayers or extracts from scripture; and several assume the availability of the consecrated sacraments. All this suggests very strongly that these are very far from being the informal healing practices of uneducated individuals, as well as suggesting once again that the criteria applied by historians may not be the same as those used in the medieval period.

The first striking thing about both collections is that, whilst many of their component parts were derived from classical sources, the texts themselves were written down in Old English. This makes Anglo-Saxon England in some ways precocious in having a vernacular terminology for medical ideas, classifications of disease, and lists of medical substances, and yet raises the question of why medical practitioners did not use Latin, like those everywhere else in Europe. The titles given are those applied by modern editors to the surviving collections, both now in the British Library. The *Leechbook*, at least, has evidence of being intended for consultation by medical practitioners, since its remedies are arranged in order of the part of the body upon which they are to be used, starting with the head and going down to the feet (London, British Library, MS Royal 12 D xvii). They are further subdivided into conditions affecting the external parts of the body and those relating to internal disorders. Given this very practical approach, it is perhaps all the more surprising to find apparently supernatural cures, such as the following instruction for treating a headache which has lasted for a very long time – swallow chicks are to be caught, and three tiny stones extracted from their stomachs. These stones must not be allowed to come into contact with earth or water, but must be wrapped up and then applied to the sufferer. They are so powerful that they will work not only on headaches but also eye pain, typhus, seizures, goblins, bewitchment, enchantments and the temptations of the devil himself. However, if the headache affects only one side of the head, then plantain is to be dug up before sunrise and without using any iron implement, and its roots are to be tied to the head with a damp, red cloth.

Although puzzling, such cures are presented in very practical language, as a series of instructions for the healer to follow. However, some of the entries in the collection called by its editors *Lacnunga* (that is, 'Remedies') appear far more poetic and even openly pagan and magical (London, British Library, MS Harley 385). Most famous is the 'charm' known as the 'Lay of the Nine Twigs of Woden'. This is written in metrical, poetic style, giving the strong impression that it is to be recited or chanted, and refers to the pagan god Woden as the source of the 'nine powerful twigs' which can defeat both disease and its supernatural causes. These causes are called poisons, but are also linked to serpents and to the 'bewitchments' of enemies, and are to be dispelled by the recitation of the poem, including its invocations of the power of Woden, God and Christ, whilst applying a very complex herbal salve, whose preparation is also described (Jolly, 1996: 125–7). This might suggest that the collection is a lightly updated version of pre-Christian Anglo-Saxon remedies; yet other remedies in the collection could only be carried out by a priest (or even a monastic community). Particularly complex is the 'holy drink against the devil's temptations and the power of elves', which involves the use of sanctified wine; five herbs; quotations from the Bible written out on a patten; water collected from a flowing stream by a 'spotless' person; and performance in church of psalms, prayers, blessings and complete masses. In a text such as this it becomes almost impossible to separate magical, medical and liturgical elements; yet the manuscript itself appears to have been produced by a scribe who wrote in a formal, learned hand, and its user must at least have been able to secure the services of priests even if he was not one himself.

A similar problem arises with the more formally scientific diagnostic tool known as the 'Sphere of Apuleius', which is also preserved in manuscripts from a wide range of ecclesiastical institutions (in this case from across Europe) [Doc. 24]. The core of this was a diagram, usually set out in and around a circle, which offered numerical equivalents for the letters of the alphabet, together with a set of instructions for their use. At its simplest, the user took the name of the sick person, and used the diagram to turn the letters of the name into a numerical sum. In some cases this was also combined with the numbers rendered by the date on which the person fell sick, or by the day of the week. The number thus reached was then divided, according to the rules given in the diagram. What was crucial was the number remaining after a long division had been carried out. This remainder had to be found in the diagram, and its location, together with accompanying symbols or images, would reveal whether the sufferer was going to live or to die – and how long either process would take. To a modern reader this appears clearly magical, or at least superstitious; however, the issue was not so simple in the medieval period. The name of Apuleius, applied to the diagram in a number of surviving medieval copies, helps to explain this, since Apuleius was a figure from the early Christian period, discussed by St Augustine, and believed to have been a Christian and an expert on pagan medicine and magic. Similarly ambiguous was the competing attribution to Pythagoras, who was a less Christian figure, but one whose scholarly and scientific credentials were still more impressive. That the 'sphere' itself was taken seriously is demonstrated by the high number of surviving copies, which are found in manuscripts produced as late as the fourteenth century (Chardonnens, 2007: 181–222; Siraisi, 1990: 183–5; Voigts, 1986).

NATURAL MAGIC AND MEDICAL MAGIC

As was shown in the previous chapter, leading theologians of the thirteenth century guardedly accepted the idea that natural objects and substances had occult powers which could be identified and used by those with the necessary knowledge and expertise, and that the problematic term 'magic' could be applied to this process. The key point was that the practitioner of such magic was manipulating a complex set of interacting forces, but that none of these involved the power or the presence of demons. Thus this was magic, but not in the negative, Augustinian sense of contact between humans and demons. Nevertheless, as the account of lapidaries, herbals and bestiaries in Chapter 4 also made clear, it proved very difficult to define and apply clear boundaries between the relatively simple, manifest, powers possessed by almost all of nature and the occult powers of the same stones, plants or animals. Certainly, the information provided by the expensive reference works listed, many of which were copied and illustrated for secular patrons rather than for scholars, made almost no attempt to make such a separation. Their approach was primarily practical, and their information was presented as purely factual, with almost no attempt to explain or analyse the powers listed. Additionally, different parts of one plant or animal could be effective in relation to quite separate problems, and again, the reasons for this were not discussed. The relationship between natural magic and medicine was thus strong, and yet very difficult to pin down. The overlap of interest is most clearly demonstrated by the fact that substantial parts of the text to be found in lapidaries, herbals and bestiaries, including descriptions of what were regarded as occult powers by the medieval period, were excerpted from classical treatises on medicine and on medicinal substances.

An example of this difficulty in neat classification is provided by the information in circulation about the mandrake plant, whose root was believed to have the shape of the human body. Its powers were confirmed both by the Bible (especially the Book of Genesis and the Song of Solomon) and by Greek medical experts such as Hippocrates. This was reinforced by Dioscorides, who warned that it could be poisonous, but also cited its powers in relation to love and sexual activity, as well as providing more information on its variant forms and its growth pattern (Dioscorides, 2005: Part IV, 75). Pliny followed Dioscorides, but added that mandrake could relieve depression, cause delirium, and cure sleeplessness, eye inflammations and gout (Pliny, 1991: XXV, 147). Isidore discusses it in his influential *The Etymologies*, stressing its value as an anaesthetic in surgery (Book 17, 9.30). Another Greek author, Theophrastus, was the first to recommend that anyone who wished to dig up a mandrake in order to acquire its powerful root should follow a special ritual. This involved using a sword of 'virgin iron' to draw circles around the plant, then using an ivory rod to loosen it, before using the sword to cut it whilst reciting special incantations about love. Related to this was the information set down in an influential early-medieval herbal, attributed to Apuleius Platonicus, which linked the mandrake to supernatural entities. Apuleius wrote that the mandrake shone at night, signifying that it was possessed by a supernatural force which made it even more powerful and dangerous. For this reason, the would-be collector should use not only the sword and the ivory rod to dig up the plant but also a dog, which would then suffer the ill effects which the plant inflicted upon those who disturbed it (Arber, 1953/2010: 39–40).

This range of information, and more besides, was available to the educated in medieval Europe and, as has been shown, carried the authority of both the Bible and the classical world. The range of powers attributed to the mandrake were of a sort which made it desirable to a wide range of users, not just to specialist doctors, but the fact that these powers were attested to by trusted medical authorities clearly added to its value. Medical experts would know from Latin translations of Dioscorides that the fruit of the mandrake brought on sleep, whilst new leaves could be used in a poultice for inflamed eyes and ulcers. The bark of the root itself should be removed while fresh and pounded to extract the juice, which had significant effects as a purgative, painkiller and anaesthetic. However, over-use would kill the patient. University scholars would be informed by works such as the thirteenth-century encyclopaedia *On the Properties of Things*, by Bartholomew the Englishman, of the mandrake's powers as a drug which brought sleep and killed pain. To this medical information Bartholomew added that anyone who wanted to dig up a mandrake must first draw three circles with a sword, then wait until sunset, and take care that the wind was in the correct direction. The powers of the plant were increased if it was dug up whilst the moon was rising (Bartholomew the Englishman, trans. John of Trevisa, ed. Seymour *et al.*, 1975–88: Book 17).

The approach taken by monastic physicians may be represented by extended versions of Apuleius's medical herbal produced for monastic libraries. From the twelfth century onwards this work was copied together with medical treatises, demonstrating how its information was regarded. It stated that the juice of the leaves could be made into a salve which would cure headaches when rubbed on the forehead, or mixed with lavender oil and poured into the ears to cure earache. For gout, the right 'hand' and right 'foot' of the root should be ground to powder, which should be drunk with wine for seven days; this would reduce swelling and take away pain in the muscles. The 'body' of the root, powdered and drunk with hot water, would cure fits or spasms; while mixed with oil and used as an ointment it would cure cramps and muscle pains. Even more impressive was the fact that even a tiny portion of the plant could drive away virulent colds simply by its physical presence. For the laity, a twelfth-century French translation of the Bestiary recommended that the plant be pulled up by a dog, since it would emit a shriek during the process which would kill any living creature close enough to hear it. The risk was worth taking, however, since mandrake root was such a potent medicine that it could cure all sicknesses (Philippe de Thaon, ed. and trans. Wright, 1841: 30–1). After what has been covered here this statement seems like a fair summary; and it is hardly surprising that the wealthy would pay enormous sums for whole mandrake roots, especially if they were markedly humanoid in appearance.

Were the powers of the mandrake magical? Some were, it would seem, not magical at all, but purely medicinal. When the more mysterious of these were enhanced by careful attention to the additional powers of the moon and the winds then the category of natural magic would seem to have been reached. But the supernatural light, the ability to affect emotions such as love, and the power to kill by emitting a scream were far more worrying. All these strongly suggested a connection between the mandrake and the powers of demons; and this latter was clearly all the more likely to be present when the plant was used in a sexual context. That possession of a mandrake root, at least by someone who was not a doctor, was associated with trafficking with demons is suggested by the evidence of the accusations made against Joan of Arc at her trial in 1431. Having been closely questioned as to the nature of the invisible beings who spoke to her and gave her information about the future, Joan was also questioned on whether she had a ring which could bring about cures and whether she owned a mandrake. Joan was perfectly sure, both that the voices she heard were those of saints and angels, and that she possessed neither a powerful ring nor a mandrake. The accusation was not pursued, presumably because there was sufficient evidence against Joan on other charges; but the association of the mandrake with demonic magic is clear (Hobbins, 2005: 75, 127).

ASTROLOGY AND MEDICINE

As the account of learned astrology has already shown, the study of the planets and their powers was not considered magical in itself, nor was the attempt to understand the ways in which these powers affected earthly phenomena. As so many of them affected not only the earth but also the human body and the illnesses which afflicted it, it is hardly surprising that the study of astrology played an ever-greater part in medicine. This process was so far-reaching and so long drawn out that it actually reached its peak in the sixteenth and seventeenth centuries, but it began in the eleventh and twelfth centuries, as with so much discussed in this book. The key was the arrival in western Europe of the tables and instruments which made it possible to draw up detailed and accurate charts of the positions of the planets on specific days, and to calibrate them for specific locations or latitudes. With this expertise, a medical practitioner who knew the day on which an illness began could cast a 'horoscope' for the disease, and could analyse what forces were acting upon it when it first affected the sick person (Wallis, 2010: 318–25). With such information, a scientific prognosis as to the likely strength and duration of the illness would be possible. If needed, calculations could also be made as to which planets were likely to play a major part in the course of the illness, and which might be capable of weakening it. This is clearly far more scientific and sophisticated than the simple procedures associated with the Sphere of Apuleius [Doc. 26].

Practitioners would be guided by textbooks, which set out the medical effects of the planets, themselves related to the Greek **medical** theory of **humours**. In this system, the qualities of heat, cold, dryness and moistness played a fundamental role; in a healthy body these qualities, and the bodily 'humours' associated with them, were well balanced. The treatment of illness was largely a matter of re-balancing the humours in the body of the sick person, a process aided by the use of the medicines derived from natural substances already described. Both the manifest and the 'occult' powers of these medicinal substances could intervene in this way. However, the power of planets such as Jupiter or the sun could do a great deal to strengthen the effect of medicines; and perhaps the most crucial force of all, according to the new medical theory, was that of the moon. Central to this theory was the principle that the moon strongly affected processes of change on earth, as it moved rapidly through its phases and through the signs of the Zodiac. This did not mean in any simple way that the moon caused or cured illness. However, illnesses clearly change as they grow stronger or weaker, and it was this which linked the course of an illness to the effects of the moon. This principle was asserted by the highly influential *Pantegni* of Constantine the African, a Latin compilation of medical theory and doctrine from Greek and Arabic sources, written in Italy in the late eleventh century (Burnett and Jacquart, 1994).

Constantine explained that the moon affects the earth, and everything on it, in ways which change as the moon's position changes in relation to the sun and the earth; and that some days are more powerful in their effects than others. These occur roughly every four days, when the moon is at 45, 90, 130, and 180 degrees to the sun as it waxes, and then at the corresponding points as it wanes. For example, on the fourth day of the lunar month the moon is at 45 degrees to the sun, and has the shape of a sickle or razor-edge when viewed from the earth; and on the eleventh day it is 'gibbous' and at 130 degrees or 'above trine'. In all there are eight such days when the moon is particularly powerful and four when it is particularly influential over the course of an illness. To apply the theory one needed also to understand the theory of critical days, as set out in the works of Galen. This was the doctrine that acute (as opposed to chronic) disease was marked by points

Medical humours: according to Hippocratic theory these were the four main fluids of the human body, i.e. blood, phlegm, yellow bile and black bile. They were associated with the four temperaments, the sanguine, phlegmatic, choleric and melancholic; and also with the qualities of heat, cold, moistness and wetness.

of rapid and important change, or crisis, often identifiable by the discharge of bodily humours such as sweat or blood. There were different views as to the periodicity of such 'critical days'; but there was general acceptance that their outcome could be greatly affected by the moon in particular, and by the other planets in addition. In relation specifically to the moon, a thirteenth-century medical textbook explained that the moon's power for change was strongest on the four days already discussed, and that its power also created a link between the zodiac sign in which the moon was positioned on significant days and the course of the illness. For instance, if a patient becomes ill when the moon is in Libra then the illness is especially likely to go through a critical day when the moon passes through a sign at 90 or 180 degrees to Libra (that is, Cancer, Capricorn or Aries) (Wallis, 2010: 320–1).

Even this theory was simple, however, in comparison to the calculations required to cast the kind of 'disease horoscope' already mentioned, or to relate such a horoscope to the astrological factors particular to a specific patient. As the treatise on 'critical days' also explained, particular zodiac signs had varying significance for individual patients, depending upon their status at the time of the patient's birth. For instance, Jupiter was a fortunate planet, and the sign in which it was located at the time of someone's birth would therefore be fortunate for that individual. Thus, when the individual was ill, the presence of the moon in that sign, or in those at 90 and 180 degrees to it, would mean that help against the illness would be forthcoming. However, the 'malefic' planet, Saturn, would have the opposite effect. Thus the presence of the moon in the sign occupied by Saturn at the individual's birth (or in the three related signs) would bode a time of danger for the patient. Given all this it is scarcely surprising that the famous Italian physician, astrologer and philosopher, Peter of Abano, took the view that only a skilled astrologer could accurately calculate critical days for an individual patient. He went even further than the text already discussed, arguing that the positions of all the planets, including their inter-relations with one another, should also be considered; although he did agree that the moon was the most important factor in determining critical days. Peter made enemies, and came to the attention of the Inquisition when he was accused of sorcery and heresy. Sadly, he died in prison during his long trial (Thorndike, 1929: vol. II, 875–947). However, whilst this illustrates again the risks involved in the link between medicine and astrology, it certainly does not show that the two were separated in the fourteenth century.

It was in this century that the teaching of medicine was established as an accepted and reputable part of the syllabus of the University of Paris, as well as at the more specialised universities of Montpellier and Salerno (Jacquart, 1998). Medicine was not one of the Liberal Arts, and so its teaching took place outside of, and at a higher level than, the arts subjects discussed in Chapter 3; however, it never challenged the status of theology as the highest of all subjects in the medieval world of knowledge. Royal patronage seems to have helped establish the serious study of medicine in late-medieval Paris, and also to have reinforced the status of astrology as an essential component of the subject. Lists of textbooks and of subjects for examination begin to include works on astrology from the middle of the fourteenth century onwards. Nevertheless, it is not easy from this evidence to tell just how many practising doctors and physicians would have the ability to draw up and to interpret the kind of detailed horoscope which Peter of Abano believed to be necessary. The very fact that late-medieval kings of both France and England, like the rulers of fifteenth-century city states in Italy, took pains to acquire and to keep the services of astrologer-physicians suggests that they were few in number. It would also follow that, like Peter of Abano himself, they charged high fees for consultations. However, although this placed their skills beyond the resources of the great majority of people, it does not mean that only the very privileged would be interested in what medical astrology could offer.

THE ZODIAC MAN

A means by which the basics of medical astrology reached a fairly wide audience in the late Middle Ages was the image known as the 'Zodiac Man'. This is found not only in works on medicine and astrology but also, more surprisingly, in many Books of Hours. The latter were perhaps the most popular and widely owned books of the time, and were in such heavy demand that they were a mainstay of early printing presses. Some 789 manuscript copies, and several thousand printed ones, survive from England alone. Their main purpose was religious, since they offered a course of prayers and readings (in Latin) to take the user through a sequence of religious services each day. The Zodiac Man was thus by no means a required part of a Book of Hours, so that his presence in so many surviving examples is in itself evidence of the level of demand for the information offered by the diagram. The link between the services of the Hours and the medical guidance of the Zodiac Man seems to have been the calendar. Books of Hours, like other medieval service books, came equipped with a Church calendar, showing the dates of religious feasts like major saints' days. These calendars also contained notes and tables making it possible for educated users to calculate the dates of 'moveable feasts' like Easter Sunday and Ascension Day each year. The key point here is that the date of Easter was (as it still is) determined by the timing of the first full moon after the Spring equinox.

Such calendars therefore routinely gave information on the timings of full and new moons. However, these were complicated to use, because of the calculations required to adjust them for actual years. By the late fifteenth century it had therefore become customary for the calendar to be accompanied by tables showing the dates of the moveable feasts for a whole run of years. These were frequently accompanied by tables of the movements of the moon, the planet just as crucial for medical calculation as it was for the liturgical calendar (Lawrence-Mathers, 2010: 34–48).

That these tables were used for do-it-yourself medical calculations is shown by the fact that they were often accompanied by charts setting out good and bad times for treatments such as blood-letting and purging. What these tables did was to make it possible for the user to calculate the sign in which the moon was placed on any particular day. The process was laborious but still much simpler than using an astrolabe or set of astrological tables. And the accompanying image of the Zodiac Man is simpler still. It consists simply of a drawing or painting of a human body, usually male and usually naked, with the symbols of the signs of the Zodiac placed over the relevant body parts [Doc. 25]. Thus Aries, the first in the astrological sequence because it begins at the time of the Spring equinox (the beginning of the astrological year) corresponds to the top of the body – in other words, the head. Similarly, the last sign, Pisces, is linked to the feet. It should be noted that signs which ruled the central portions of the body, had power over the relevant internal organs also (thus, for instance, Virgo ruled the stomach). The owner of a Book of Hours thus equipped, or indeed of the smaller and cheaper 'almanacs' which were also produced in large numbers from the fifteenth century on, would be able to calculate the current sign-position of the moon and to check instantly whether that was linked to the site of any illness affecting them. Equally significantly, it had become established medical doctrine by the fourteenth century that blood should not be let, or surgery performed, when the moon was in a sign connected to the affected body part. It is worth emphasising that, despite the modern view of such calculations as bordering on the magical, the presence of this material in such contexts as Books of Hours shows its acceptance as part of a 'scientific' understanding of the links between the human body and the workings of God's creation.

MEDICINE, MAGIC AND POPULAR PRACTICE

Much more troubling than the scientific and calendar-related information to be found in Books of Hours is material apparently aimed at a wider audience, and made available for transmission to the relatively poor by being included in pocket-sized, illustrated almanacs. Even books like these would be beyond the means of the majority of people, at a time when books were luxury possessions, and when the great majority of people were illiterate. However, relatively inexpensive, small pamphlets, or the medieval equivalent of paperbacks, would be owned by the barber-surgeons who provided more affordable medical services to their customers. What makes these troubling, in relation to the increasing anxiety of the Church about how easily the unwary could fall into the clutches of demons, is that they often contain simplified versions of astrological predictions. These are based both on lists of lucky and unlucky days which can be traced all the way back to the early medieval 'prognostics' discussed in Chapter 2 and on simplifications of Latin versions of Arabic astrological treatises. The astrological theory to which they related was that of elections – the teaching that astrologically propitious times for all sorts of human activities could be calculated by those with sufficient skill. The simplified versions found in the small almanacs draw upon the theory that each day of the week is linked to one of the seven planets, as is each hour within the day. More contentious is the connection made from this to the activities and medical data associated with each planet (in medieval theory the sun and moon were both classed as planets). Thus not only can forthcoming risks to body and health be identified, but the likely constitution and occupation of new-born children can be predicted (Carey, 2003).

Even the more learned versions of such teaching, found in works on astrological elections, such as those of Abu Ma'shar and Zahel, could very easily be seen as providing definite predictions as to the future actions of affected individuals (Wallis, 2010: 320–5). This is where the material became dangerous. Whilst it was accepted that the stars could affect the material parts of the human body, just as they affected all earthly things, it was heretical to argue that the stars could dictate human actions and thus negate the key doctrine of free will. What Abu Ma'shar's treatise did was to set out some 600 sets of astrological relationships between the moon and other planets. Each was then given brief interpretations as to their impact on human affairs. As with the medical ideas already discussed, the key element was to know the position of the moon. The next step, which required the skill of an astrologer, was to identify whether any other planet was at a significant angle (or 'aspect') to it. Thus, if Mars was in trine (at 120 degrees) to the moon in Aries, then it was a propitious day for both medical blood-letting and fighting. But if Mars was in opposition (at 180 degrees) to the moon in Cancer then the individual must not enter water. Equally, if Venus was in trine with the moon in Gemini, then one was 'permitted' to employ servants and to enter into marriage contracts. Clearly, at this more sophisticated level, the argument could easily be made that these were no more than recommendations which an individual could ignore, meaning that there was no infringement of free will. Related issues were carefully discussed by another medieval practitioner, Abraham Ibn Ezra, who expressed criticisms of Abu Ma'shar (Ibn Ezra, trans. Sela, 2011: 10–4 and 45–91). But when turned into diagrammatic predictions at a more popular level such information takes on a very different appearance. Does this mean that it was necessarily magical, in a negative sense? The answer is that it was not, but it could certainly lead the unwary into heresy and thus into the clutches of demons, so that this distinction also was easily blurred.

Still more worrying for medieval churchmen, and extremely difficult for historians to reconstruct, were the healthcare practices of the poor. People who could afford neither a book nor the services of a physician (or even a barber-surgeon) had two sources of help in illness. The first, entirely reputable, one was to appeal for the help of a saint. Those fit and free enough to undertake a journey could go on pilgrimage to a shrine such as that of St James at Compostela, or to a more local centre if that was all that could be managed. No medieval writer considered cures achieved in this way to be magical and so, whilst they are fascinating in themselves, they are outside the concerns of this book. Much more troubling were those forms of attempted protection against disease, or cure of actual illness, which Church writers referred to as 'incantations' and 'sorceries'. The manuals for confessors which were the thirteenth-century successors to the early-medieval penitentials provide information on these, and confirm once again how complex was the boundary between the acceptable, the dangerous and the downright sorcerous. In theory, the definitions offered by St Augustine remained fundamental, and appeared to offer certainty. Augustine had condemned amulets and medical cures which took the forms of 'incantations', 'marks and characters', and things hung up or tied onto the body, and had stated that such things were not only superstitious but also magical and demonic. In practice, however, this left various types of behaviour recorded in medieval Europe very difficult to define.

The scale of the problem is suggested by a question which thirteenth-century confessors were to ask those who came to them. This was 'Do you know any of the incantations against fevers and illness which are called blessings?' This question accepts that for the confessing sinner this type of remedy was a 'blessing', even whilst categorising such things as 'incantations' and thus posing a real risk of inadvertently opening the way for demons. Even the written texts of prayers, when superstitiously misused, could be dangerous. Thus another thirteenth-century confessors' manual stressed that written copies of prayers in Latin were acceptable possessions for the illiterate; but that written prayers which included supposedly secret names of God, and whose owners were promised protection from illness and misfortune, were to be emphatically condemned (Rider, 2011: 92, 96; Rider,

2012: 25–45). As Thomas Aquinas warned, such names were at best superstitious, and were all too likely to be the names of demons rather than of God. This type of literature also contains valuable references to secular practitioners, referred to as 'enchanters' and 'enchantresses' who sing charms over the sick. Such behaviour was not forbidden in itself; but it is clear that educated priests were very anxious about it, since the negative term 'enchanter' is applied even to people who recite only standard prayers.

Even more troubling was that many such people apparently attempted to affect the illness directly by issuing commands as if it were a sentient being. We are told that they commanded or 'adjured' the diseases and threats, but that even this was acceptable as long as they invoked only well-known and safe powers, such as those of Christ's Passion or Cross. The laying of hands on a sick person whilst reciting a prayer was cautiously accepted even when performed by a lay person, as it had biblical support. However, reciting prayers over inanimate objects, such as 'an apple, a pear or a belt' was forbidden. This prohibition is not explained. However, such objects were presumably intended to be placed upon the body of the sick or endangered person, and would thus fall into the forbidden category of things superstitiously tied onto someone. Further evidence of just how difficult this area of behaviour was to keep safe is that if an object such as a belt was lent by the guardians of a saint's shrine (for instance to a woman experiencing a difficult childbirth) that was entirely safe. But a lay person superstitious enough to recite words over inanimate objects could clearly not be trusted to stick only to established, standard prayers. Thus both they and their clients were in terrible danger of demonic influence and must be stopped.

The Church's 'front line' against popular superstition and magic was those clergy who had direct contact with the laity; and these included the friars as well as parish priests. Friars in particular were given thorough training in preaching and teaching before being sent out, and it is clear that many of them were extremely effective in reaching and educating large audiences, especially in the growing towns and cities of medieval Europe. Such preachers played an important role in carrying the ideas expressed in the confessors' manuals to the urban masses, but there is evidence that they themselves were sometimes shocked by the ideas and behaviour they encountered. The best evidence has been left by St Bernardino of Siena, whose 'mission' took place in the early fifteenth century and whose sermons had great effects upon the large audiences who came to listen. Many of them bear witness to the strength of his concern, both about the superstition rife amongst the people and about the influence of demons. His sermon 'Of the Scourges of God' was preached in Siena in the 1420s, and warns of the coming punishment of God upon those who use charms and divinations (St Bernardine of Siena [sic], ed. Orlandi, trans. Robins, 1920: 163–76). Popular practitioners seem to have been called upon to help in cases of theft and illness but Bernardino casts aside the careful discriminations set out in the confessors' manuals. Any divinations and charms are adorations of the devil, and users are just as guilty as suppliers. Bernardino also warns that those who can break charms can also make them, and they also are guilty of the same crime. He tells his audience that, when any maker of charms says they are going to cure someone, they should be seized and burnt as a witch or sorcerer. To emphasise the point he goes on to tell of how, when he preached the same message in Rome, enormous numbers of accusations and arrests were made. Other members of the clergy expressed concern at the number of arrests, but Bernardino was unshakable in his belief that anyone who tolerated such practices was as guilty as those who directly used them, and that society must be saved from this enemy within. The cities of fifteenth-century Italy were clearly not a safe place for popular healers or their clients, and the evidence suggests that the situation was similar across the whole of late-medieval Europe. Those who could afford the services of qualified physicians, and those with access to the shrines of saints, were safe, but those who turned when ill to makers of charms and incantations were placing themselves in several sorts of danger. This hardening of opinion will be discussed in more detail in the final chapter of this book.

Plate 1 Caladrius bird, reputed to foretell the fate of a sick man, above a man in bed, from a bestiary based on the fifth century *Physiologus*, Durham, c.1200 (vellum), English school, (thirteenth century) / British Library, London, UK / The Bridgeman Art Library

Plate 2 Demon tempting a woman, exterior figure, thirteenth century (stone) / Chartres Cathedral, Chartres, France / The Bridgeman Art Library

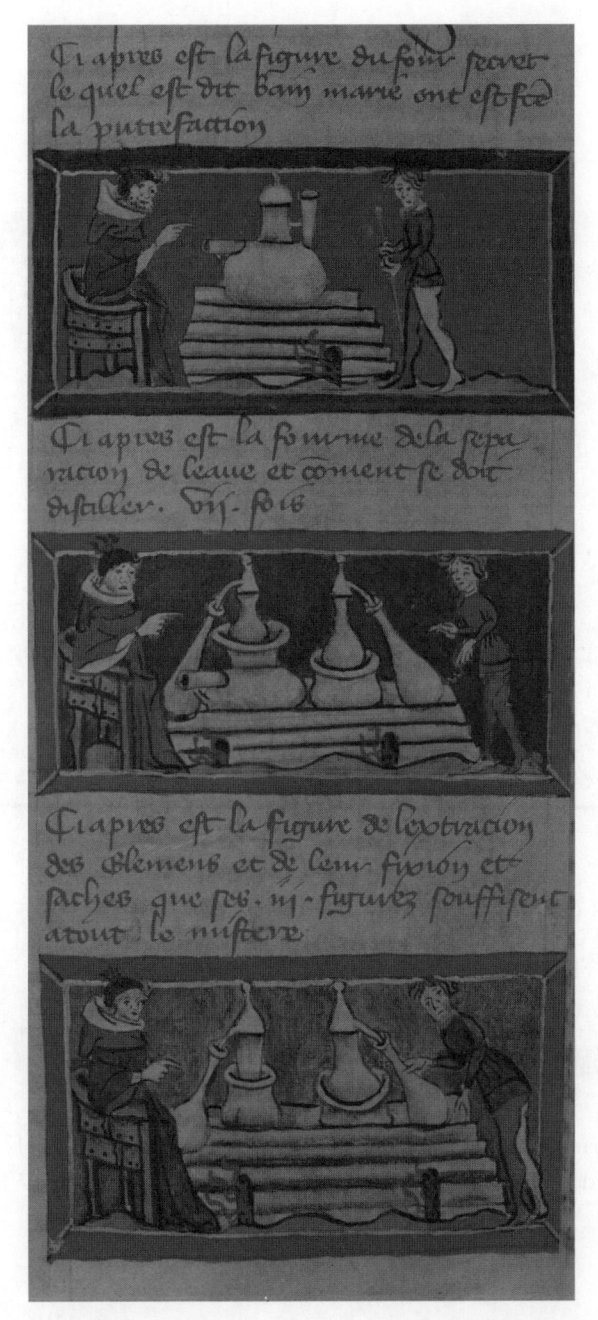

Plate 3 Alchemists at work, from a manuscript of alchemy (vellum), French school, (fourteenth century) / Bibliothèque de L'Arsenal, Paris, France / Archives Charmet / The Bridgeman Art Library

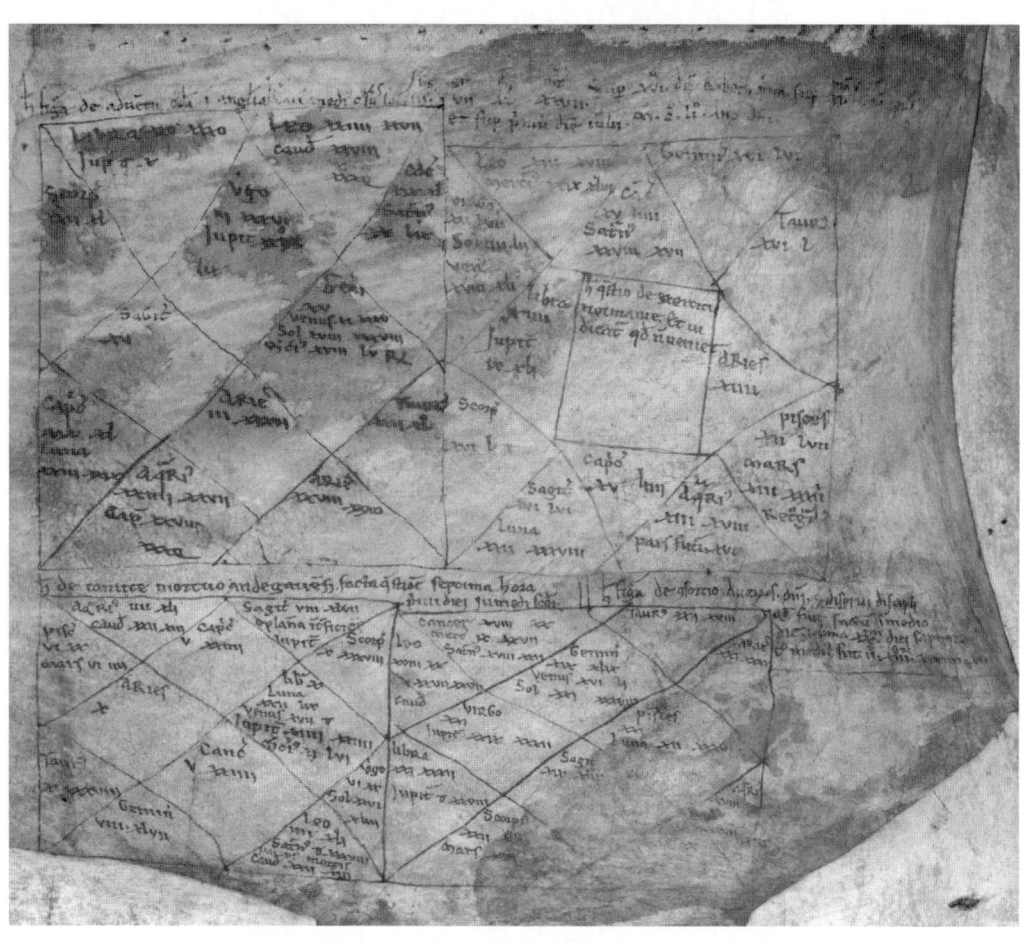

Plate 4 Anglo-Norman horoscopes, 1151 (vellum), Adelard of Bath (fl.1151) (attr.to) / British Library, London, UK / © British Library Board. All rights reserved / The Bridgeman Art Library

Plate 5 Mandrake, from *Tacuinum Sanitatis* (vellum), Italian school, (fourteenth century) / Osterreichische Nationalbibliothek, Vienna, Austria / Alinari / The Bridgeman Art Library

Plate 6 Moorish astrolabe, from Cordoba, 1054, Spanish school, (eleventh century) / Jagiellonian Library, Cracow, Poland / Giraudon / The Bridgeman Art Library

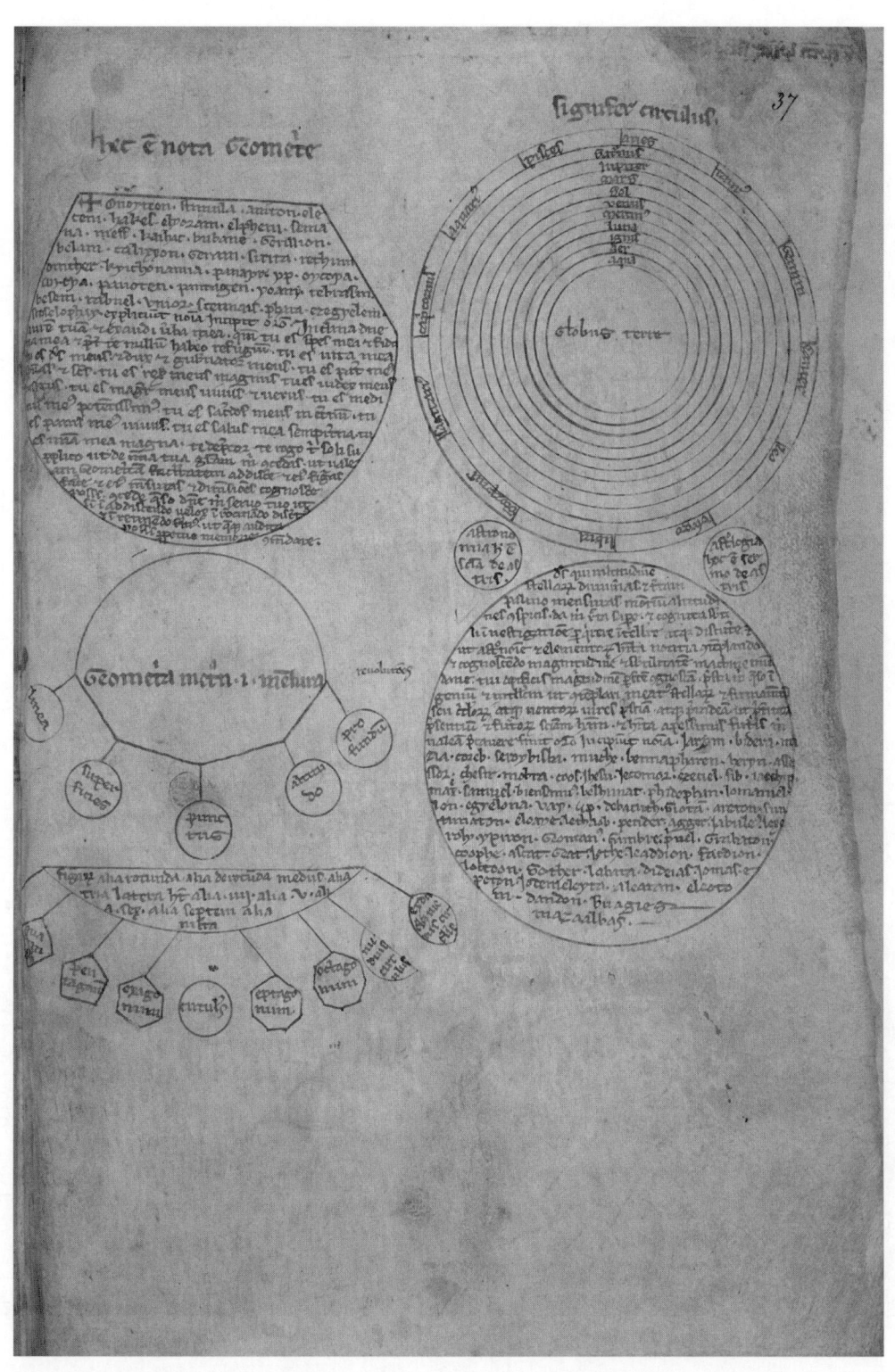

Plate 7 BL Sloane 1712, fol. 37; an image for astronomy and astrology, in a fourteenth-century English manuscript of the *Ars Notoria* © The British Library Board

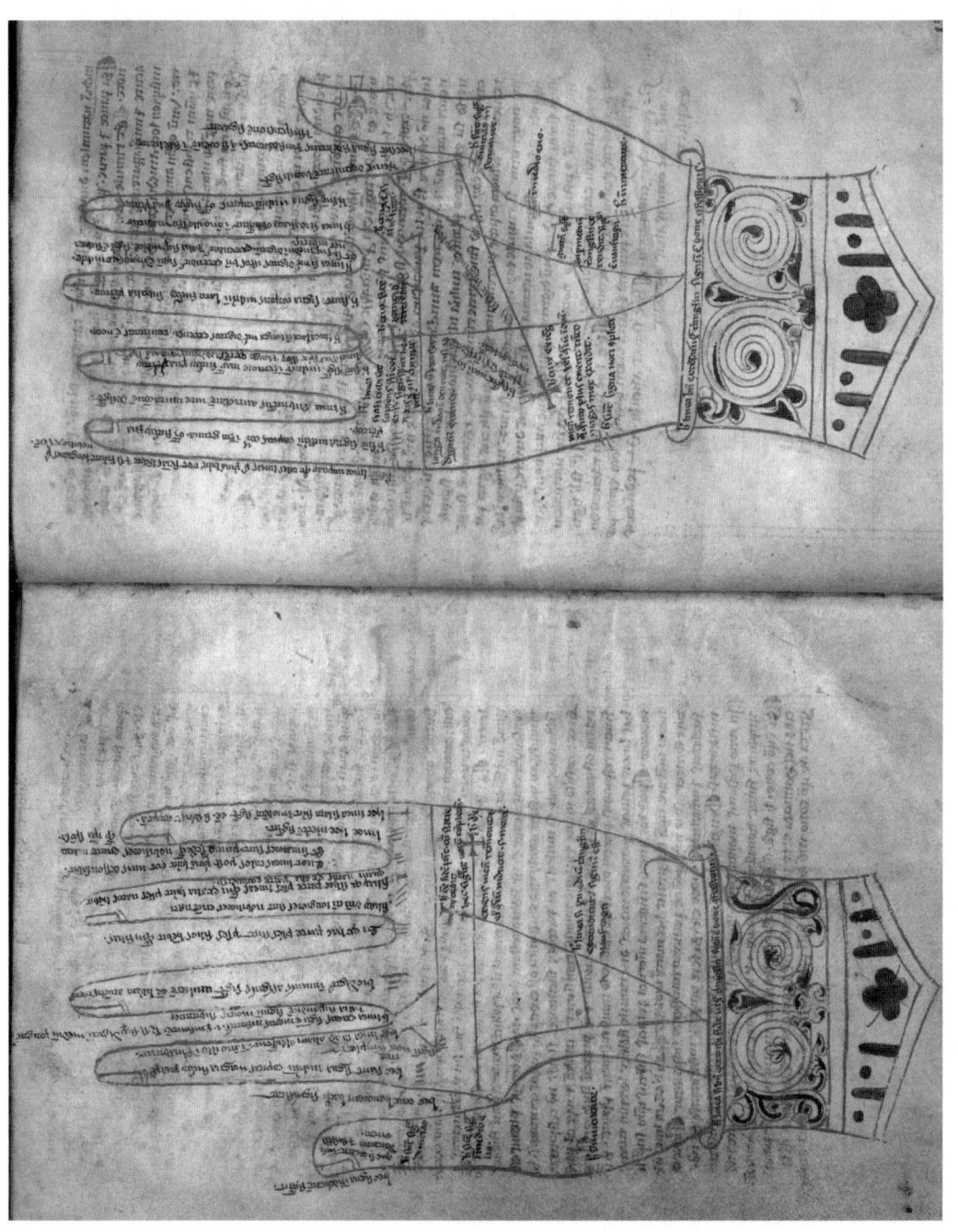

Plate 8 BL Sloane 2030, fols. 125v-126r; illustrations for a treatise on palmistry, in a thirteenth-century English collection of theological, scientific and prognostic texts © The British Library Board

6

Conclusion: the rise of magical crime

As this book has shown, it proved very difficult in the twelfth and thirteenth centuries to classify and control the rapidly expanding knowledge of the earthly world, the stars and the cosmos. There was no challenge to the basic views on the demonic origin of magic which had been laid down by the Fathers of the Church in the fifth century; yet defining what was actually magical within the new knowledge proved complex. Even an activity as clearly magical and problematic as the deliberate summoning of spirits could be, and was, defended as a virtuous expansion of established practices of prayer and meditation. Nevertheless, great steps forward in the systematisation of theological and legal terms were taken in the twelfth century. Specialists emphasised that magical practices not only endangered the individual human soul, as had been argued by early authorities like Augustine, but also posed a threat to Christian society. Tainted transactions between humans and demons could have very real effects. In Chapter 2, on the Church, the important role played by twelfth-century lawyers and theologians like Gratian and Peter Lombard was discussed. These great scholars introduced the concept of demonically inspired magical crime into their textbooks, and thus into increasingly technical discussions about magic. Central to this was the use of their works in university environments, where most professional members of lay and ecclesiastical courts were trained. The newly systematised collections of theological and legal propositions meant that, from this point on, those in authority had a clear set of established definitions at hand, ready for use when needed. Particularly fundamental for future developments was the fact that Gratian and Peter Lombard agreed in treating magical practices as both demonic and deceptive.

This basic theological and legal work was added to during the thirteenth century when, following the influx of Arabic material into western Europe, Church writers increasingly focused on the problem of demons. A key question was that of the influence of demonic powers over supernatural phenomena, including attempts to harness the marvels and wonders found in the natural world. Within the learned environment of the universities, theologians like William of Auvergne and Albertus Magnus produced fuller, even more systematic analyses on the issue. As seen in Chapter 4, they both accepted that there were occult powers in nature which, if properly studied and understood, could be harnessed by highly trained individuals [Doc. 28]. However, such work required a correct balance of natural-scientific and religious knowledge. As in all areas of learning where advanced Arabic knowledge was being juxtaposed with more traditional ideas, the central concern was to define what was acceptable. One of the results of this huge undertaking was the development of a new terminology, expanding and defining the category of the marvellous. This was especially important since this concept offered an alternative to the opposition between negative demonic magic and divine miraculous revelation.

WILLIAM OF AUVERGNE

Pioneering this process, as has been seen, was the influential theologian and Bishop of Paris, William of Auvergne. His theory, mostly contained in *On the Universe* (*De universo*) and *On the laws* (*De legibus*), introduced a new categorisation of magical practices. He upheld the traditional condemnation of practices like divination and astrology as demonically inspired, but he also allowed for the manipulation of the occult properties of nature by learned individuals. It was also necessary for William to set out a careful and comprehensive discussion of the nature of demons, and the scope of their operations, within the accepted model of the universe. This posited a universe operating under God's natural laws, some of which are apparent, and others occult. Occult properties can be manipulated by both learned individuals and demons, and the latter remain bound by natural law despite their greater powers. The laws that govern the universe can only be superseded by God, their creator [Doc. 29].

William clearly respected the discipline of natural philosophy, and its scientific observation of nature. Accordingly he set natural magic clearly apart from demonic manipulation of nature (William of Auvergne, *De legibus*, Cap. 14). He ties the latter closely to negative forms of magical practice, such as the superstitious observance of the stars; manipulation of images, figures, words and names; and superstitious ways of choosing times and seasons or finding lost objects (William of Auvergne, *De legibus*, Cap. 23). Divination from dreams, auguries, constellations, sneezes, figures, marks, characters and images is condemned (William of Auvergne, *De legibus*, Cap. 14); as are incantations. For William, magicians do not always realise that lying behind their wonder-making is nothing other than demonic manipulation, and thus they are involved in idolatrous transactions. Demons can avail themselves of the forces of nature to deceive naïve humans. Here, William is reasserting both patristic and twelfth-century views, whilst giving a fuller sense of the dangers presented by such demonic activity. In natural magic, William sees an alternative to demonic magic (William of Auvergne, *De universo*, II-iii-21). Natural magic is the eleventh part of all knowledge of the natural world. William attempted to distinguish between *magi* (harmless magicians) and *malefici* (workers of evil magic). Thus natural magic is harmless, although its works may appear so marvellous to the ignorant that they could seem to be the works of gods or demons [*Doc. 29*]. As examples of natural magic William offers the power of the magnet, the sudden regeneration of animals such as frogs and worms, or the ability of the soul of the basilisk to work marvels outside its body.

William not only provides a philosophical framework for analysing new knowledge on natural phenomena; he also shows a remarkable familiarity with magical texts. He makes reference to works ascribed to Aristotle, Hermes Trismegistus and Solomon. He mentions the *Sacred Book* and also the 'cursed book' of Cocogrecus on 'stations to the cult of Venus' (probably a thirteenth-century treatise on ritual magic) (Thorndike, 1929: vol. 2, 279). He writes of Artesius, or Arthesius, whom he calls a magician and philosopher, identifying him as the author of a book on the powers of words and characters (William of Auvergne, *De legibus*, Cap. 27). In the same work, he describes how in his youth he examined books of judicial astrology together with books of magic and sorcery [*Doc. 18*]. He also criticises the error of magicians and sorcerers who believed there were armies of spirits in the sky. He could even describe necromantic operations like that of the 'The Major Circle' which supposedly summoned four demon-kings, accompanied by hosts of phantom horsemen, jugglers and musicians (William of Auvergne, *De Universo*, II-iii-7). According to these same books of 'experiments', says William, water can be made to appear out of nowhere as can wonderful castles with gates, towers, walls and citadels which then vanish without a trace. William ascribes these wonders to demonic intervention and condemns the magicians as idolaters. Such magicians attempt the subversion of nature, as when they claim to bind fire so that it cannot burn, or prevent robbers from stealing, or stop water from flowing downhill. For William, such things can only truly be accomplished through miraculous intervention [*Doc. 29*].

William especially attacks the magicians' use of images and characters, words, names and incantations, and especially of wax images to harm people or things. He states that he does not believe that Nectanebus (legendary father of Alexander the Great) could sink ships by submerging wax images of them. Moreover, magic images do not possess intelligence or will and when an image appears effective it is only due to demonic deceit. Claims that there is divinity in stones or herbs are as false as the belief that men can make gods, for minds and souls cannot be put into statues. There is no divinity in the angels of Solomon's pentagon, and those who believe this are idolaters. William appears to be referring here to works like the *Ars Notoria*, an idea further confirmed when he says that such idolatrous cults distinguish between four kinds of figures: seals, rings, characters and images and that such are the rings and seal of Solomon (William of Auvergne, *De legibus*, Cap. 23). William also denies that there is magic power in mere words or incantations, including supposed names of God, thus if sorcerers use them they are calling upon demons (Thorndike, 1929: 338–71).

RITUAL MAGIC AND AQUINAS'S DEMONOLOGY

William's account of thirteenth-century magical practices accords with surviving evidence on what ritual magic was actually like. In the *Sworn*, or *Sacred*, *Book* of Honorius of Thebes we find instructions on how to obtain a beatific vision by constructing a magic circle and summoning an 'angel' (or demon) (Mathiesen, 1992). The text also promises knowledge of all the heavens, control over all the angels, knowledge of all the sciences, of someone's death, and of all things present, past and future, including of plants, stones and stars. The work was translated into vernacular languages and was still of interest in the sixteenth century, as proven by an ownership inscription in one of the manuscripts to John Dee, the famous magician of the Elizabethan court. As noted in Chapter 3, it is likely that William actually knew the work. Its claims of an official assault on magic and magicians, aimed at exterminating both the magic art and its practitioners, are not without substance; although the assertion that ritual magic was genuinely devout is more problematic. Whether or not these claims are true, down to the fourteenth century actual magical practices were not widespread and represented less of a problem for the Church than heresy. Awareness of magic, however, was growing. As we have seen, writers were struggling to come to terms with new paradigms and challenges. Another influential attempt at dealing with this problem was led by the thirteenth-century theologian Thomas Aquinas, who believed that parts of magic could work [*Doc. 30*]. However, this is only because of the actions of demons; human beings on their own are incapable of producing wonders. If such wonders are produced by means of divine powers then we are witnessing a miracle. He acknowledged the presence of hidden powers in natural substances, but these are subtle and not of the type that bring about the wondrous effects promised by magicians and necromancers. Such powers could be active and useful in the art of medicine, but when stronger effects occur, they do so because of demonic intervention.

In the hierarchy of creation, according to Aquinas, demons are placed somewhere between God and human beings. There was still plenty of space for speculation, however, and medieval writers took the issue to heart, producing all sorts of speculative treatises on fallen angels in particular. They posed questions such as: what kind of angels were the ones who fell? Are all demons fallen angels? Was there something in their essential nature that predisposed them to fall? If so, would this have been unfair on the part of God? The story of the Fall could at least provide some clues, because the leader of the rebel angels, Lucifer, the bringer of light, was one of the most powerful angels and closest to God. It was Lucifer who committed the unforgivable sin of refusing to accept the superiority of God; he challenged God directly despite the fact that He had created him together with all the other angels. The story of this Fall is not included in the book of Genesis or anywhere else in the Bible; however, it was part of a separate category of sacred texts, the Apocrypha, which circulated with the Bible (Anderson, 1997: 105–34). Genesis is not clear on whether the serpent which tempted Eve was Satan himself, but theologians were definite that demons could make their way from hell to earth and affect the physical world.

Demons were not believed to possess physical bodies, and hence could pass through a wall and be invisible to humans. However, they were not above the laws of nature, for they were part of God's creation. Moreover, the Bible told of demons being cast out of infirm bodies, where their presence had caused harm, by Christ's miracles. Thus, whilst they were frequently linked to illnesses like epilepsy and melancholy, their attacks could be defeated (Caciola, 2006; Kieckhefer, 1997: 57–64). A question which arose for thirteenth-century theologians was whether demons could make bodies for themselves that were perceptible to human beings. Since demons did not possess divine powers, Aquinas was clear that they could not create matter by themselves, and thus their ability to create bodies was limited. They did, however, possess the power to manipulate matter, and thus could create thunderstorms, for example, by producing the movement of moist air [*Doc. 30*]. Another example from Aquinas provides details of how demons could impregnate a woman. They would make for themselves a fake female body, with which they would seduce a man and steal his seed. They would keep this seed and then make a male body and thus use the seed to make a woman pregnant. The seed would be affected by the power of the demon and the result would be a child that was not simply human (Thomas Aquinas, trans. K. Foster, 2006: vol. 9, 39–44). By allowing demons to intervene in human affairs, God was testing the resilience of human beings; to make the battle fair He allowed his angels to help people resist the power of demons. Increasing emphasis was placed on the belief that for every person there was a guardian angel to help ward off the negative influence of the devil (Keck, 1998, 161–5).

This world-view suggested that all around human beings there were imperceptible angels, spirits and devils, who could draw upon special powers and affect life on earth. Ritual magic offered a promise that by tapping into that power, a mere human could gain power over angels, demons and spirits. As has been seen, surviving texts assert that, contrary to the allegations of the Church, magicians were observant religious men, but for historians, as for medieval theologians, evidence is problematic. As the propositions of theologians like William of Auvergne and Thomas Aquinas have shown, the response of the Church was to discredit these beliefs as demonically inspired illusions, associating them with idolatry at best and with heresy at worst. An additional example comes from the *Book of Angels, Rings, Characters and Images of the Planets*, a fifteenth-century compilation of earlier texts dating to the thirteenth century, mostly containing psalms and prayers (Lidaka, 1998: 32–75). This text includes instructions for the production of magical rings. These instructions frequently involve sacrificial rituals, which could take the form of animal sacrifice or the offering of stones. If you wish for armed soldiers to appear, for example, you should have access to the ring of Mars. As part of the procedure, you must sacrifice a bird of prey in the fire, then write with its blood on its skin the name of the relevant angel and its character. Using this ring will also allow you to make a castle or mock swordplay appear (Lidaka, 1998: 46–9). Since this work also offers the means to impose pain, disability and death on specific individuals, it appears to support the negative views of the theologians discussed here. The fact that users of the book might attempt to cause such effects also makes it unlikely that they could genuinely believe that the beings whose powers they harnessed were truly angels. William of Auvergne and Thomas Aquinas were responding to genuine problems, even if only a learned elite could attempt such magic.

FOURTEENTH-CENTURY SHOW TRIALS

The Church's interest in magical practices developed further during the fourteenth century, and it is not a coincidence that this period saw an outburst of show trials for magic in France, the Papal court in Avignon, and England. The people accused in these trials were rich and powerful individuals, with close connections to lay and ecclesiastical courts, suggesting that the accusation of magical crime was a tool in the political game. During the reign of Edward I in England, in 1301–3, Walter Langton, Bishop of Coventry and king's treasurer, was accused of trying to gain the favour of the king and of amassing a large fortune with the use of sorcery and necromancy (Jones, 1972: 119; Beardwood, 1964). The accusation was not brought forward by the king or a member of the court, but by a member of the minor aristocracy, Sir J. Lovtot. The long list of charges included accusations of simony, nepotism and adultery, and also of hiring a magician to murder Lovtot's mother, with whom Langton was perhaps having an affair. The charges also included the accusation of having made a pact with the devil, involving words and 'obscene kisses'. Edward I defended Langton and was unconvinced by the accusations. These, however, gained currency and the then pope, Boniface VIII, summoned Langton to the papal court to discuss the charges. The whole affair resulted in an incredibly expensive legal process, and an inconclusive one too; Langton eventually came back to England without being condemned, but not being absolved either. The business was settled when in 1303 the king found Langton innocent on all charges under his own authority and that of the Archbishop of Canterbury. A few years later another English royal official was accused of using magic to improve his position at court and to attack his enemies; this was the chamberlain of the exchequer, Adam Stratton (Peters, 1978: 119).

These cases introduced something new into the history of magic, and are indicative of a series of legal developments that were taking root especially around the figure of Boniface VIII. Ironically, Boniface himself was the posthumous victim of similar accusations levied by the French king, Philip IV, 'the Fair' (Peters, 1978: 121; Coste, 1995). From 1300 onwards, both Edward I and Philip IV were increasingly at odds with Boniface over the issue of whether kings were under the international authority of the pope and whether they had the right to tax Church property. Boniface's view was that he was the sole and universal source of power in western Europe, and that as head of Christ's church he had the authority to delegate such power to lay rulers. This position assumed that kings were bound to do the pope's will, including on the issue of property held by the Church in their own kingdoms. Boniface's position brought him into conflict with lay rulers, especially the King of France. In Italy itself, and more or less at the same time that Langton was being accused by Lovtot in England, one of Boniface's own cardinals, a member of the Colonna clan, accused the pope himself of being in league with the devil and of being a sorcerer. Colonna's accusation was only later committed to writing. The cardinal accompanied a French expedition against Boniface which ultimately cost the pope his life. Boniface's career as pope was troubled from the very start, because he was elected while his predecessor was still alive. Colonna's accusations referred back to the moment of Boniface's election, and alleged that on that day he was wearing a collar which actually hissed and moved. Moreover, cunningly concealed in Boniface's ring was a demon to which he spoke. However, it was only after Boniface's death that Philip IV brought accusations of sorcery against him. The case dragged on from 1309 to 1311, when Boniface's successor, Clement V, effectively sacrificed the Order of the Templars to persuade the king to drop the case against the dead pope.

It was Philip IV who also brought the accusations against the Order of the Templars which resulted in the complete destruction of the order. The charges brought against the Templars did not explicitly include sorcery, but provide an interesting list of things the accusers considered evil (Barber, 1978, 1994). The timing of this attack was no coincidence. It gathered pace on 24 August 1307 with a letter from Pope Clement V to Philip, stating that the pope had decided to act on the accusations that the king had levied, as they were now being levied by others as well (Barber and Bate, 2002: 249–50). The Master of the Templars himself, convinced of the innocence of the order, had also asked the pope to deal with the accusations. Thus, the pope proposed to begin with a careful investigation at Poitiers, and asked Philip to wait for the proceedings. On 14 September, however, Philip issued an order for the arrest of all the Templars in his kingdom. There is no mention in the order of the actions already taking place at Poitiers. The terms of the order express the king's inconsolable grief at the wickedness that was corrupting the order and his kingdom (Barber and Bate, 2002: 244–8). Sensationally, the whole order was accused of being transformed from Christian knights into heretical devil worshippers. The charge of heresy was based upon practices that were supposedly taking place within the order, including spitting on the crucifix, sodomy, idol worship, denial of Christ, obscene kissing and secret rites, allegedly beginning with a ritualistic ceremony of initiation. Clearly, devil worship was part of a broader package of horrible crimes in this case, but the case was followed across Europe, and the successful destruction of the Templars can only have helped to spread fear about demonic influences.

HERESY AND WITCHCRAFT

The charges levied against the Templars were built around concepts of idolatry and of illegal forms of intercourse, and extended later to abominable forms of cannibalism and infanticide. Being charged with heresy was by far more serious at this point than any accusation of magical crime. In 1233 a decretal letter by Gregory IX, *Vox in Rama* (*A Voice in Rama*), mentioned practices associated with a sect of heretics from the Rhineland (Peters, 1978: 158–60); the similarities with the accusations levied against the Templars almost eighty years later are striking. This German sect was accused of denying true religion, gathering together in secret at night, swearing in new members by means of an idolatrous ritual, and engaging in orgies and illicit sex. Apparently they would not hesitate to attack their enemies and bring about their deaths, using the powdered corpses of murdered infants as magical ointments. The focus here was less on idolatry than on demon worship. The sect not only worshiped an image or a statue, but a living creature, allegedly a demon in the form of an animal or a male human being. If an animal it might take the shape of a frog or a toad, and ritual kissing on its mouth would follow; the demon could also take the form of a monstrously large goose, duck or black cat, which would descend upon its followers to be ritualistically kissed in the hindquarters. If a man, he would have black eyes and an emaciated face, with only mere skin over his bones. Ritualistic kissing would also follow in this case, but it would feel cold as ice and erase all memory of the catholic faith from the heart of the worshipper. This list of charges was sent to the pope by regional inquisitors, with the intention of impressing upon him how very serious the threat of heresy was. The question of whether inquisitors should also be concerned with magic was addressed in the 1250s to Pope Alexander IV, who instructed them not to undertake investigations into divination or sorcery unless manifest heresy was involved (Kors and Peters, 2001: 116–18). Nevertheless, this paved the way for future inquisitorial trials of magical crime. Curiously, as a crime against state and church, sorcery or *maleficium* could already be tried in both ecclesiastical and secular courts, which raises the question of why the Inquisition became increasingly concerned with it.

It was in 1327, in Florence, that the first university master was burnt alive by the Inquisition on charges of heresy. This was Francesco d'Ascoli, a master of astronomy and astrology. He was accused both of casting a horoscope for Christ and, in at least one of his books, expressing heretical views on the powers of demons (Peters, 1978: 123). These charges clearly combine heresy and magic; and it is important to note that by this point there had been a string of trials for magic, including not only those discussed above but also those of cardinals, bishops and archbishops at the papal court of Avignon. In 1320, Pope John XXII had allegedly survived three magical attacks by members of his own papal court (Peters, 1978: 129–31). In 1317 Hugues Geraud, Bishop of Cahors, was accused and convicted of having hired professional magicians to perform harmful magic against the Pope; he was burnt alive. In 1320 Matteo and Galeazzo Visconti were charged with a plot to kill the pope by means of poison and ritual- and image-magic. They hired a professional magician who later claimed that he was forced to do the Milanese bidding through kidnapping and torture, and after escaping he chose to present his evidence to the pope rather than take his chances with the Visconti back in Milan. By this point the attitude of the papacy had shifted, and in a letter to inquisitors in the south of France, John XXII explicitly asked them to turn their attention to criminal magic. He stated that practitioners of evil magic must be dealt with, for 'they are infecting God's flock', and 'they need to flee from the midst of the house of God'; the rhetoric here is strongly reminiscent of earlier condemnations of heresy [*Doc. 31*]. By this point there was a clear fear that society in general, and its highest representatives in particular, were liable to magical attack. However, these attacks were believed to require the skills of specialists in learned ritual magic.

Records of actual accusations for witchcraft do not start to appear consistently until the fifteenth century (Kieckhefer, 1976: 106–47). In England, for example, there appears to be a sudden shift in the attitudes towards accusations against witches. Whereas legal records of the thirteenth century attest the failure of accusations of magic in lower places, proving that raising a charge of magical crime was not in itself sufficient to secure a conviction, the situation by the fifteenth century appears to have changed. During the reign of King John, at the court of the King's Bench, a woman identified as 'the wife of the merchant' accused another woman of sorcery. No additional details are provided, but it is clear from the records that the accusation failed, and the accuser was herself placed under the mercy of the king, who decided on a penalty, probably a heavy fine. In the fifteenth century, on the other hand, the old English term witchcraft appeared again, used predominantly in association with female criminals.

In the fourteenth century, handbooks of church or canon law were written by experienced inquisitors for the benefit of junior colleagues. The key document is perhaps Bernard Gui's *Manual for Inquisitors* [*Doc. 32*]. Gui had practised as an inquisitor for many years, based in Toulouse, during the period of the rise of inquisitorial activity against sorcery. His text, dating from c.1327, is contemporary with the papal decretal *Super Illius Specula* (*Upon His Watchtower*). However, there is no evidence of a special interest in magic in Gui's manual; as would be expected, his main interest was in heresy. Gui tried about 1,000 individuals during his time in Toulouse (Turning, 2010: 10), all of them for heresy and none of them for magic. His handbook includes only a small section on magic, which nevertheless expands the existing legal definition of sorcery. Gui was up to date with canon law and decretals. When referring to necromancy, Gui describes the performance of complicated and learned rituals, involving expensive objects and the use of Church liturgy. The implication is still that only someone literate in Latin and familiar with church services could be realistically considered as a practitioner. However, the text also mentions another type of magic, related to unlearned people who were not priests, and particularly to the practice of medical magic. The emphasis is on muddled medical cures, which had been forbidden as magical since the time of Augustine. As shown in Chapter 5, these seem to have been widely used by the fourteenth century and were strongly condemned. It is telling that similar practices are unhesitatingly condemned by Gui, who identifies them with very serious magic and equates their threat to that of learned sorcery. Thus, without much ado, the traditional practitioner of cures is equated with a learned necromancer. At this point, the blueprint for the witch is taking shape.

Other categories in Gui's handbook also attest to the widespread use of popular magic, including rituals to locate lost or stolen properties, in which even priests were indulging. Gui provides the example of a priest who was accused and found guilty of misusing liturgical materials, including the consecrated host itself, in such rituals (Peters, 1978: 133). By the end of the Middle Ages, there are corresponding records of individuals thought to possess special abilities and to harness particular powers through the use of formulae and strange things. They were believed to cure people, identify wrong-doers and locate stolen property. Another category is that of fertility magic. Early medieval Penitentials show concern about love or erotic magic, thought of by the Church as being carried out by women. Such practices were used to gain the love of men, to secure a pregnancy or to bring about an abortion [Doc. 19]. All these were treated in the Penitentials and in later canon law as very serious issues. Gui shows evidence of having come across these strange folk practices too; but he does not make any distinction between them and the learned liturgical rituals of the priest.

From Aquinas onwards, the proposition that occult properties in nature could manifest in natural physical effects, though only in a rather limited way, was generally accepted. Where an effect exceeded the power of a natural substance it could not be attributed to that substance; hence, the underlying power causing the effect must have some other cause. In most cases that other power was identified with demons. Therefore, even if the practitioner thought he was just channelling occult virtues found in nature, as in natural magic, the likelihood was that he was actually harnessing demonic powers. Even in ignorance, the use of non-standard prayers, the suffumigation of herbs and the imitation of church services, could actually imply worshipping and offering sacrifices to demons. Thus, such practitioners were considered to be committing very serious religious crimes. In the minds of those in official positions, like Gui, these practices were not very different from those of the learned clerical sorcerer, and claims of benevolent intent did not make them harmless.

Whether Gui's intention was to innovate is not clear, but he did so nevertheless. Any inquisitor using his text as a guide would be left without any doubt that neighbours who carried out informal practices such as these in their communities posed a serious threat. These more common practices then became as worthy of attention from the Inquisition as learned clerical practices already were. From the Lateran Council of 1215 onwards there was something else in place too, and that was the devotion of more attention to the welfare of common Christians. Until the twelfth century, detailed enquiry into common people's behaviour and ideas was not necessary, and perhaps not even possible. Dutifully, the Church made the necessary sacrifices to God on behalf of wider society, and as long as everyone observed the Sabbath, turned up to the required services and paid the requisite dues, common people were fulfilling their primary Christian duties. After 1215, much more detailed attention was given to the spiritual welfare of all members of the Church, both lay and clerical. From here on, it was expected that everyone, and not just the wealthy, should go to confession at least once a year, so they would receive penance and absolution. It is this effort that lies behind the production of confessional manuals for priests during the thirteenth century, with their probing questions. In this way, the Church gained a profound insight into the ideas and practices of ordinary people (Rider, 2012: 17–23). It is no coincidence that the new, itinerant orders of friars, both Franciscans and Dominicans, could go anywhere and bring the services of the Church to people who would have previously escaped attention. Their work made the information available to Church officials even greater. One of the results appears to have been an increasing number of bishops worrying about behaviour in their dioceses. This coincided with the ever-increasing concern within the Church about a perceived international rise in heresy, which lay behind the founding of the Inquisition in the thirteenth century. These novel, mobile and highly skilled arms of the Church were responses to this growing tide of heresy, and, as has been seen, magic was increasingly included in their concerns.

The final layer comes with new developments in the Church's concept of heresy itself. Heresy was not believed to be the affliction of isolated individuals; it was dangerous because it was taught and learned collectively, passed from one person to another. The language that the Church applied to heresy made it equivalent to a disease or an infection, transmitted from one person to another. Thus, where you find one heretic you will also find a teacher or leader, spreading heresy in the community. In the case of the German sect of heretics discussed earlier, the reference was not specifically to sorcery but rather to demon worship – but the step from that to ritual magic is a short one. From the 1250s, the popes introduced changes to the legal system of the Church which meant that inquisitors could try cases of sorcery, if that sorcery was manifestly heretical (Kors and Peters, 2001: 116–18). By the late fourteenth century, bishops, priests and inquisitors, and even the pope himself, believed that they were facing a new sect of magical heretics, both heretical demon-worshippers and practitioners of sorcery. Thus, we witness different strands coming together, where members of these new sects followed the teachings of a leader, just as heretical groups had been thought to do since the Roman period. The new focus, however, falls upon women. The *Canon episcopi*, as seen in Chapter 4, was included in canon law, bringing with it an instruction to bishops that they were likely to discover groups of deluded women, gathering together to worship a pagan goddess and indulge in strange rituals which led them to believe they could fly together at night. The implication of the original text was not that the women could actually fly, but rather that the bishop should punish the women for believing it was possible and for being worshippers of a false goddess. This document was included in Gratian's collection of Church law, the textbook that all Church lawyers studied at university, as part of the canonical texts relating to magic and divination. Thus, inquisitors going to places like the Rhine Land would have been familiar with it and, when confronted with practices such as the ones described earlier, would have found them all too recognisable. The fact that idolatry and superstition were included in the text also helped to strengthen the growing association between heresy and magic.

THE ONSET OF THE WITCH CRAZE

Evidence of a further key shift comes in the early fifteenth century in Switzerland, where papal letters contain statements referring to cases where the night flight is believed to be actually real. By the end of the fifteenth century, in the *Malleus Malleficarum* (*Hammer of Witches*), written by two trained German lay inquisitors, the assumption was that it was heretical not to believe in all the details of this new sect of heretical witches, including that they were enabled to fly by the power of the devil. In this text, witches were portrayed as completely evil: they were also expected to be women, as they were less rational and more physical than men, so it should not be surprising that they even enjoyed having sex with the devil (Peters in Jolly et al., 2002: 238–45). The Latin term for female, *femina*, was here broken down into *fe* and *mina*, and translated as 'less faith', the implication being that the very word woman means that her faith is lower and weaker than a man's. It follows logically then that, given their weaker nature, the devil would prefer to target women. Traditional histories of the witch craze have traced the evolution of the concept of witchcraft largely in legal material, making it appear as primarily a construct of the Church. But was the Church the only group involved in this transformation and combination of established ideas and practices into the concept of witchcraft? It is worth noting that in England, for example, inquisitors and inquisitorial trials were not allowed. However, charges for witchcraft and the accusation of being a witch were brought against the Duchess of Gloucester for an alleged attack on Henry VI (see Chapter 1). Her assistant, Margery Jourdemayne, was also unproblematically identified as a witch. In England the Inquisition was not needed for the development of a stereotype of the witch. Furthermore, if spread by the Church, the expectation would be that the new attitudes and ideas about witches would appear across Europe at roughly the same time, but this is not the case. Large-scale trials for witchcraft affecting secular groups occurred in the dioceses of southern France following the letter by John XXII. By the end of the fourteenth and the beginning of the fifteenth centuries, similar trials were moving to a new geographical location in the Rhine Land, Bavaria and parts of Switzerland. Furthermore, lay magistrates were also conducting cases of witchcraft. Written in about 1436/7, a treatise of magic reveals actions in the Dauphiné by a lay magistrate on more than 100 accusations of witchcraft. By this point, medieval Europe held a strong belief in an organised international attack, designed to bring down the whole of Christian society. By the early fifteenth century all the elements needed for the take-off of the witch craze were in place – yet large-scale accusations are only found in a relatively small number of areas of Europe (Kieckhefer, 1976: 106–47). Another 100 years would be necessary for the witch craze to take off, and by that time the Middle Ages were over.

This book has traced, not the presence of witches in medieval society, nor even the activities of clerical sorcerers. Rather, it has attempted to explore the wide range of areas within which different traditions and forms of what can be viewed as magic were present. Magic was at least as widespread in medieval society as it was in the early-modern period, but the various strands which made it up were far from unified. Equally importantly, it took time for the learned, ritual magic of the clergy to be equated with the regrettable errors of the uneducated. Finally, it also took time for theologians and natural philosophers to explore the new theories involved in the concept of natural magic, and to conclude that naturally occurring occult powers were generally weak unless boosted by an external power. As has been seen in several chapters of this book this did not lead to a rejection of the reality of magic. Instead, it placed ever more emphasis on the diabolical origin, and thus terrible threat, of magical activity and power.

DOCUMENTS

Document 1   SIBYLLINE PROPHECIES

The Sybils are described in The Etymologies *of Isidore of Seville (c.560–636), an impressive compilation of classical knowledge completed in the early seventh century. It was 'arguably the most influential book, after the Bible, in the learned world of the Latin West for nearly a thousand years' (Barney et al., 2006: 3). The Sybils are placed in Book 8 (On the Church and Religious Sects) and between Poets and Magicians.*

Female prophets are all called Sybils in the Greek language. They interpret the divine will to men, and make statements on things to come. The most learned authorities report that there were once ten sibyls. The first of them was the Persian sibyl, the second the Libyan, and the third the Delphic sibyl, who was born in the Temple of Apollo at Delphi. This sibyl began to prophesy before the Trojan War, and Homer used her verses. The fourth was the Cimmerian sibyl, in Italy. The fifth was the Eritrean, or Babylonian, sibyl, who was named after the island of Eritrea where her prophetic verses were discovered. She prophesied to the Greeks that Troy would fall and that Homer would lie about it. The sixth was the Samian, named after the Greek island of Samos. The seventh is Amaltheia, the Cumaean sibyl, who brought to Rome nine books containing what was laid down for the Romans. She is the sibyl whom Virgil called Cumaea, when he wrote that the final age of the prophecy of Cumaea had come. She is named after the city of Cumae, in Italy, and her tomb in Sicily can be visited to this day. The eighth, the Hellespontian, was born outside Troy, and is recorded to have lived in the time of Solon and King Cyrus. The ninth is the Phrygian, who prophesied at Ancyra. The last, Albumea, is known as the Tiburtina. Verses by all of them are recorded, declaring to the peoples many truths about God and Christ.

Source: Isidore of Seville, *Etymologies*, Book VIII, Ed. W. M. Lindsay, Oxford: Oxford University Press, 1911.

Document 2   JOACHIM OF FIORE AND RICHARD I

The chronicler Roger of Howden (d.1201/2) was a clerk in the service of Henry II and then of Hugh du Puiset, Bishop of Durham (1153–95). Roger probably began his Chronica (Chronicle) c.1192, shortly after finishing his Gesta Henrici II (Deeds of Henry II), which covered the years from 1169 to 1192. The Chronica deals with the history of England from the eighth century to 1201.

In the same year (**1190?**) Richard, king of England, heard the rumour, discussed by many, that there was a certain religious man in Calabria, an abbot of the Cistercian order, called Joachim. It was said that this man had a prophetic spirit and foretold to the people what was to come. The king sent for him and listened with pleasure to the words of his prophecies, and his wisdom and teaching. He was learned in the Holy Scriptures, and he especially interpreted the visions of Saint John the Evangelist, which John himself related in the Book of Revelations. The king of England and his companions were greatly interested by what they heard, including the interpretation of the revelation by Saint John the Evangelist: 'There are seven kings, five have fallen, and one is, and one has not yet come'.

Elsewhere in the Book of Revelations is this vision: 'A woman was clothed with the sun, and with the moon under her feet, and on her head a crown of twelve stars, and being about to give birth, she suffered agony to deliver. And behold! a great red dragon, having seven heads and ten horns, and with seven crowns on its heads. His tail moved a third part of the stars of heaven, and hurled them into the earth; and he stood before the woman who was about to deliver, so that when she delivered he could devour her child. And the woman brought forth a son, who was to rule all nations with an iron rod, and her son was carried off to the Lord, and to his throne. The woman fled into the wilderness of Egypt, where she had a place prepared by God, so that there they would feed her for one thousand, two hundred and sixty days.'

The interpretation of this vision, according to abbot Joachim, is as follows: 'The woman clothed with the sun and with the moon under her feet' signifies the Holy Church, the sun of justice, who is Christ our God, overshadowed and veiled; under her feet is this world, always trampled down with its vices and concupiscence. And 'on her head was a crown of twelve stars' signifies Christ as the head of the Church; his crown is the Catholic faith, which the twelve Apostles have preached. 'The woman suffered to deliver', and just so the Holy Church, which always rejoices in new offspring, suffers day by day, so she may gain souls for God, which the devil attempts to snatch away, and to drag with himself into hell. 'And behold a great red Dragon, having seven heads and ten horns', this dragon signifies the devil, who is rightly said to have seven heads, for all the heads of the Devil are hostile, and he sets seven as if it were finite when it is infinite; for the heads of the Devil are infinite, that is, the persecutors of the church, and the unjust. Amongst these persecutors, although they may be infinite, the said Joachim expounded seven as the greatest, whose names are these: Herod, Nero, Constantius, Mahomet, Melsermut, Saladin and Antichrist.

On Saint John's saying, in the Book of Revelation, that: 'There are seven kings, five who are fallen, and one is, and one is yet to come', Joachim expounded thus: 'The seven kings are certainly Herod, Nero, Constantius, Mahomet, Melsemutus, Saladin and Antichrist. Of these five are fallen, namely Herod, Nero, Constantius, Mahomet and Melsemutus; one is, namely, Saladin, who is oppressing the Church of God at present, and with it the Sepulchre of the Lord, and the Holy City of Jerusalem, and the land on which stood the feet of the Lord keeps occupied; but he shall shortly lose it'. Then the King of England asked him: 'When will this be?' Joachim answered: 'When seven years have elapsed from the day of the capture of Jerusalem'. The king of England said: 'Then, have we come here too soon?' Joachim answered: 'Your arrival is very necessary, because the Lord will give you the victory over His enemies, and will exalt your name over all the princes of the earth'.

Source: Roger of Howden, *Chronica Magistri Rogeri de Houedene*, Ed. W. Stubbs, Rolls Series 51, V. III, London: Longman, 1870.

———◆———

Document 3 REPORT OF ASTROLOGICAL FEARS AND PREDICTIONS IN 1186

Letter of the astrologer Corumphiza on the conjunction of the planets
In the name of the Father, the Son and the Holy Spirit, Amen. Almighty God knows, and the rule of number makes known, that the planets both superior and inferior are inevitably to converge in Libra in September, in the year of the incarnation of our Lord Jesus Christ, eternal and true God, 1186. This is the year 582 according to the Arabs. This conjunction will be preceded in the same year by a partial solar eclipse, of fiery colour, at the first hour of the 22nd day of the month of April, and by a total eclipse of the moon in the same month of April. . . . Therefore, in the aforementioned year the planets, by God's command, will come together in Libra, which is an airy and windy sign. Moreover, *cauda draconis*, the tail of the dragon, will also be in that very place. A terrible earthquake will affect the places most vulnerable to such things, and they will be destroyed, and their air and water made foul. In the Western regions, a violent wind will rise and will most strongly blacken the air and corrupt everything with a poisonous stench. Thereupon, much death and sickness will take place and crashes and voices will be heard in the air and will terrify the hearts of those listening. The wind will lift up the sand and dust from the surface of the earth and the cities of the plains will be buried, especially in sandy regions. In the 5th climatic zone, Mecca, Barsara, Baldac and Babylon will be destroyed. They will be buried in the earth, brought down by sand and dust, and the regions of Egypt and Ethiopia will be left almost uninhabitable. And these misfortunes will extend from west to east. In the Western regions discord will grow and sedition will break out amongst the people; and some will join into a great army. They will make war by the shore of the sea, and so much slaughter will be brought about that the outpouring of blood will overcome the waves.

It is certain that the coming conjunction will bring changes to kingdoms, pre-eminence to the Franks, destruction to the Saracens, greater piety and the greatest exaltation of the law of Christ. Those born afterwards will live longer. Whatever others may say, this is what it means to me, if God wills it.

Similarly, William the astrologer, the cleric of John constable of Chester, (and other astrologers) wrote about the same conjunction of the planets.

Source: Roger of Howden, *Chronica Magistri Rogeri de Houedene*, Ed. W. Stubbs, Rolls Series 51, V. III, London: Longman, 1870.

ROGER BACON, INTRODUCTION TO THE *GREAT WORK*, 1266   **Document 4**

Roger Bacon (c.1214–c.1292) was a Franciscan philosopher and theologian active in Oxford and Paris in the thirteenth century. His most famous work, the **Opus Maius***, is divided in seven parts, which explore in detail all areas of natural knowledge. The following extract addressed to Pope Clement IV, discusses the place of pagan prophecies in Christian theology.*

The Church should study the prophecies in the Bible, the inspired sayings of the saints, the predictions of the sibyl, and the prophecies of Merlin and of pagan soothsayers. These should be put together with astrological data and knowledge gained from experience and experiment. Such work would give vital protection against the coming of Antichrist. It is important for us to know his origin and identity, and I believe that God would grant us a greater revelation if the Church were to make a greater effort. It would help if a special prayer were composed and read in all churches. For certain prophecies can be averted, and much of what is said about Antichrist by the prophets will be fulfilled only if Christians are negligent. Therefore Christians should work hard to discover when Antichrist will come, and make use of all the knowledge which he himself will seek to use.

Source: F. A. Gasquet, 'An unpublished fragment of a work by Roger Bacon', *The English Historical Review* 12 (1897), pp. 514–15.

JOHN OF SALISBURY, *POLICRATICUS*   **Document 5**

The **Policraticus** *was written between 1156 and 1159 by John of Salisbury (c.1110–80), while he was in the service of Theobald, Archbishop of Canterbury, and Thomas Beckett was Chancellor. As a moralist, John* *opposed much that he saw in fashionable, courtly life. The* Policraticus *has been called 'a manual of government, a mirror of princes, a moralizing critique of life at court; and also an encyclopaedia of letters and learning'. (Luscombe, ODNB)*

Chapter 28. On crystal-gazers; and how malignant spirits can sometimes foresee the future through the subtlety of their nature, their long experience, or by receiving information from higher powers; and how they deceive, or are themselves deceived; and how evil things follow the activities of the crystal gazers.

Crystal gazers lie to themselves that because they offer no forbidden sacrifices, and harm no one, they are useful in uncovering theft and cleansing the world of sorcerers. They claim to seek only true and useful things. But these wicked people are deceivers. God said: 'who is not with me, is against me'. If they practise arts which are forbidden by God, what else are the crystal gazers doing, but scorning Him?

Nothing is more effective against their wiles than to refuse to listen to such vanities. I thank God who showed me favour and protected me against the attacks of such evil enemies, when I was very young. For as a boy still learning the psalms, I was handed over to the care of a priest; and this priest practised powerfully magical crystal-gazing. For this reason he forced me and a boy a little older than me into this sacrilegious art. After a few preliminary magical rites, we would sit at his feet, with our fingernails wetted with holy water or oil. His intention was to use us, or the polished surface of a basin, to gain visions to be interpreted.

And so we would pronounce names which, even though I was a young boy, I understood to belong to demons, because of the horror they inspired in me. The priest would utter adjurations, of which I know nothing, thanks to God. My companion indicated that he saw certain misty and yet delicate figures; but I appeared blind to this and saw nothing, except for the nails, the basins and the other objects that I had seen there before. Therefore, I was judged useless for these purposes thereafter, and, as an impediment to this sacrilegious art, I was forbidden to come anywhere near it. Whenever they decided to practice this art I was kept away, as an impediment to their divinations. Thus God protected me at that tender age.

But as I grew older I became increasingly terrified by such things, and my horror was only confirmed as I saw what befell all who practised this art, including many whom I had come to know. They were deprived of sight before they died, either by the failure of nature or by the hand of the Lord, not to mention other disasters, which I saw inflicted upon them by God. I have known only two exceptions – the priest whom I have mentioned and a certain deacon. They, seeing the misfortunes of the crystal-gazers, fled – one to an Augustinian priory, the other to a cell of Cluny – and took the protection of the monastic habit. Yet, I am sorry to say that even they endured many adversities afterwards, in comparison to others in their congregation.

Source: John of Salisbury, *Ioannis Saresberiensis Policraticus*, Ed. K. S. B. Keats-Rohan, Corpus Christianorum Continuatio Mediaevalis 118, Turnhout: Brepols, 1993.

MICHAEL SCOT AND THE EMPEROR FREDERICK II | Document 6

Salimbene de Parma (c.1221–88), also known as Salimbene di Adam, was a Franciscan chronicler in thirteenth-century Italy. In his Cronica *(Chronicle) he relates events between 1168 and 1287, some of which he witnessed first-hand. He was a follower of Joachim of Fiore and a believer in his teaching about the Apocalypse and the impending coming of Antichrist.*

On Michael Scot, who was an honest astrologer
The Emperor Frederick's seventh and last curiosity and superstition was, as I mentioned in another chronicle, that on a certain day and in a certain palace he asked Michael Scot, his astrologer, how much distance there was between the heavens and this palace. The astrologer said what appeared to him to be the case. Frederick then deliberately ordered him to go to other places in the kingdom, and thus detained him for several months. Meanwhile, architects, workmen and carpenters were instructed to move that palace and to lower it in such a way that no one would be able to tell. And when this was done, the emperor came again with the astrologer into the same palace. Starting as if afresh, Frederick asked him again how far it was distant from the sky and whether it differed from his previous calculation. Having made his account, the astrologer said that either the sky had risen or the earth had certainly sunk; and thus the emperor learnt that this astrologer told the truth.

The words of Michael Scot about things to come in the cities of Lombardy, Tuscany and Romagna

> Fearing the banner of the king, Brescia will take cover and will
>   not be able to protect her own sons, but will stand strong in
>   the following battle with the king . . .
> Afterwards the walls of the Griffin of Milan will be laid low.
> Milan, terrified by the hot blood of death, will rise again
>   covered in the gore of death.
> Wanderers and wild men in great numbers will come to
>   Vercelli, Novara and Lodi.
> The days will arrive when Pavia will be sick . . .

> Fearful Piacenza will be subject to the commands of the king;
> after being oppressed and suffering ruinous slaughter she
> will spring back. . . .
> Piacenza will lie open to attack under a heavy weight of blood.
> Obedient Parma will flourish, though all her leaves will burn;
> The swelling serpent slyly leaves the dragon.
> Parma, obedient to the king, will rise up and strike him
> Like a viper striking at a dragon, and will blossom and flourish.
> You, Cremona, I predict, will in the end suffer the pain of the
> flame, having shared in such great evil
> And the factions of Reggio will hold evil words against each
> other.
> The sons of Padua will cry over the harsh and dreadful death of
> its great men, caused by the whelp of Verona.
> The March will fall compelled under the heavy burden of
> slavery . . .
> Rome will fall and will no longer be head of the world.
> The fates warn, and the stars and the flight of birds show us,
> that Frederick will be the hammer of the world.
> The great dragon will bring immeasurable storms to the world.
> The fates are silent, the stars and the flight of birds do not
> reveal
> Whether Peter's vessel will cease to be the head.
> The mother will revive and will hammer the head of the
> dragon.
> Not for long will stubborn Florence flourish with blossoms
> She will fall into decay, will live by dissimulation.
> Venice will open her veins, and will strike the kingdom on
> every side.
> After one thousand two hundred and sixty, the great tumult of
> the world will be stilled.
> The griffin will die, its feathers sent spinning.

Anyone can see that the prophecies in the verses above were true. For I myself saw several realised 'and my mind had contemplated many things wisely, and I have learned', and I know that they were true, except for a few. For clearly Frederick was not the hammer of the whole world, although he did much evil. Nor did the ship of Peter, in fact, ever cease to be the head, except perhaps at the time when the papacy was vacant because of the disagreement of the cardinals. It is also not true that in the year 1260 the immense turmoil of the world was stilled, for there are still many wars and disagreements and evils in various parts of the world. Nevertheless, in that year of 1260 the devotion of the Flagellants began, and men made peace with enemies, and war diminished and much good came about, as I saw with my own eyes.

Source: Salimbene de Parma, *Cronica*, Ed. G. Scalia, Corpus Christianorum Continuatio Medievalis 125, Turnholt: Brepols, 1988.

TWELFTH-CENTURY ANGLO-NORMAN HOROSCOPES **Document 7**

From a set of twelfth-century horoscopes written in an Anglo-Norman hand, now in British Library, Royal App. 85.

Chart for an 'Interrogation'; drawn up on 15 September 1151
Heading: 'Concerning the Dead Count of Anjou'
(Geoffrey Plantagenet, Count of Anjou, died suddenly on 7 September 1151)

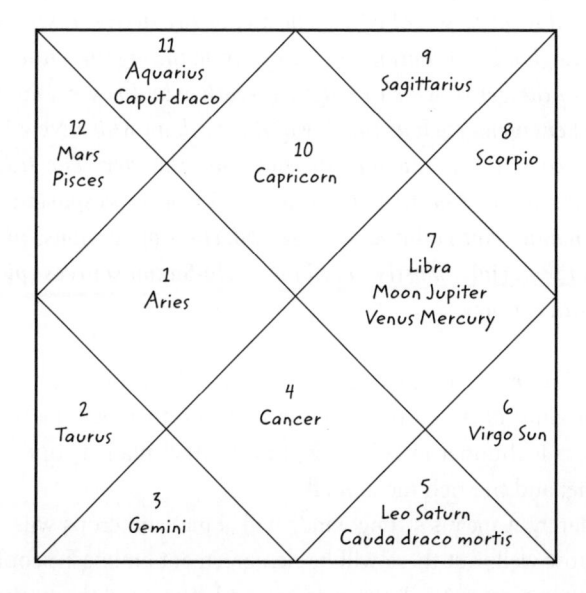

```
          11                    9
       Aquarius             Sagittarius
      Caput draco
   12                              8
  Mars           10             Scorpio
  Pisces      Capricorn
                                  7
                                Libra
            1                Moon Jupiter
          Aries             Venus Mercury

                  4
   2           Cancer            6
 Taurus                       Virgo Sun

          3                    5
        Gemini              Leo Saturn
                         Cauda draco mortis
```

The chart shows:

the Moon, Venus, Mercury and Jupiter all in House 7, the house of Marriage;
the positive presence of Caput Draconis in House 11, the house of Friends;
the positive presence of the Sun in House 6, the house relating to illness and health;
the ill-omened planet, Mars, in House 12, the house of Enemies;
and the very threatening combination of Saturn and Cauda Draconis in House 5, the house of Children. Significantly, the word 'mortis', relating to death, is legible in this sector of the chart.

The question actually asked of the astrologer is not given, although the heading suggests that the count's death was known when the chart was drawn up. However, his heirs apparently had cause to worry, since battle with his enemies was threatened, and children were in great danger, even though alliances and, in particular, marriages, are very positively emphasised.

Other horoscopes in the same group relate to whether an army will come from Normandy (presumably to England, though possibly to Anjou), and whether a king will succeed in his attempt to force his barons to swear fealty to his son.

Source: London, British Library, Royal App. 85.

Document 8 PROGNOSTICATION BY THUNDER

This is one of a set of so-called Prognostic, or predictive, texts which were popular in England and continental Europe from the eighth century onwards. It belongs to the genre which predicted weather and key events for a year based on phenomena such as the day of the week on which New Year's Day fell; in this case, the predictions depend upon thunder. The text is based on that found in London, British Library, MS Cotton Vespasian D xiv, fol. 75v. This manuscript contains a large collection of sermons, prayers and educational materials, mostly based on Anglo-Saxon sources, put together in the twelfth century.

> If it thunders in January, great winds are likely, but the produce of the earth will grow well; and there will be battle.
> If there is thunder in February, it means that many people will die; and the rich most of all.
> In March, it means strong winds will come, and crops will grow well; but there will be no agreement amongst people.
> If it thunders in April, the year will be happy, and the wicked will die.
> Thunder in May means a year of hunger.
> In the month of June, thunder warns of strong winds, and madness amongst lions and wolves.
> Thunder in July means good growth for crops, but that animals will die.
> In August, it means a good year, though many will suffer sickness.
> In September also it means a good year, but the killing of powerful men.

> In October, it means strong winds, and crops to come, but a poor harvest from trees.
> In November, it means a happy year and good crops.
> In December, a good year for the land, with peace and harmony.

Source: London, British Library, Cotton Vespasian D xiv.

EXCERPTS FROM THE *DREAM-BOOK OF THE PROPHET DANIEL* — **Document 9**

At least 73 medieval versions of this text have been identified, from almost all European countries and in several vernacular languages as well as Latin. The shortest has only about 50 entries, whilst the longest have over 300. The seriousness with which they were treated is shown by their alphabetical organisation, and the care with which they were copied. This short selection follows the version in British Library Ms Cotton Tiberius A iii, a manuscript produced c.1050 for the monks of the Cathedral Priory of Christ Church, Canterbury, which also contains the Rule of St Benedict *and other important religious texts. A full edition and translation of the Prognostics in this manuscript is given by R. M. Liuzza, in* Anglo-Saxon Prognostics; An Edition and Translation of Texts from London, British Library, MS Cotton Tiberius A iii, *(D. S. Brewer, 2011).*

> If you dream of birds, and that you are fighting them, it means that conflict is coming.
> If you dream of trees full of fruit, some wealth which you want very much will come to you.
> If you dream of drinking vinegar, you are about to be ill.
> If you dream that you are washing yourself in a bath, it means something worrying is coming.
> If you dream of rain, it signifies coming joy.
> If you see two moons in a dream, joy and happiness are coming.
> If you dream that a dragon flies over you, you will gain treasure.
> If many dogs appear, you are in danger from your enemies.
> If many bees fly into your house, you are about to be forsaken.
> If you see yourself praying, great joy is coming.
> If you build a house in your dream, your wealth will increase.

Document 10   PETER LOMBARD, *SENTENCES*

Written in the mid-twelfth century by the Italian theologian Peter Lombard, the Sententiae (Sentences) became the standard textbook of theology in medieval universities in the thirteenth century. The work is divided in four books. The issue of magic is discussed in the second book, dealing with the creation and sin.

Book II, Distinction VII

Chapter 5: How evil angels can know the truth about temporal things
And although evil angels have been hardened through their wickedness, yet they are not wholly deprived of the power of their senses. For, as Isidore records, demons are strengthened by threefold knowledge, through: the subtlety of their nature; long experience; and the revelations of higher spirits. St Augustine also said: 'Evil spirits are allowed to know certain truths about temporal things . . . partly from what God almighty reveals to them by his will. But sometimes these abominable spirits also make false "predictions" of things they know they themselves are going to do'.

Chapter 6: That the magical arts work by the power and knowledge of the Devil, which is allowed by God
The magical arts and those who use them are granted knowledge and power by God, either to deceive the deceitful, or to warn the faithful, or to test the patience of the just. St Augustine in *On the Trinity* says: 'To those whose reasoning is feeble, even miracles may take place through the magical arts. For the magicians of Pharaoh made serpents and other wonders. But it is more remarkable that these powerful magicians, who could make serpents, entirely failed when it came to the tiny flies which constituted the third plague by which Egypt was smitten. This demonstrates that the magical arts, like the wicked angels and spirits of the air which give them whatever powers they possess, . . . cannot do anything except through a higher power than their own.'

Chapter 7: That the substance of visible things does not obey evil angels
It must not be thought that the matter or substance of visible things serves the will of these evil angels except through the judgement of God, by whom this power is given.

Chapter 8: That evil angels are not creators, although through them magicians produce frogs and other things
Nor can evil angels justly be called creators, although through them Pharaoh's magicians made frogs and serpents; for they did not actually create them. Within all corporeal and visible things which make up this world there lie hidden certain seeds with which God originally endowed them. He is the

creator of all things, and the creator of these invisible seeds. Everything which our senses can perceive, is imprinted by these hidden seeds with the fundamental rules which govern its magnitude and distinctive form. Therefore, just as we do not say that parents are the creators of human beings, or that farmers are the creators of fruits . . . it is against divine law to think of evil angels, and even of good ones, as creators. Through the subtlety of their senses and bodies they can perceive the seeds within things which are hidden from us, and they can scatter them secretly, and in accordance with the harmonious rules which govern the elements, and thus they appear to create things and to make them increase in size. But neither the good angels nor the evil angels truly do such things, unless God himself permits.

Source: Peter Lombard, *Doctoris seraphici S. Bonaventurae opera omnia* (2 vols), Florence: Typographia Collegii S. Bonaventurae, 1885.

GRATIAN, *DECRETUM (DECRETALS)*   Document 11

*The **Decretals** of Gratian constitute an encyclopaedic collection of c.4,000 texts on canon law, collected and organised in the mid twelfth century, which became the standard legal text studied in thirteenth-century universities. The work is divided into three parts, covering 'distinctions' in part I and 'cases' in part II. Magic is mainly discussed in Cases 26 and 33. Case 26 discusses the case of a priest found guilty of lot-casting and divination.*

Part II, Case 26 (Extracts designed to illustrate Gratian's procedure, and the key points made here)

Question 1: What are lot-casters?
Canonical text (from Isidore of Seville): Casters of lots are those who practise the false rituals, which they claim to be religious, known as the lots of the saints or the apostles. They also claim to foretell the future by scrutinising the scriptures.

Question 2: Is this a sin?
Gratian's conclusion (based on texts from St Augustine): this is clearly a sin, and necessarily entails the invocation of demons.

Question 5: Should persistent lot-casters and diviners be excommunicated?
The canonical texts: The texts assembled here by Gratian provide details and definitions of the sorts of magical practice considered to be related to lot-casting and divination, all of whose practitioners are to be excommunicated, according to the decisions of Church Fathers, early popes and Church Councils.

Text 2, attributed to the Council of Ancyra, also condemns those who consult magicians or diviners.

Text 3, from the collection of Martin of Braga, condemns Christians who give reverence to the Moon or to 'the courses of the stars'. It adds that, when collecting medicinal herbs, no ritual practices or incantations may be used, except for making the sign of the Cross and saying the Lord's Prayer.

Text 5, from the Council of Toledo, condemns anyone in holy orders who consults magicians of any sort. The list specifies: 'soothsayers, enchanters, practitioners of divination, augurs, lot-casters, and all who use the magical art'.

Text 12 is the long 'Canon Episcopi', here attributed to the Council of Ancyra.

Text 14 is also long, and provides proof that the works of magicians are tricks and illusions, first citing the examples of Pharaoh's magicians and of the sorceress Circe, who appears in the Odyssey. Paragraph 1 says that: 'magicians are called malefici (evil-doers) by many people because of the crimes they commit. With the permission of God they disturb the elements and try people's faith; and they are capable of killing with their incantations.' Their power is actually provided by demons, 'and they use blood and the bodies of the dead'. The subsequent definitions of necromancers and other practitioners of divination largely follow Isidore. Paragraph 6 states that 'magical illusions are said to have been first invented by Mercury'; while paragraph 7 attributes the discovery of augury and entrail-reading to the Etruscans, 'whose books were translated into Latin by the Romans'.

(The overall emphases are: that all forms of magic relate to demonic power; that magicians can operate only with the permission of God; and that no true Christian should believe that they themselves have power. The punishment recommended is excommunication.)

Source: Gratian, *Decretum magistri Gratianii*, Ed. A. L. Richteri, Corpus Iuris Canonici 1, Tauchnitz, 1879.

Document 12 MAGICAL CIRCLES, DEMONS AND NECROMANCY

Cesarius of Heisterbach wrote his* Dialogus miraculorum *(c.1219–1223) as a work of instruction for the young novices at his monastery, where he occupied the position of Master of novices before becoming prior.

Chapter 2. On Henry the knight, who did not believe in demons, but saw them through necromancy

A knight named Henry, from Falkinstein castle, was cupbearer to our own monk Cesarius, then abbot of Prüm. And, as I learnt from the words of this

Cesarius himself, Henry did not believe in the existence of demons. Whatever he heard about them he judged frivolous; until one day he sent for a certain clergyman called Philip, a most famous necromancer, and earnestly asked to be shown some demons. Philip replied that the sight of demons is both horrible and dangerous, and that it is not given to all men to see them. When the knight insisted, he added: 'if you assure me that no harm shall come to me either from your relatives or your friends, if it happens that you are deceived, terrified or hurt by the demons, I will agree'. Philip assured him of this.

On a chosen day at noon (for demonic power is much greater at midday) Philip led the knight to a certain crossroads. Here he made a circle around him with his sword, and warned him about the law of the circle within the circle. He then said: 'if you extend any of your limbs outside this circle before I return, you will die, because you will immediately be dragged out by the demons, and be killed.' He also warned the knight to give the demons nothing, regardless of their pleas, to promise them nothing, and to avoid making the sign of the cross. And he added: 'the demons will tempt and terrify you in many ways, and yet they will not be able to harm you, if you take heed of my commands'. And he left. Sitting alone in the circle, suddenly Henry saw coming at him floods of water; then he heard the grunting of pigs, the blowing of the wind and other similar phantoms with which the demons tried to terrify him. But because of the fore-warnings he found the courage to resist them.

At length, he noticed in a nearby wood a foul shadow, almost human in shape, yet taller than the trees, which was hurrying towards him. He realised at once that this might be the devil himself – and it was. When this being arrived at the circle he stood still and he asked the knight what he wanted of him. He had the appearance of an enormous man, the colour of shadow, dressed in blackened garments, and so terrifying that the knight could not look back at him. Henry said: 'you did well to come, for I wanted to see you'. 'Why?' asked the devil, and the knight replied: 'I have heard a lot about you'. When the devil asked: 'what have you heard of me?' the knight replied: 'little good and much evil'. The devil said: 'frequently men judge me and condemn me without cause. I have hurt no one, have struck no one down unless provoked. Philip your master is a good friend of mine, and I of his; ask if I have ever offended him. I do what pleases him, and he obliges me in all things. When he called me, I came to you here'. Then the knight said: 'Where were you when he summoned you?' The demon replied: 'I was as far across the sea as this place is distant from the coast. And therefore it is fair that you should compensate me for my trouble with a gift.' . . . The knight said: 'I will give nothing to you', but asked the devil to reveal the source of his power. The demon replied: 'No evil in the world is hidden from me: and to prove that this is true, I can tell you in what town and in what house you lost your virginity, and just what sinful acts you performed'. And the knight could not contradict him for he spoke the truth.

For some time after this the devil would ask for other things, but Henry refused to concede. Then the demon snatched at him as if to drag him out of the circle, and he terrified the knight so much, that Henry cried out and fell backwards. Hearing his voice, Philip rushed back, and at his arrival the phantom immediately disappeared. From that time on the knight was always pale, never regained his natural colour, and lived free from errors, believing earnestly that demons exist. It was not long ago that he died.

Chapter III – Of a priest who was dragged out from the circle and so injured that he died within three days

At that same time there was a certain stupid priest who asked for this same clergyman, Philip, and paid him to show him also some demons. So Philip placed him in a circle and instructed him in the manner described above. This priest was frightened by the devil and was dragged out of the circle, and before Philip could arrive he was so beaten and broken that he died within three days. His house was confiscated by count Walter of Luxembourg. I saw this same Philip myself, and have heard that he was killed a few years ago by his master and friend, the devil.

Source: Cesarius of Heisterbach, *Dialogus Miraculorum*, Ed. J. Strange, Cologne: J. M. Herbele, 1851.

Document 13 WILLIAM OF MALMESBURY ON GERBERT OF AURILLAC

The influential Gesta Regum Anglorum (Deeds of the Kings of England), written by the English Benedictine historian William of Malmesbury, presents an account of English history from 735 until 1142. As part of a digression on Church history, following his account of the reign of King Aethelred (c.968–1016), William discusses the life of Pope Sylvester II. This controversial pope, born Gerbert of Aurillac, was esteemed as a great scholar, but after his death was claimed to have been a magician and necromancer.

After Pope John XVI came Sylvester, who is also called Gerbert; and I should not be blamed, I think, if I set down in writing what is said by many about him. Born in France, he grew up from childhood as a monk at St Benoit sur Loire. When he reached the age of decision, whether because he was tired of the monastic life or because he lusted for glory, he escaped by night to Spain, intending to learn astrology and other similar arts from the Saracens . . .

And just as the Christians have Toledo as capital of their kingdom, so the Saracens have Hispalis, which they commonly call Seville, and here they busy themselves with divinations and incantations, as is the custom of their nation. So Gerbert, arriving amongst them, as I said, obtained what he wanted. There, he excelled Ptolemy in skill with the astrolabe, Alhandreus in charting the stars, and Julius Firmicus Maternus in judicial astrology. There he learnt to make predictions from the song and flight of birds, and how to summon misty forms from hell. He studied all the hidden things, whether harmful or healthful, that human curiosity has uncovered. The established liberal arts, arithmetic, music and astronomy and geometry, he treated casually, as if they were unworthy of his talents. Through great industry he revived in his own country arts that had fallen entirely into disuse long before. He was the first to grasp the Saracen skill with the abacus, and passed on rules which are still barely understood by hardworking mathematicians.

In Spain he lodged with a certain philosopher of the Saracen religion, whose help he purchased with much gold and many promises. The Saracen was willing to sell his knowledge, and they frequently sat down together, talking sometimes about serious things and sometimes about trivia; and sometimes Gerbert was given books to copy. There was, however, one volume which gave knowledge of the Saracen's whole art, and Gerbert could never get hold of this, despite being desperate to see it. As Ovid says: 'we always strive for what is forbidden, and place the highest value on whatever is denied us'. Gerbert pleaded, and begged the master in the name of God and of their friendship, offering much and promising more. When that failed, he tried treachery under cover of darkness. He flattered and seduced the man's daughter, then got her to help in plying her father with wine. This made it possible for Gerbert to remove the book from under the Saracen's pillow, and to run off with it. The Saracen philosopher, however, woke from his sleep and, through expert study of the stars, followed the runaway. Gerbert, discovering the pursuit through the same science, hid himself under a wooden bridge that was nearby. He cunningly hung there, clasping the bridge in such a way that he would touch neither water nor earth. This hid him from the searches of his pursuer, who then returned home. Gerbert then travelled fast to the coast, and there invoked the devil by using incantations. He promised perpetual homage if only the devil would protect him from the Saracen, who had renewed his pursuit, by carrying him across the sea. And so it was done.

Some may think this a lie, for the ignorant underestimate the powers of the learned, and think that all skill in science is learnt from the devil. But the story of Gerbert's death, which I shall tell elsewhere, confirms his crimes.

Source: William of Malmesbury, *Gesta Regum Anglorum, The History of the English Kings*, Ed. R. A. B. Mynors *et al.*, Oxford: Clarendon Press, 1998.

Document 14 HUGH OF ST VICTOR, *DIDASCALICON*

Written in the late 1130s by the Parisian theologian and philosopher, Hugh of St Victor (c.1096–1141), the Didascalicon is an exposition of the arts, selecting and defining all of the relevant areas of knowledge. It includes a chapter on magic (drawing in part on Isidore of Seville).

Book 6, Chapter 15 – On magic and its parts
Zoroaster, king of the Bactrians, is said to have been the first discoverer of magic. Some say that he was Cham, the son of Noah, under a different name. Ninus, the king of the Assyrians, conquered him in war, then killed him and had his books of magic and sorcery burnt. Aristotle writes on him that his books preserved for posterity no less than two million, two hundred thousand verses on the magical arts, all composed by him. Later, Democritus wrote more on this art, at the time when Hippocrates was celebrated for his practice of the art of medicine. Magic is not accepted as part of philosophy, but left outside despite its false claims. It produces nothing but iniquity and wickedness, distorts the truth and actually injures men's minds. It leads its students away from true religion and into the worship of demons, it corrupts morals, and it turns the minds of its followers towards crime and sin.

It is generally considered to include five kinds of sorcery: *mantike*, or divination; false mathematics; lot-casting; destructive magic; and illusions. Moreover, divination contains five sub-types. The first is necromancy, which translates as divination by means of the dead, for *nekros* in Greek means 'dead', from which comes the term 'necromancy'. This sort of divination takes place through the sacrifice of human blood, for which demons thirst, delighting in it when it is shed. The second is geomancy, that is, divination by means of the earth. The third is hydromancy, that is, divination by means of water. The fourth is aeromancy, or divination by means of air. The fifth is divination by fire, which is called pyromancy. Varro affirmed that the four elements of earth, water, fire and air are used for divination. In this way, the first, necromancy, appears to relate to hell and its inhabitants, the second to earth, the third to water, the fourth to air, and the fifth to fire.

False mathematics, or Astrology, is divided into three types. Practitioners of the first type are called *aruspices* because they consider the hours or *horas* at which things should be done, or examine the entrails of animals sacrificed at altars or *aras*. The second type is called augury, and entails either observing the flight and movement of birds with the eyes, or using the ears to listen to the sounds made by birds. Divinations are made from both. Horoscopy, or observation of the stars, involves reading men's fates in the stars. This is what the *genethliaci* do, when they calculate birth horoscopes, which are also called nativities. They were once called *magi*, and are the sort of magician we read about in the gospels.

Lot-casters are those who divine the future by casting lots.

Practitioners of destructive magic, or sorcerers, are those who bring about abominable things by means of demonic incantations, or ligatures, or other forbidden types of cures, through their own wickedness and the cooperation of demons.

Magical illusions fool human senses by pretending to change one thing into another, through demonic arts.

Thus it can be seen that there are altogether eleven parts which make up magic: five under *mantike*; three under false mathematics; and finally lot casting, sorcery and magical illusions. Mercury is said to have been the first to discover magical illusions; the Phrygians discovered augury; Tages the Etruscan was the first soothsayer; and hydromancy originated amongst the Persians.

Source: C. H. Buttimer, *Hugonis de Sancto Victore Didascalicon de Studio Legendi*, Studies in Medieval and Renaissance Latin 10, Washington: The Catholic University Press, 1939.

ADELARD OF BATH, TREATISE ON THE ASTROLABE

Document 15

De opere astrolapsus *is a short treatise by the English natural philosopher and translator, Adelard of Bath (c.1080–c.1150). The treatise opens with a section on cosmology before proceeding to describe the astrolabe and to offer precise instructions for its use.*

Here begins the treatise of master Adelard of Bath on the workings of the astrolabe. I believe most strongly that those who are noble and of royal descent should apply themselves to the study of the liberal arts. I also recognise that it must be balanced with their duty to govern. Thus I understand that you, Henry, as a relative of the king, have taken in the lessons of philosophy. For it is said that public affairs are blessed either if they are given over to philosophers, or if those in charge are governed by philosophy. Your infancy was imbued with such wisdom and it has remained with you, and however much you are weighed down with external cares, you will take equal time away from them. So it comes about that you have not only read and understood the works of western writers, but are also willing to study the teachings of the Arabs concerning the sphere of the universe and the orbits and the movements of the stars. For you say that if anyone living in a house is ignorant of its matter and composition, its size and strength, position and prominence, he is not worthy of such lodging. Thus, anyone born and brought up in the palace of this world should if possible be thrown out of it if, after reaching the age of discretion, he were to refuse to study the rules which govern such beauty and wonders.

Since you have told me with some force that I should add something to the philosophy of our own age, although I doubt my ability, I shall do my best to do this. I shall write down in Latin what I learnt from the Arabs about the world and how to understand it, with the provision that, since the world is neither square nor rectangular nor any shape other than spherical, whatever I say about the sphere will be understood to apply to the world also.

[Definitions of a sphere, its surface, its hemispheres, its axes and poles are given, with other information on the earth as a globe.]

[Part II] . . . I shall first set down what an astrolabe should be like, then I shall explain what it does. It is a flat disc of copper, which can be hung from a chain and examined on both sides. One surface is called the face and the other the back. And the face has a border running round it, inside which engraved plates calibrated for zones of the earth [known as 'climates'] and other such things are held in place. Onto the back is placed the alidade, which is called the 'radius' by Boethius, into which may be cut a groove, or onto whose ends may be fixed two protruding pieces, each pierced through the centre. This alidade is fixed at its centre with a pin, which is called the axel-pin in Arabic, and which also holds in place the plates or tables. This pin has a hollow end, into which is inserted what the Arabs call the alferaz, that is, the horse.

That is what an astrolabe should look like; now I shall explain what it can do. . . .

In the first place, it can show the position of the sun on any day at any hour, that is the altitude, or in Arabic 'artifa'. And it can do the same at night for the stars.

Secondly, it shows which sign, and which degree of that sign, the Sun occupies on any chosen day.

Thirdly it can give an exact measurement of anything on the earth to which it is applied: the longitude and latitude of a flat area; the height of something vertical; or the depth of something submerged.

Fourthly it will give the measure of bodies and their shadows in relation to one another.

Fifthly, it can calculate the longitude and latitude of any zone of the earth.

Source: Adelard of Bath, *De opera astrolapsus*, Ed. B. G. Dickey, Toronto: Unpublished PhD thesis, 1983.

ARS NOTORIA: GENERAL INSTRUCTIONS, AND TEXTS RELATING TO ASTRONOMY

Document 16

Probably originating in the twelfth century, the Ars Notoria *is a treatise of Solomonic magic which promises the acquisition of advanced academic learning through the ritual use of orations and figures or diagrams that receive the name of* notae. *The* Ars Notoria *was very popular in university environments during the central Middle Ages.*

(These extracts are taken from the introductory section and from that on astronomy, and are brought together to illustrate the ways in which the book could be used)

Opening statement:
Here begins the most holy Art of all Knowledge, which was revealed to Solomon at the altar of his Temple by the holy angels of God the creator of all. Through it Solomon learnt at once all the Arts, and also the Sciences, and all the parts which compose them. This knowledge was infused into him, together with great wisdom, and mastery of holy words and their sacred mysteries.

The preparatory prayer:
Almighty God, Alpha and Omega, the source of all things, who has no beginning and no end, hear my prayer on this day! . . . I humbly pray that you will illuminate my mind with the light of your Holy Spirit, so that I may be able to reach perfection in this holy Art. I pray that I might gain knowledge of all science, art and wisdom, and attainment in memory, learning, understanding and intellect, through the power of the Holy Spirit and in your name. Oh God, who in the beginning made heaven and earth, and created all things out of nothing, who transforms and makes new all things through your Holy Spirit, grant me a full and strong and complete understanding, so that I may glorify you and all your works, through my thoughts, words and deeds. Oh God my Father, who lives and reigns forever, grant me this prayer, strengthen and increase my capacity to understand and to remember, so that I may fully grasp and retain all knowledge, eloquence and perseverance in all branches of learning. Amen.

The first part of the art:
Here begins the first treatise, which is the general introduction to all the Arts, as approved by Solomon, Manichaeus and Euclid. Behold!

I, Apollonius, Master of Arts, have been granted the knowledge of the Liberal Arts, and shall expound them, together with Astronomy. . . . I shall teach all the mysteries of Nature, both high and low, together with the skill to divide them and to allocate them to the proper times. It is necessary to know how to choose the proper days and hours for all actions to be started and finished. You must also know what knowledge and preparation are required, in order to master this Art; and how to observe and understand the course of the Moon. . . . Parts have been taken from the ancient books of the Hebrews, set out here in writing and providing marvellous effects. You should respect their miraculous powers, even though their words have been forgotten and are no longer understood. The power of words upon the works of nature is truly a wonder.

Certain Names of God, and certain holy words, have such great virtue and power that simply to read them out will immediately make you eloquent in speech. This will help you to advance to the more powerful and sacred Names of God. And the source and nature of their power will be revealed to you in the sequence of prayers which follows.

On the Ars notoria:
This Art is divided into the General Rules and the Special Rules; and the Special Rules are divided into a set of three and a set of four. These are followed by Theology. Mastery of all these will be granted, if you follow the rituals and the prayers set out here, reading them as directed. The Art is based upon *Notae* which are here shown, whose power the human mind cannot comprehend. The first *Nota* draws its meaning from the Hebrew, and uses only a few words; but when properly used they retain their power. Their power is such that particular effects are produced when they are spoken, and this is a great wonder.

On astronomy:
Truly, Astronomy has six *Notae*, each with its own prayers; and these must always be said while the image is fixed in your vision. In each chapter this work will deal with the different arts and their magical figures, perfectly explaining each in turn, including all of theology and philosophy, with the knowledge and the *Nota* of each. In the case of the mechanical arts [hydromancy, pyromancy, necromancy, chiromancy, geomancy, geonogia and neonogia] their exposition is mainly contained within their *Notae*.

There are ten prayers which, if uttered in sequence, immediately bestow the power to remember all knowledge, with the eloquence to expound it and explain it, and the strength of mind to retain it always and clearly. The third of these prayers should be recited on its own before meditating upon the third *Nota* of any art or science which you want to attain, uttering it with the figure in front of you. In particular, this prayer is the special prayer for the first *Nota* or figure of the Art of Astronomy. Therefore, whilst looking closely at this image, you must say this special prayer. Then, after resting but without interruption, you must move on to the second figure of astronomy. [The prayer asks for the speaker to be cleansed of evil deeds, and to be granted clear understanding, and the knowledge which is reserved for true believers. 'Breathe into me, Oh Lord, the breath of life, increase my reason and understanding, send me your Holy Spirit, so that I may be perfect in all knowledge . . . and understand those things I desire.' There is no specific mention of astronomy.]

Caption to the Nota:
This is the first figure of the six belonging to the art of astronomy. This truly is the first figure, and it must be first used on the first day of the new moon in any calendar month. After this must come the second figure and then the third, and so on, all six in order, on subsequent days of one month. The days of the month do not matter. You must apply yourself to each figure four times in the day: firstly from the first hour of the morning until the third hour; then from the third hour until midday; then from midday until the ninth hour; finally from the ninth hour until vespers. Each of the prayers must be recited twice.

Source: J. Véronèse (ed.), *L'Ars Notoria au Moyen Âge, Introduction et Édition Critique*, Florence: Sismel-Edizioni del Galluzzo, 2007; and *Ars Notoria: The Notory Art of Solomon, Englished by Robert Turner*, London, 1657.

THE EMERALD TABLE   Document 17

Part of the so-called Hermetic corpus, its author was supposedly the legendary Hermes Trismegistus. The Emerald Table is a short text, which cryptically outlines the fundamental principles of alchemy. The first surviving copies date from c. eighth century (in Arabic); the first surviving translations into Latin are from the twelfth century.

The Emerald Table of Hermes, as translated into Latin from the Phoenician, and so made known
Statement in words of the secrets of Hermes Trismegistus:

1. This is true, without lies, certain and most true.
2. What is below is as that which is above, and what is above is as that which is below, to accomplish the miracles of the one thing.
3. And as all things were made from one, through the mediation of the one, so all things were born from that one thing, through adaptation.
4. Its father is the fiery sun, its mother the watery moon. The wind carried it in its womb, its nurse is the earth.
5. The father of all perfect and sacred things in the world is here.
6. Its power is complete, if it is turned upon earth.
7. You should separate the earth from the fire, the subtle from the dense, smoothly, and with great mastery.

8. It ascends from the earth into heaven, then descends again to the earth, and takes into itself the power of higher and lower things.
9. Thus, you shall have the glory of the whole world. All darkness shall flee from you.
10. This is the force of all forces, the power of all powers, which shall overcome all that is subtle and penetrate all that is solid.
11. This is how the world was created.
12. From this there will be wonderful adaptations, and it is the means.
13. For this reason I am named Hermes Trismegistus, the Triple Magus, since I have three parts of the wisdom of the whole world.
14. That which I have spoken on the working of the Sun is finished.

Source: J. Ruska (ed.), *Tabula Smargadina, ein Beitrag zur Geschichte der hermetischen Literatur*, Heidelberg: Carl Winters Universitätsbuchhandlung, 1926.

Document 18 MAGICAL BOOKS IN UNIVERSITIES

In his theological treatise De fide et legibus (On faith and laws), the theologian and philosopher William of Auvergne (c.1180–1249) offers a careful and comprehensive discussion of the nature of demons, including their role in magical practices and idolatry. In the short extract below, while discussing the errors of the pagans, he offers a glimpse of the material available to contemporary students at the University of Paris.

And this is why the pagans rendered honours and holy sacrifices to the planets. They believed the sun and the moon, and the rest of the planets, to be gods and rulers over the world. They shared out the whole of the earth, allocating it amongst them.... Germany was assigned to Mars, Italy to Saturn, Cyprus to Venus. And they also distributed faiths, laws and crafts, virtues and vices, in the same way. Again, they shared out every ornament and instrument, colour, scent and flavour, not to mention the animals, and also the locations of human trades, such as ovens, mills, and so on. The animals were distributed between them also, so that pale-coloured animals were assigned to Venus, and birds of reddish colour to Mars, and dark birds to Apollo. Letters and numbers were similarly divided, and finally the human body itself, with its limbs and organs, was shared between them. All this is written in books of judicial astrology, and in the books of magicians and sorcerers, which I remember reading when I was young.

Source: William of Auvergne, *Opera Omnia*, Venetiis: Ex officinal Damiani Zenari, 1591.

PENITENTIALS   Document 19

Early medieval Penitentials were collections of instructions for priests designed to guide them in deciding what the correct penance should be for a given sin. Penitentials first appear to have been compiled in Ireland and Wales, before being taken up in Anglo-Saxon England and the Carolingian Empire. Later versions were also produced in Spain and eastern Europe. What follows are selected clauses from the ninth-century Spanish Penitential attributed to Vigila of Alveda.

Selected clauses

136. Whoever commits murder by means of a drink or by any other art, must do ten years of penance.
138. If a woman kills her unborn child by means of a drink or by any other art, she must do penance for fifteen years.
     This applies equally to those who kill their newborn babies.
     But if the woman who does this is very poor, she should do penance for ten years.
141. For helping someone who wants an abortion, the penance is four years.
143. For killing an unborn child, before it has received its soul, the penance is four years, since this does not count as murder.
145. But a woman who accepts a potion, to help her to conceive or to give birth, should know that she has committed a sin equal to murder.
146. If a Christian pays heed to diviners, enchanters, sorcerers, auguries, lot casters, those who observe the elements, or other similar things, he must do penance for five years.
181. Anyone who performs an incantation, or perverts himself in any similar way, must do penance from three to fifteen years.

Source: 'Penitentiale vigilanum' in F. W. H. Wasserschleben (ed.), *Die bussordnungen der abendländischen kirche*, Halle: C. Graeger, 1851.

LAPIDARY   Document 20

The following descriptions of stones come from a thirteenth-century Castilian Lapidario, produced for the future King Alfonso X (1221–84), 'the wise'. Lapidaries were books on stones, describing their physical and occult properties. This Spanish lapidary is unique in preserving both Jewish and Arabic elements, and including astrological details in its descriptions of stones.

On the stone known as Camorica:
Of the third degree of the sign of Taurus is the stone called Camorica, whose name means 'vinegary' in both Chaldean and the vernacular. And this is because when it is placed in liquid, the result will be a strong vinegar flavour. Its nature is cold and dry, it is red in colour, and rough and porous in texture, though very difficult to break.

It is found in Meçanbor, in the mountain caves of that city. Some stones are large and others small. Men from that land grind them and mix the powder with water, and after 6 days it turns into a very strong vinegar, and they use it in their food. The physicians put this liquid in their medicines and in other things used to moderate the humours, because it acts better and faster than ordinary vinegar. And if it is placed on linen or woollen cloths, it eats through them. Because it dissolves solid bodies, and cleans them by removing dirt, this stone is used by those who practise alchemy.

The two stars in the constellation of Azoraza, at the ends of the row called 'the seven kids' (near the centre of Taurus) have power over this stone, and send it strength and virtue. And when these powerful stars are in the ascendant, this stone works more effectively.

On the stone called Abarquid:
Of the fifth degree of the sign of Taurus is the stone called abarquid. It is found in Africa, in the sulphur mines. It is light and hard to break. And on the outside its colour is green with some yellow. It is flat in shape, and when men observe it carefully, it appears to have the form of a scorpion. If it is broken, the same scorpion shape is found inside. Its nature is cold and dry.

If a woman carries it, its power will make her so lust for a man that she will restrain herself only by a great effort of will; and it has the same effect on any female animal. And those from India who practise the art of necromancy work with this stone very often, for if it is given to a woman, as a powder dissolved in drink, its power will make her belly swell gradually as if she were pregnant. However, when she is due to give birth, this 'pregnancy' vanishes. The necromancers pretend that their art and knowledge are the cause of the pregnancy and its termination.

The twinkling star that is on the right side of the star-group of Perseus has power over this stone, and gives it its virtue. When this star is in the ascendant, this stone works more powerfully.

On the stone that appears over the sea when the moon sets:
Of the ninth degree of the sign of Cancer is the stone that appears over the sea when the moon sets, and ascends when the moon rises. It is found in the dark sea, with other stones connected to the powers of the planets. Its nature is cold and moist, it is light in weight and very black in colour. When the moon

comes out, the stone sinks to the sea-bed; and when it sets, the stone rises up and floats. Even when removed from the sea, it continues to go dark when the moon is above the earth, and goes clear again when the moon sets. It is a great wonder that this darkest of stones can be transparent to the sight like crystal. It has a very marvellous and strange virtue, that whoever hangs it between their eyes can see as well at night as during the day, without any candle or other light.

And the right-hand star of the two at the front of the shell of the constellation of Cancer, the crab, and the other on the front claw of this same figure, these rule over the stone, and from them it receives its virtue. And when they are in the ascendant, this stone is at its most powerful.

On the stone called Militaz:
Of the ninth degree of the sign of Libra is the stone known as Militaz. This stone is strong and so hard that nothing but diamond and fire can damage it. It is found in the land of India, in mines but not in caves, or other deep places. It shines powerfully and its colour is similar to fine gold. It can be large or small and takes diverse shapes. Its nature is hot and moist, and its power is such that it drives away flies and harmful reptiles. Furthermore, learned men say that devils flee whoever carries it, and he will be protected from necromancy or any spells cast against him. And the star . . . called Cantoriz has power over this stone, and gives it strength and virtue, especially when it is in the ascendant.

Source: M. Brey Mariño (ed.), *Lapidario, según el manuscrito Escurialense H.I.15*, Madrid: Castalia, 1980.

HERBALS   Document 21

Medieval herbals dealt with the medicinal properties and with the occult hidden properties of herbs. Belonging to an ancient literary tradition, these often beautifully illustrated texts survived in an almost unbroken tradition from Late Antiquity to the later Middle Ages. The first extract is from De herbis femininis, *a herbal that was probably compiled in southern Europe before the sixth century.*

Heliotrope:
This plant keeps away witches, and those possessed.

For Warts: take its leaves and rub the warts with them. Crush the same leaves and mix them with vinegar; bind the mixture on the warts. The warts will fall out immediately and will not return.

For rash over the whole body: burn the heliotrope on clean roof-tiles and collect its ashes. Combine them with vinegar. Have the affected person take a hot bath; while he is sweating, rub him thoroughly and vigorously with the ashes, then bandage him with greased linen and give him a hot drink. He will mend.

Whoever carries this herb will not be harmed by any demon or witch.

You should gather this herb thus: search it out early in the morning, before sunrise, on the sixteenth day of the moon. Wrap it with gold, silver or ivory before you dig it up, and invoke the Father Almighty and Christ, saying: 'I offer this herb, that it may be a remedy to me and to all those to whom I shall give it'. Then dig it out with a wooden implement, using no iron, and separate the fruits from the beans. Then level the ground.

Source: H. F. Kästner, 'Pseudo-Dioscorides de herbis femininis', *Hermes* 31 (1896), pp. 578–636.

The following extracts belong to the most important illustrated herbal in the Latin West, the Herbarius, attributed to Apuleius Platonicus, and compiled between the second and fourth centuries CE. It survives in c.60 manuscripts dating from the sixth to the fifteenth century.

The basilisk herb:
This basilisk herb grows in the places where you find the basilisk snake.

There is not one variety of it, but three. The first is tufted, the second glitters with a golden head, the third has the colour of red lead but also has a golden head. All three varieties are easily obtained. Whoever carries one will have the power of all three, and cannot be harmed by the evil eye.

However, anyone who looks at the first variety will puff up and burn. And if it is of the type called 'glittering', or starry, they will wither up and die. And the third makes whoever sees or pierces it disappear, leaving only his bones behind. This herb obtains all of its violence from this basic principle. But anyone carrying this herb will be protected from every generation of serpents.

The leaves of this herb resemble those of the willow, but are squarer and narrower, and sprinkled with dark spots. Its root resembles a bear's paw; it has golden sap, like the swallow-wort; but its flower is like a red berry.

Whoever wishes to pick it should trace a delicate line around it and place gold, silver, ivory, a wild boar's tooth, the horn of a bull or a stag, and sweetened fruits, on the line; then they can safely gather it. The Italians call it a royal herb.

Mugwort:
Anyone making a journey should carry mugwort in their hand, and they will not feel the toil of the journey. It also puts demons to flight, and if placed in the house it keeps away poisons. It protects from the attentions of evil men.

Mugwort, beaten with axle grease and rubbed on the feet, will remove pain.

Mugwort, once reduced to a powder, can be given as a drink with water and honeyed wine; this calms intestinal pain.

This herb is called *toxotis* by the Greeks . . . and by the Romans, Artemisia. It grows in stony and sandy places.

Source: E. Howald and H. Sigerist (eds), *Antonii Musae de herba vettonica liber. Pseudoapulei herbarius. Anonymi de taxone liber. Sexti Placiti liber medicinae ex animalibus, etc.*, Lipsiae: Berolini, 1927.

THE BESTIARY **Document 22**

The Bestiary, or Book of Beasts, presents short descriptions of all sorts of animals, both real and imaginary. The basic bestiary material was probably translated into Latin in the sixth century, from the Greek* Physiologus, *and sought to give an explicitly Christian interpretation of the natural world. Its descriptions are usually accompanied by illustrations, sometimes simple drawings and sometimes fully painted miniatures. The accounts of the hyena and the magpie are two of many which include occult but natural powers.

Hyena
There is an animal called the hyena, which lives in the tombs of the dead and feeds on their flesh. By nature it is sometimes male, and sometimes female, and it is a foul animal. It has a stiff spine, all in one piece, so it cannot turn around, unless it rotates its whole body. Solinus records many marvellous things about it: that it follows shepherds to their stables; that it circles the houses of men at night and by constant listening learns their speech; that it can imitate the human voice; and that through its cunning it can lure out men at night and fall on them. It can also imitate human vomiting and sobbing, and lures dogs out and devours them. If hunting dogs come under its shadow, they lose their voices and are unable to bark.

The hyena opens up tombs in which bodies are buried. . . . Those among us who serve luxury and greed are like this beast, for they are neither male nor female, neither faithful nor faithless, but are those of whom Solomon said: 'a double-minded man, is fickle in all things' (James, 1:8). The Lord says, 'you cannot serve both God and Mammon' (Matthew, 6:24). This beast has a stone in its eyes, called 'hyenia', and anyone holding it under his tongue is believed to foresee the future. Any animal at which a hyena has looked three times is not able to move. It is said that the hyena possesses magical arts.

In Ethiopia it mates with the lioness, from which the monstrous crotote is born, which can also imitate the human voice. It never changes territories, but it strives to avoid change. It has no gums in its mouth and one everlasting tooth, which never becomes blunted.

Magpie

Magpies are like poets, because they can utter words like men. Indeed, perching on the branches of trees, making annoying chattering noises, even if they cannot conduct a real conversation, they can still sound human. As the poet said: 'I, the talkative magpie, greet you with the voice of a lord. If you do not see me, you will deny that I am a bird' (Martial, Epigrams, 14: 76). The magpie is also called picus, after the son of Saturn, who used them in foretelling the future. They say that this bird has something divine about it; the proof is that if a magpie builds its nest in any tree, a nail or anything fixed in its trunk will not be able to stay there for long, but will fall out immediately after the bird alights in the tree. However, you can think what you wish of this story. The magpie, with its false voice, can signify either the false teaching of heretics or the vain talk of philosophers, as is also said about the jackdaw.

Source: Oxford, Bodleian Library, Bodley 764, ff. 15r–16r.

Document 23   ON ANIMALS

The following extract on the powers of the wolf comes from a medical text attributed to the fifth-century Roman writer Sextus Placitus, the **Liber Medicinae ex animalibus.** *Not unlike the* **Herbal of Apuleius Platonicus,** *this work describes the various properties of medicinal substances, though here they are derived from animals. There is an Old-English translation of this text dating from the tenth century, and it was used by medical authorities from the eleventh century onward.*

On the wolf:

Whoever eats the preserved flesh of a wolf will not be troubled by any demon, ghost or phantom that may appear.

Place the head of a wolf under the pillow, and the infirm will sleep.

A wolf whose tracks you have followed will do you no harm if you see it first, and if you carry the tip of a wolf's tail. In this way you can travel without fear. By this same method a wolf can be frightened off.

For recurrent fevers bind on the right eye of a wolf, and it will dissipate both nocturnal and daytime fevers.

When rubbed vigorously over cataracts, the wolf's eye will diminish them, pull them away and remove the mark, and it will remove them completely, if they have first been punctured.

Source: E. Howald and H. Sigerist (eds), *Antonii Musae de herba vettonica liber. Pseudo-apulei herbarius. Anonymi de taxone liber. Sexti Placiti liber medicinae ex animalibus, etc.*, Lipsiae: Berolini, 1927.

SPHERE OF APULEIUS   Document 24

This popular medical prognostic combined a diagram, usually circular, with sets of numerical equivalents for the letters of the alphabet, and instructions for their use. It was widespread in early medieval Europe, and remained popular in some regions, including England, beyond the end of the medieval period.

[What follows is a compound text]

The sphere of the philosopher Pythagoras, recorded by Apuleius, is used to discover whatever you may wish to know, for instance the outcome of an illness. This is how it should be used.

Calculate as numbers that which you wish to be ascertained, thus: add together the figures for the letters of the sufferer's name, the day of the week, and the day of the moon. Divide the total by 30. The remainder will be found in one half of the circle, or placed by the image of life or that of death. If it is in the upper half, and in the place of life, the patient will live. But if it is in the place of death, they will die.

A. 3   B. 3   C. 28   D. 24   E. 15   F. 3   G. 7   H. 6   I/J. 15   K. 15   L. 21
M. 23   N. 15   O. 8   P. 14   Q. 21   R. 13   S. 9   T. 8   U/V. 5   X. 6   Y. 3   Z. 3

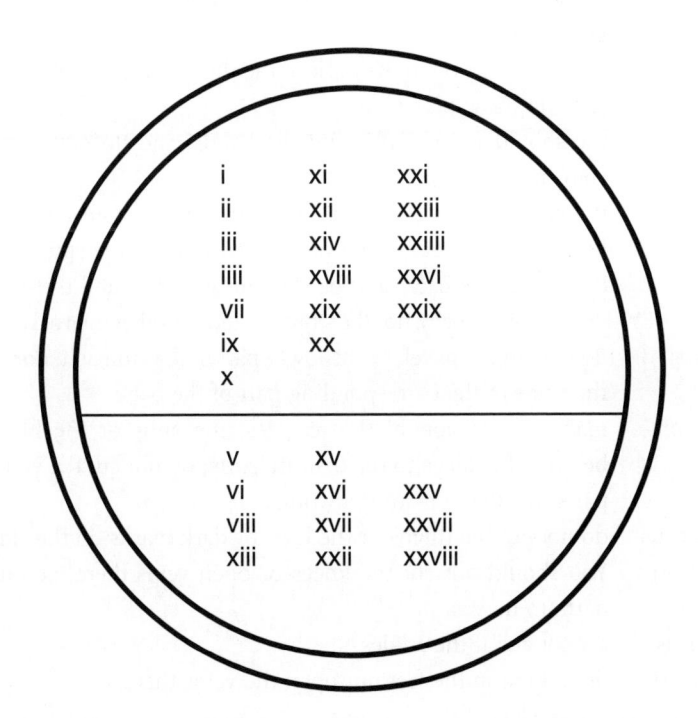

```
        i      xi     xxi
        ii     xii    xxiii
        iii    xiv    xxiiii
        iiii   xviii  xxvi
        vii    xix    xxix
        ix     xx
        x
        ─────────────────────
        v      xv
        vi     xvi    xxv
        viii   xvii   xxvii
        xiii   xxii   xxviii
```

For the weekdays: Sunday, 12; Monday, 18; Tuesday, 15; Wednesday, 25; Thursday, 11; Friday, 15; Saturday, 17.

To ascertain the outcome of a combat, you should add the number of the hour to the day on which you ask the question. Then proceed as before. If the remainder is in the higher portion the subject will conquer; but if in the lower, the subject will be defeated.

Source: L. S. Chardonnens, *Anglo-Saxon Prognostics, 900–1100; Study and Texts*, Leiden and Boston: Brill, 2007.

Document 25   ZODIAC MAN

Medieval medical theory, drawing on Greek and Roman models, stated that the human body, like most matter, was subject to the influence of the heavenly bodies. Thus, it is not surprising that diagrams setting out the links between the parts of the human body and the houses of the Zodiac were highly regarded. This knowledge became more widely available during the central Middle Ages, as images of the 'Zodiac Man' appeared in Books of Hours and illuminated calendars.

Instructions according to the sign of the moon

Aries:	do not cut the head or the face; and it is madness to open the great vein.
Taurus:	make no incision in the neck or the throat, and do not open the veins in those places.
Gemini:	the shoulders, the arms and the hands; and do not open the veins in those places.
Cancer:	the chest and sides; beware of harm to the stomach and the lungs, and do not cut the vein which leads to the spleen.
Leo:	do not cut the back, and beware of the nerves and the lungs.
Virgo:	do not cut the belly, nor the stomach and the other internal organs.
Libra:	do not cut the navel, or the lower part of the stomach, nor open the veins in the corresponding part of the back.
Scorpio:	make no incision in the testicles, the anus or the bladder; beware of damage to the delicate parts; do not cut the venereal parts in either a man or a woman.
Sagittarius:	do not cut the thighs or the legs, or dark marks on the skin.
Capricorn:	You should not cut the knees or open veins there, beware of harm to nerves.
Aquarius:	do not cut at the ankles.
Pisces:	do not cut in the feet nor open the veins there.

Source: London, British Library, Sloane 2250, section 12.

SPECULUM ASTRONOMIAE

Document 26

The Speculum astronomiae, a thirteenth-century text generally attributed to Albertus Magnus, has long been recognised as important evidence for the historian. Apart from including a list of texts on astronomy, astrology and magic, which are criticised according to their degree of theological error, the work also includes an informed discussion of astronomy, astrology and magic. The following extracts are taken from the section on astrological medicine.

On horoscopes:
All natural philosophers agree that if we know the hour of conception, we may know from that what will happen with regard to the foetus until it receives its soul, and until it is born, and perhaps what will happen throughout its life. . . .

On medicines:
We should choose the hour to give a medicine, taking into account, for instance, that if Capricorn is in the ascendant, or is the house of the patient's particular star, then vomiting is likely. And we should also note whether there is any significant aspect between these and a malefic planet, that is, Saturn or Mars. For Saturn slows medicine and Mars draws up the blood. We should also know that when the Moon is in conjunction with Jupiter then purging will be easier and more effective.

On surgery:
Again, when carrying out surgery, one should avoid making an incision in a limb when the Moon is in a sign which rules over that limb. For at that time the limb will be affected by the rheumatic humour, and pain will be worse. And I myself have seen infinite problems caused by neglect of this. I have seen a man expert in medicine and in the stars, who due to urgent heart problems bled himself in the arm, even though the moon was in Gemini, which rules the arms. There was no evident harm, except for a small inflammation of the arm, yet he died on the seventh day. I also know of a patient who had an ulcer near his rectum. He was cut open by a so-called surgeon, who was ignorant of both medicine and the study of the stars, with the moon in Scorpio, which rules over those parts. Without the opening of a vein, or some other clear cause, he died within the hour, in the arms of those treating him. His death was attributed to the effects of the heavens, since no other cause of sudden death, such as the blocking of the ventricles of the brain, or a lesion or blockage of the airways, was apparent.

Source: P. Zambelli, *The Speculum Astronomiae and its Enigma*, London: Kluwer, 1992.

| Document 27 | GUIBERT DE NOGENT, *MONODIES (MELANCHOLY MEMOIRS)* |

This account, by the Benedictine historian Guibert de Nogent (c.1055–1124), is part of his Memoirs, and describes a case of impotence, caused by magic (affecting his own parents). The account is interesting, both because it demonstrates belief that magical practitioners were widespread in medieval society, and because it illustrates the influential view that magic was especially likely to be used in relation to fertility and conception.

At the beginning of my parents' marriage, their marital relations were affected by the sorceries of certain people. Rumour said that the marriage was affected by the malice of my father's stepmother. She had nieces of great beauty and nobility, and was planning to place one of them in my father's bed. Seeing that she had not succeeded in her plan, she is said to have used wicked arts in order to prevent the consummation of the marriage. The wife's virginity remained intact for several years, and during that time she endured this great misfortune in silence. At last, encouraged by his relatives, my father was the first to reveal the facts. In all imaginable ways his relatives then exerted themselves to bring about a divorce. . . .

The sorcery, by which the bond of lawful marital intercourse between my parents was broken, lasted for seven years and more [and throughout this time my mother lived a virtuous and restrained life]. It is clearly plausible that, just as the faculty of sight may be deceived by tricks and illusions, and magicians may appear to produce something out of nothing, or to make certain things out of others, so the faculties directed at sexual activity may be inhibited by much simpler arts. Indeed this is now frequently done, and is understood even by common people. These vicious arts were finally broken by a certain old woman, and from that time my mother devoted herself faithfully to the dutiful intimacies of marriage, just as she had previously guarded her virginity whilst being so greatly attacked.

Source: Guibert de Nogent, *Guibert de Nogent: Histoire de sa Vie*, Paris: A. Picard et fils, 1907.

| Document 28 | ALBERTUS MAGNUS ON PRECIOUS STONES |

Albertus Magnus's* De mineralibus *(On Minerals) deals with the physical properties of precious stones, minerals and metals, both apparent and occult, as is evident from the following passage.

Part II, Section 1
Chapter 1. Here we shall discuss precious stones individually, considering the causes of their power, their characteristics, and the images which are

found upon some. We shall not enquire beyond this into the study of the physical nature of stones, for the cause of their power is very difficult, and natural philosophers have felt differently about it. Many have doubted that there is in stones any of the powers that are claimed, such as curing ulcers, driving out poisons, soothing human feelings, granting victory, and similar things. These philosophers say that there is nothing in the makeup of stones beyond the compounds formed by their component parts, and that these are responsible only for physical characteristics such as heat or moistness or hardness or receptivity. Those who deny that stones can possess powers also argue that living things have a higher nature than stones, and are more likely to possess the sorts of powers attributed to stones. This argument, however, is contrary to experience, for we know that a magnet attracts iron, and that adamant reduces the power of the magnet. Experience also shows that some sapphires can cure ulcers, and we ourselves have observed one such. Moreover this is widely believed by everyone, and it is impossible that there should be no truth in it at all.

However, some of the philosophers called Pythagoreans, while they have attributed special powers to stones, say that these powers come from the presence of a spirit or soul in the stone. They believe that such powers belong to the spiritual level, and not to things which are merely material, and that they exert their effects upon other things by their living force. This can be compared to the way in which the human intellect can work upon those things which it can comprehend, and the imagination can work upon what can be imagined. They also say that, in the same way, the soul of a human or another living creature can go out and enter another, holding it fascinated and weakening its force. . . .

On this, we say that it is absurd to state that stones have souls. As to fascination, the magicians can judge whether it is true or not. . . .

We state, without ambiguity, that stones have powers which bring about marvellous effects, and that these powers come not from their components but from their combination together. And it is untrue that only living beings can have such powers, for in every natural thing we see that something taken over by higher powers is thereby blocked against lower ones. Proof of this is provided by the fact that creatures with intellectual powers, such as humans, do not notice changes in the elements as clearly as brute beasts do. . . . And every natural thing has its own specific power, including herbs, roots, wood and even human flesh and dried wolf's dung. These can be helpful against poison and illness. Thus it is clear that stones also have powers, even if our knowledge of many is incomplete.

Source: Albertus Magnus, *Opera Omnia* 5, Ed. A. Borgnet, Paris: Ludovicum Vives, 1890.

Document 29 ON NATURAL MAGIC

In the theological treatise De fide et legibus, *the theologian and philosopher William of Auvergne (c.1180–1249) offers a careful and comprehensive discussion of the nature of demons, as part of which he discusses forbidden magical practices and idolatry. He also develops the new concept of 'natural magic', a category allowing for the expert use of the occult properties in nature.*

The Lord wished to protect His people from all things harmful . . . and for this reason He ordered sorcerers and enchanters to be killed. For all enchantments are idolatrous incantations, and true wonders are natural works, like the generation of frogs and worms, and these do not depend upon incantations. Indeed, these are natural manifestations, and knowledge of them is one eleventh part of the knowledge of nature, and needs no help from demons. For the same reason the consultation of diviners, dream interpreters and augurs is forbidden, and no evil magician, or enchanter, or consulter of diviners, is to be found in the land of Israel; for all these things lead to idolatry. This is also why anyone who is possessed by a prophetic spirit should be killed. . . .

This idolatrous worship of demons, which is manifestly promoted by the same demons, can be divided into seven forms. Those deceived by such errors believe that demons have power, not only over men and human affairs, but also over the elements. They were led into this error, because demons, by illusion, seemed to heal bodily injuries and to settle the disturbances of human affairs, such as quarrels and wars, and also to calm storms at sea and on rivers. Evil beings cannot cause war, avert it, or end it, still less bring water or good health, except when they are permitted to do such things by the hidden or manifest judgement of God. . . .

The third type of error is caused by certain marvellous phenomena. These are in reality works of nature, but because their natural elements, or their combination, or mixing, or some other aspect, appears to be produced by deliberate intervention, they are believed by the ignorant to be the work of demons. And natural magic, which some philosophers call necromancy or false philosophy (*philosophica*), is concerned with such works. These terms are inaccurate, for it constitutes the eleventh part of natural philosophy. The wonders of this science, which are the result of powers imbued in nature by the creator, are believed by ignorant men to be the work of demons. On account of this such men attributed not only great and marvellous powers, but even omnipotence, to those demons. Through this error they inflict a double injury upon the creator: firstly by denying that the power of demons depends upon the will of that same creator; and secondly by denying the truth of nature.

Source: William of Auvergne, *Opera Omnia*, Venetiis: Ex officinae Damiani Zenari, 1591.

ST THOMAS AQUINAS ON DEMONS

Document 30

One of the greatest figures of scholasticism and medieval theology, St Thomas Aquinas discusses the question of demons in his influential Summa Theologica, *written in Paris, 1265–74. The work is divided into three parts: the existence and nature of God; morality and law; and the incarnation and the sacraments.*

Part I, Question 114 – Preamble
Next we should consider the assaults of demons. And there are five points to be examined about this. First, whether men may be assailed by demons. Second, whether it is characteristic of the devil to tempt humans. Third, whether all the sins of men come into being through the attacks and temptations of demons. Fourth, whether demons are able to work real miracles for the purpose of leading humans astray. Fifth, whether demons which are overcome by men such as saints may be hindered from further attacks.

Article 4: whether demons can work real miracles to lead men astray
Objection 1: It seems that demons should not be able to lead men astray by means of any true miracle. For the work of demons will be strongest amongst the works of Antichrist. But as the Apostle says in the second Epistle to the Thessalonians, his coming is in accordance with the works of Satan, and with all his powers, and his false signs and wonders. Therefore it is even more the case at all other times that magicians cannot produce their false wonders except through demons.

Objection 2: It is also true that genuine miracles may involve some bodily change; but demons are not able to change the nature of bodies. Augustine says (*On the City of God*, XVIIII): 'I shall certainly not believe that the human body might for any reason receive the limbs of a beast through the art or power of demons'. This proves that demons cannot work true miracles.

Objection 3: Besides, an argument has no force if it can be turned against itself. If true miracles could be worked by demons practising deceit, they would not be effective in confirming the faith. This is not possible, since it is written (in Mark xvi. 20) that the Lord worked with the Apostles, and confirmed their teaching through miraculous signs.

It is the case that Augustine says that the magical arts can produce miracles similar to those which are worked by the servants of God. But I counter that, as was said above, an actual miracle cannot be worked by a demon, or by any creature, but only by God. This is because a miracle, in the strict sense, is something which exceeds the natural order of the created universe, which governs the powers of every creature. However, the term 'miracle' can also be understood in a broader sense, meaning something which exceeds human power and understanding. And demons are able to work this sort of miracle, that is, things which are marvellous to men, and exceed their power and understanding. . . . Nevertheless, although demons may perform works of this sort, which appear miraculous to us, these are not true miracles, although they may be real acts. This applies, for instance, to the magicians of Pharaoh who, by the power of demons, produced real serpents and frogs. And when fire fell from heaven and consumed all of Job's possessions, and when the storm destroyed his house and killed his sons, these were real works by Satan, not illusions, as Augustine says (*On the City of God*, XX).

Comment on Objection 2. As was said above, corporeal matter does not obey the will of good or bad angels, so demons cannot by their own power fully change matter from one thing into another. However, they can manipulate certain seeds found in natural, material things to produce such appearances, as Augustine says (*On the Trinity*, III). And therefore such transformations of corporeal things as can be produced through natural powers, including the said seeds, can be produced by demons using these seeds. Similarly, certain things were transformed into serpents and frogs, just as great changes can also be produced by putrefaction. However, transformations of corporeal things which cannot be produced by the power of nature cannot truly be accomplished by demons. For example, they cannot change a human body into the body of a beast, or bring the body of a dead man to life again. If sometimes such things appear to be done by demons, this is not truly real, but only a change in appearances.

This can happen in two ways. Firstly a demon can alter a man's internal thoughts, and even his physical senses, so that something appears to be other than it is, as was said above. Indeed, even certain material substances can have such effects. Secondly, external appearances can be changed. For a demon can shape a body out of air, and use it to appear physically. By the same power, he can also manipulate the appearance of one natural form into that of another. As Augustine says (De Civ. Dei xviii), an imagined image of a man may be affected by thoughts or dreams, and thus changed into the imagined likeness of an animal. [This applies also to the works of demons, which are illusory.]

Source: St Thomas Aquinas, *Opera omnia iussu impensaque Leonis XIII*, Roma: Polyglotta, 1889.

SUPER ILLIUS SPECULA

Document 31

Papal Decretal issued in 1326 by Pope John XXII, and directed 'against making offerings to demons, to solicit their answers and assistance; and against owning or using books about such errors'. **Super Illius Specula** *followed previous condemnations of magic and alchemy by John XXII, who believed himself to have been attacked three times by political enemies, using magic.*

Carefully considering how the sons of men know and serve God through the cultivation of the Christian religion, we looked down from the watch-tower upon which, however undeserving, we have been placed by the favouring compassion of God . . . With grief and turmoil of heart, we noted that there are many who are Christian in name only, and who, abandoning the light of truth, have strayed into the darkness of error. Thus they make themselves the allies of death and hell. They offer sacrifices and worship to demons, and they make or commission images, rings, mirrors, phials, and suchlike things, within which demons may be bound by magic. From them they seek and receive replies and help in satisfying their perverse desires. For a foul purpose they thus offer up their foul slavery. This is grievous, and even worse is the fact that this plague is at present gaining in power in this world, and seriously threatening the flock of Christ.

1. We are bound by our office to care for souls, and to bring back to the fold the lost sheep, whilst protecting them from infection by banishing from the flock of the Lord those who are diseased. We therefore, by this perpetual edict, and in accordance with the counsel of our brother bishops, . . . under threat of anathema enjoin upon all who have been born again in the fountain of baptism that they must not teach, study, or – still worse – practice, any of the said perverse doctrines.
2. And . . . we make known by this public proclamation the sentence of excommunication against all those who presume to act against our most salutary warnings and commands. And we firmly decree that, in addition to the above penalty, a trial must be held before competent judges. Anyone found guilty of the practices listed above, and who does not amend their behaviour within eight days of the formal warning, is to suffer the appropriate legal punishments for such heresy, except only confiscation of goods.
3. Since it is necessary also that no opportunity should be given for such abominable practices to spread, we, in agreement with our brother bishops, instruct and command further that no one shall presume to possess, keep or study any booklets or writings of any kind containing any of the said condemned errors. We greatly wish, and by the power

of holy obedience we order, that anyone who possesses any of the said writings or booklets shall, within the space of eight days after hearing of our proclamation in this matter, destroy and burn them, in their entirety, absolutely and completely. Anyone who infringes this command is automatically to incur the sentence of excommunication, and also such other, heavier penalties as shall be deemed appropriate.

Given at Avignon, etc.

Source: (1859) *Bullarum diplomatum et privilegiorum sanctorum romanorum pontificum Taurinensis edition* 4, Seb. Franco et Henrico Dalmazzo.

Document 32   BERNARD GUI, *MANUAL FOR INQUISITORS*

Bernard Gui offered his Manual for Inquisitors *for the edification of his junior colleagues in c.1327. The text is the result of his years of experience as an inquisitor in Toulouse, during the period of increasing inquisitorial activity against sorcery. Although most of the text deals with heresy, the question of magic and sorcery is discussed briefly, as shown by the following extract.*

VI On sorcerers, diviners and invokers of demons
The plague and error of sorcerers, diviners and invokers of demons is found in various and numerous forms in different lands and regions, according to the varying inventions and false testimonies of superstitious men who believe in erroneous spirits and the doctrines of demons.

Suspected sorcerers, diviners, or invokers of demons should be questioned on the number of sorceries, divinations or invocations they know, and how they learnt them. First, going into concrete detail, consider the suspects' quality and condition of character, because not everyone should be questioned in the same way ... Then you may question them as to: what they themselves know; what they have been taught; and what they have actually done.

These questions may be used, for instance, on the subject of infants or children who have been attacked by sorcery or freed from it.

> Likewise, on the souls of the dead or the damned
> On impediments between married couples
> On the impregnation of sterile women
> On those who provide potions and such things
> On foretelling future events

On women who summon spirits which they call good, and which they say come at night

On reciting incantations to conjure up fruit, herbs, laces and other things

On the teaching of enchantments and incantations

On the treatment of sickness by conjurations or incantations

On collecting herbs on bended knees, facing East, while reciting the Lord's prayer

On the pilgrimages, masses, offerings of candles and lavish alms which are demanded

On the discovery of things stolen or hidden

Special enquiry should be made about what the accused knows about any superstition, disrespect or injury to the sacraments of the Church, and especially to the sacrament of the body of Christ, and everything relating to divine worship and to sacred places

Likewise, on retaining the consecrated bread, and stealing chrism or sacred oils from the church

Likewise, on baptizing waxen or any other images and about how the baptism takes place, and what are its uses and effects

Likewise, on the making of images of lead, and how they are made, and how used

You should ask from whom they learnt or heard such things; and when they began to use them

You should also ask how many people came to consult them, and who these were, especially if they came within the year

Likewise you should ask if they have at any time been forbidden from practicing such things, and by whom; and whether they swore never to practice again; and if so, whether they have relapsed

Likewise, if they believed in these practices, and taught others

Likewise, what goods or presents or offerings they have accepted for their services.

Source: Bernardus Guidonis, *Manuel de l'inquisiteur*, Paris: Belles Lettres, 2006.

STEPHEN TEMPIER, LIST OF CONDEMNED OPINIONS AND WORKS, 1277 **Document 33**

Stephen Tempier, chancellor of the University of Paris in 1263 and Bishop of Paris in 1268, is renowned for having issued an interdict on the teaching of 219 philosophical and theological theses in 1277. The full list of opinions and works banned by Tempier covers a wide range of teachings and ideas which are condemned as leading students of the Liberal Arts into error. It includes the following:

The book on Geomancy, which begins 'The Indians esteemed...' is condemned, as are all the books, scrolls, or pamphlets on necromancy, or which contain sorcerous rituals, invocations to demons, or conjurations which imperil the soul, and all such things which work against the true faith and against all good conduct. All who own such works, scrolls, and pamphlets are instructed to bring them to the bishop's officials within seven days, on pain of excommunication and of other appropriate punishments.

Source: H. Denifle and A. Chatelain (eds), *Chartularium Universitatis Parisiensis*, vol. 1, Paris: Delalain, 1889.

Bibliography

PRIMARY SOURCES

Abraham Ibn Ezra (2011) *On Elections, Interrogations, and Medical Astrology*. Ed. and trans. S. Sela. Leiden: Brill.

Adelard of Bath (1983) *De opera astrolapsus*. Ed. B. G. Dickey. Toronto: Unpublished PhD Thesis.

Albertus Magnus (1967) *Book of Minerals*. Trans. D. Wyckoff. Oxford: Clarendon Press.

Augustine of Hippo (1997) *De Doctrina Christiana*. Trans. R. P. H. Green. Oxford and New York: Oxford University Press.

Barber, R. (1992) *Bestiary*. Woodbridge: Boydell.

Bernardus Guidonis (2006) *Manuel de l'inquisiteur*. Paris: Belles Lettres.

Brey Mariño, M. (ed.) (1980) *Lapidario, según el manuscrito Escurialense H.I.15*. Madrid: Castalia.

Cesarius of Heisterbach (1851) *Dialogus Miraculorum*. Ed. J. Strange. Cologne: J. M. Herbele.

Chardonnens, L. S. (2007) *Anglo-Saxon Prognostics, 900–1100; Study and Texts*. Leiden and Boston: Brill.

Cockayne, O. (1864–66) *Leechdoms, Wortcunning and Starcraft of Early England* (3 vols). Rolls Series. London: Longman, Green, Longman, Roberts and Green.

Constantinus Africanus (1539) *Theorica Pantegni*. Ed. Henricus Petris. Basel: Henricus Petris.

Coste, J. (ed.) (1995) *Boniface VIII en Procès: Articles d'Accusation et Depositions des Témoins 1303–1311*. Rome: Fondazione Camillo Caetani.

Denifle, H. and Chatelain, A. (eds) (1889) *Chartularium Universitatis Parisiensis*, vol. 1. Paris: Delalain.

Dioscorides (2005) *De materia medica*. Trans. L. Y. Beck. Hildesheim: Olms-Weidmann.

Fairweather, J. (ed.) (2005) *Liber Eliensis: A History of the Isle of Ely from the Seventh Century to the Twelfth*. Woodbridge: Boydell.

Gasquet, F. A. (1897) 'An unpublished fragment of a work by Roger Bacon', *The English Historical Review*, 12, pp. 514–15.

Geoffrey of Monmouth (1973) *Vita Merlini (Life of Merlin)*. Ed. and trans. B. Clarke. Cardiff: University of Wales Press.

Geoffrey of Monmouth (2007) *Historia Regum Britanniae*. Ed. M. Reeve, trans. N. Wright. Woodbridge: Boydell.

Gerald of Wales (1978) *The Journey through Wales and The Description of Wales*. Trans. L. Thorpe. Harmondsworth: Penguin.

Gerald of Wales (2000) *The Topography of Ireland*. Ed. T. Wright, trans. T. Forester. Cambridge, Ontario: In Parentheses Publications, Medieval Latin Series.

Gervase of Tilbury (2002) *Otia Imperialia (Recreation for an Emperor)*. Ed. and trans. S. E. Banks and J. W. Binns. Oxford: Clarendon.

Gratian (1879) *Decretum magistri Gratianii*. Ed. A. L. Richteri, Corpus Iuris Canonici 1. Tauchnitz.

Guibert de Nogent (1907) *Guibert de Nogent: Histoire de sa Vie*. Paris: A. Picard et fils.

Guido Bonatti (2007) *Liber Astronomiae (Book of Astronomy)*. Trans. B. Dykes. Minneapolis: Cazimi Press.

Haddan, A. and Stubbs, W. (eds) (1965) [1869–78] *Penitential of Theodore*, (1869–78) *Councils and Ecclesiastical Documents Relating to Great Britain and Ireland*, (3 vols). Oxford: Clarendon Press.

Hildegard of Bingen (1990) *Scivias*. Trans. C. Hart and J. Bishop. New York: Paulist Press.

Hobbins, D. (trans.) (2005) *The Trial of Joan of Arc*. Cambridge, Massachusetts: Harvard University Press.

Howald, E. and Sigerist, H. (eds) (1927) *Antonii Musae de herba vettonica liber. Pseudoapulei herbarius. Anonymi de taxone liber. Sexti Placiti liber medicinae ex animalibus, etc.* Lipsiae: Berolini.

Hugh of Fouilloy (1992) *The Medieval Book of Birds, Hugh of Fouilloy's Aviarium*. Ed. and trans. W. B. Clark, Medieval and Renaissance Texts and Studies 80, Binghamton. New York: Center for Medieval and Early Renaissance Studies, State University of New York at Binghamton.

Hugh of St Victor (1991) *The Didascalicon*. Trans. J. Taylor. New York: Columbia University Press.

Isidore of Seville (2006) *The Etymologies*. Trans. S. A. Barney, W. J. Lewis, J. A. Beach and O. Berghof. Cambridge: Cambridge University Press.

John of Salisbury (1938) *Frivolities of Courtiers and Footprints of Philosophers*. Ed. and trans. J. B. Pike. Minneapolis: University of Minnesota Press.

John of Worcester (1998) *The Chronicle of John of Worcester, vol. 3, The Annals from 1067 to 1140*. Ed. and trans. P. McGurk. Oxford: Clarendon Press.

Kästner, H. F. (1896) 'Pseudo-Dioscorides de herbis femininis', *Hermes*, 31, pp. 578–636.

Lidaka, J. (1998) 'The book of angels, rings, characters and images of the planets: attributed to Osbern Bokenham', in C. Fanger (ed.) *Conjuring Spirits; Texts and Traditions of Medieval Ritual Magic*. Sutton: Stroud.

Liuzza, R. M. (2011) *Anglo-Saxon Prognostics, an Edition and Translation of Texts from London, British Library, Ms Cotton Tiberius A iii*. Cambridge: Brewer.

Manzalaoui, M. A. (ed.) (1977) *Secretum Secretorum: Nine English Versions*, vol. 1, Early English Text Society, 276. Oxford: Oxford University Press.

Marbod of Rennes (1977) *Marbode of Rennes' (1035–1123) De lapidibus* Ed. J. M. Riddle, Sudhoffs Archiv, Zeitschrift fur Wissenschaftsgeschichte, Beiheft 20, Wiesbaden: Franz Steiner.

Martin, J. D. (1978) *The Cartularies and Registers of Peterborough Abbey*. Peterborough: Northamptonshire Record Society.

Matthew Paris (1932) *Prognostica*. Ed. L. Brandin, 'Les Prognostica du Ms. Ashmole 304', in M. Williams and J. A. de Rothschild (eds) *Miscellany of Studies in Romance Languages and Literatures Presented to L.E. Kaistner*. Cambridge: Cambridge University Press.

McAllister, J. B. (1939) *The Letter of Thomas Aquinas 'De operationibus occultis naturae'*. Washington DC: Catholic University of America Press.

Moses Maimonides (1904) *The Guide for the Perplexed*. Trans. M. Friedlander. London: G. Routledge.

Peter Lombard (2007) *The Sentences*. Trans. G. Silano. Toronto: Pontifical Institute of Mediaeval Studies.

Petrus Alfonsi (1977) *The Disciplina Clericalis*. Ed. and trans. E. Hermes and P. R. Quarrie. Berkeley and Los Angeles: University of California Press.

Petrus Alfonsi (1993) 'Letter to the peripatetics', in J. Tolan (ed. and trans.) *Petrus Alfonsi and his Medieval Readers*. Gainesville: University of Florida Press.

Petrus Alfonsi (2006) *Dialogue Against the Jews*. Trans. I. M. Resnick. Washington D.C.: Catholic University of America Press.

Philippe de Thaon (1841) 'Li livre des creatures' in T. Wright (ed. and trans.) *Popular Treatises on Science Written During the Middle Ages*. London: The Historical Society.

Pliny the Elder (1991) *Natural History*. Ed. and trans. J. Healey. Harmondsworth: Penguin.

Richer de Saint-Rimi (2011) *Histories*. Ed. and trans. J. Lake. Cambridge, Massachusetts: Harvard University Press.

Robert de Boron (1980) *Merlin de Robert de Boron, roman en prose du XIIIe siècle*. Ed. A. Micha. Paris and Geneva: Droz.

Roger of Howden (1868–71) *Chronica Rogeri de Hovedene*. Ed. W. Stubbs (4 vols), Rolls Series 51, London.

Ruska, J. (ed.) (1926) *Tabula Smargadina, ein Beitrag zur Geschichte der hermetischen Literatur*. Heidelberg: Carl Winters Universitätsbuchhandlung.

Saint Bernardine of Siena [sic] (1920) *Sermons*. Ed. N. Orlandi, trans. H. J. Robins. Siena: Tipografia Sociale.

Salimbene de Parma (1998) *Cronica*. Ed. G. Scalia. Corpus Christianorum Continuatio Medieavalis 125. Turnholt: Brepols.

Seymour, M. C. (ed) (1975–88) *On the Properties of Things: John Trevisa's Translation of Bartholomaeus Anglicus, De Proprietatibus Rerum* (3 vols). Oxford: Clarendon Press.

Thomas Aquinas (2006) *Summa Theologiae*, vol. 40. Trans. T. F. O'Meara and M. J. Duffy, *Superstition and Irreverence*. Cambridge: Cambridge University Press.

Thomas Aquinas (2006) *Summa Theologiae*, vol. 9. Trans. K. Foster, *Angels*. Cambridge: Cambridge University Press.

Vasari (1912–14) 'Life of Leonardo da Vinci', in Gaston De C. De Vere (trans.) *Lives of the Most Eminent Painters, Sculptors, and Architects*. London: Warner.

Véronèse, J. (ed.) (2007) *L'Ars Notoria au Moyen Âge, Introduction et Édition Critique*. Florence: Sismel-Edizioni del Galluzzo.

Walter Map (1983) *De Nugis Curialium, Courtiers' Trifles*. Trans. M. R. James, rev. C. N. L. Brook and R. A. B. Mynors. Oxford: Clarendon Press.

Wasserschleben, F. W. H. (ed.) (1851) 'Penitentiale vigilanum', *Die bussordnungen der abendländischen kirche*. Halle: C. Graeger.

William of Auvergne (1591) *Opera Omnia*. Venetiis: Ex officinal Damiani Zenari.

William of Malmesbury (1998) *Gesta Regum Anglorum, The History of the English Kings*. Ed. R. A. B. Mynors, R. M. Thomson and M. Winterbottom. Oxford: Clarendon Press.

Zambelli, P. (1992) *The Speculum Astronomiae and its Enigma*. London: Kluwer.

SECONDARY SOURCES

Adamson, P. (2007) *al-Kindi*. Oxford: Oxford University Press.

Anderson, G. (1997) 'The exaltation of Adam and the fall of Satan', *Journal of Jewish Thought & Philosophy* 6, pp. 105–34.

Arber, A. (1953) *Herbals: their Origin and Evolution*. Cambridge: Cambridge University Press.

Bailey, M. (2001) 'From sorcery to witchcraft', *Speculum*, 76, pp. 960–90.

Bailey, M. (2003) *Battling Demons, Witchcraft, Heresy, and Reform in the Late Middle Ages*. University Park, Pennsylvania: Pennsylvania State University Press.

Barber, M. (1978) *The Trial of the Templars*. Cambridge: Cambridge University Press.

Barber, M. and Bate, K. (2002) *The Templars: Selected Sources*. Manchester: Manchester University Press.

Beardwood, A. (1964) 'The trial of Walter Langton, Bishop of Lichfield, 1307–12', *Transactions of the American Philosophical Society*, n.s. 54, pp. 1–45.

Boudet, J. P. (2006) *Entre science et nigromance. Astrologie, divination et magie dans l'occident médiéval, XIIe-XVe siècle*. Paris: Publications de la Sorbonne.

Burnett, C. (ed.) (1987) *Adelard of Bath. An English Scientist and Arabist of the Early Twelfth Century*. London: Warburg Institute.

Burnett, C. (ed.) (1992) 'The prognostications of the Eadwine Psalter' in Gibson, M., Heslop, T. A., Pfaff, R. W. *The Eadwine Psalter: Text Image and Monastic Culture in Twelfth-century Canterbury*. University Park, Pennsylvania: Pennsylvania State University Press.

Burnett, C. (ed.) (1995) 'Mathematics and astronomy in Hereford and its region in the twelfth century', in D. Whitehead (ed.) *Medieval Art, Architecture and Archaeology at Hereford*. British Archaeological Association Transactions, 15, pp. 50–9.

Burnett, C. (ed.) (1996) *Magic and Divination in the Middle Ages. Texts and Techniques in the Islamic and Christian Worlds*. Aldershot: Variorum.

Burnett, C. and Jacquart, D. (eds) (1994) *Constantine the African and Ali ibn al-Abbas al-Magusi: the Pantegni and Related Texts*. Leiden: Brill.

Caciola, N. (2006) *Discerning Spirits: Divine and Demonic Possession in the Middle Ages*. Ithaca, New York: Cornell University Press.

Canaan, T. (2004) 'The decipherment of Arabic talismans', in E. Savage-Smith (ed.) *Magic and Divination in Early Islam*. Aldershot: Ashgate Variorum.

Carey, H. M. (1992) *Courting Disaster. Astrology at the English Court and University in the Later Middle Ages*. London: Macmillan.

Carey, H. M. (2003) 'Astrological medicine and the medieval English folded almanac', *Social History of Medicine* 17, pp. 345–63.

Chardonnens, L. S. (2007) *Anglo-Saxon Prognostics. 900–1100: Study and Texts*. Leiden: Brill.

Cochrane, L. (1994) *Adelard of Bath. The First English Scientist*. London: British Museum.

Cohn, N. (1993) *Europe's Inner Demons*. London: Pimlico.

Collins, M. (2000) *Medieval Herbals; the Illustrative Tradition*. Toronto: University of Toronto Press.

Crick, J. (1992) 'Geoffrey of Monmouth, prophecy and history', *Journal of Medieval History*, 18, pp. 357–71.

Fanger, C. (ed.) (1998) *Conjuring Spirits. Texts and Traditions of Late Medieval Ritual Magic*. Stroud: Sutton.

Fanger, C. (ed.) (2012) *Invoking Angels. Theurgic Ideas and Practices, Thirteenth to Sixteenth Centuries*. University Park, Pennsylvania: Pennsylvania State University Press.

Flint, V. I. J. (1991) *The Rise of Magic in Early Medieval Europe*. Oxford: Clarendon Press.

Frantzen, A. J. (1983) *The Literature of Penance in Anglo-Saxon England*. New Brunswick, New Jersey: Rutgers University Press.

Freeman, J. (2004) 'Sorcery at court and manor: Margery Jourdemayne, the witch of eye next Westminster', *Journal of Medieval History*, 30, pp. 343–57.

George, W. and Yapp, B. (1991) *The Naming of the Beasts: Natural History in the Medieval Bestiary*. London: Duckworth.

Gibson, M. T., Heslop, T. A., and Pfaff, R. W. (1992) *The Eadwine Psalter: Text, Image and Monastic Culture in Twelfth-Century Canterbury*. London: Modern Humanities Research Association and Pennsylvania State University Press.

Gilchrist, R. (2008) 'Magic for the dead; the archaeology of magic in later medieval burials', *Medieval Archaeology*, 52, pp. 119–59.

Griffiths, R. A. (1968–69) 'The trial of Eleanor Cobham: an episode in the fall of Duke Humphrey of Gloucester', *Bulletin of the John Rylands Library*, 51, pp. 381–99.

Halleux, R. and Schamp, J. (1985) *Les Lapidaries Grec*. Paris: Les Belles Lettres.

Heng, G. (2003) *Empire of Magic; Medieval Romance and the Politics of Cultural Fantasy*. New York: Columbia University Press.

Holdenried, A. (2006) *The Sibyl and her Scribes. Manuscripts and Interpretation of the Latin Sibylla Tiburtina c.1050–1500*. Aldershot: Ashgate.

Jacquart, D. (1998) 'Medical scholasticism', in M. D. Grmek (ed.) and A. Shugaar (trans.) *Western Medical Thought from Antiquity to the Middle Ages*. Cambridge, Massachusetts: Harvard University Press.

Jolly, K. L. (1996) *Popular Religion in Late Saxon England*. Chapel Hill: University of North Carolina Press.

Jolly, K. L., Raudvere, C. and Peters, E. (2002) *Witchcraft and Magic in Europe. The Middle Ages*. London: Athlone Press.

Jones, W. R. (1972) 'Political uses of sorcery in medieval Europe', *The Historian*, 34, pp. 670–87.

Juste, D. (2007) *Les alchandreana primitifs. Étude sur les plus anciens traités astrologiques latins d'origine Arabe (Xe siècle)*. Leiden: Brill.

Keck, D. (1998) *Angels and Angelology in the Middle Ages*. Oxford: Oxford University Press.

Kieckhefer, R. (1976) *European Witch-Trials*. London: Routledge and Kegan Paul.

Kieckhefer, R. (1994) 'The specific rationality of medieval magic', *The American Historical Review*, 99, pp. 813–36.

Kieckhefer, R. (1997) *Magic in the Middle Ages*. Cambridge: Cambridge University Press.

Kieckhefer, R. (1998) *A Necromancer's Manual of the Fifteenth Century*. University Park, Pennsylvania: Pennsylvania State University Press.

Klaassen, F. (2013) *The Transformations of Magic, Illicit Learned Magic in the Later Middle Ages and Renaissance*. University Park, Pennsylvania: Pennsylvania State University Press.

Klaniczay, G. (1990) *The Uses of Supernatural Power. The Transformation of Popular Religion in Medieval and Early-Modern Europe*. Princeton: Princeton University Press.

Knight, S. (2009) *Merlin, Knowledge and Power through the Ages*. Ithaca, New York: Cornell University Press.

Kors, A. C. and Peters, E. (eds) (2001) *Witchcraft in Europe, 400–1700: a Documentary History*. Philadelphia: University of Pennsylvania Press.

Láng, B. (2008) *Unlocked Books. Manuscripts of Learned Magic in the Medieval Libraries of Central Europe*. University Park, Pennsylvania: Pennsylvania State University Press.

Lawrence-Mathers, A. E. (2010) 'Domesticating the calendar: the hours and the almanac in Tudor England', in A. E. Lawrence-Mathers and P. Hardman, (eds) *Women and Writing c.1340–c.1650; the Domestication of Print Culture*. Woodbridge: York Medieval Press.

Lawrence-Mathers, A. E. (2012) *The True History of Merlin the Magician*. New Haven: Yale University Press.

Lawrence-Mathers, A. E. (2013) 'John of Worcester and the science of history', *Journal of Medieval History*, 39, pp. 255–74.

Liuzza, R. M. (2001) 'Anglo-Saxon prognostics in context; a survey and handlist of manuscripts', *Anglo-Saxon England*, 30, pp. 181–230.

MacKinney, L. C. (1943) 'An unpublished treatise on medicine and magic from the age of Charlemagne', *Speculum*, 18, pp. 494–6.

MacKinney, L. and Herndon, T. (1965) *Medical Illustrations in Medieval Manuscripts*. London: Wellcome Historical Medical Library.

Mathiesen, R. (1998) 'A thirteenth-century ritual to attain the beatific vision from the Sworn Book of Honorius of Thebes', in C. Fanger (ed.) *Conjuring Spirits: Texts and Traditions of Medieval Ritual Magic*. Stroud: Sutton.

Maxwell-Stuart, P. G. (2005) *The Occult in Medieval Europe, 500–1500*. Basingstoke: Palgrave Macmillan.

McCluskey, S. (1990) 'Gregory of Tours, monastic timekeeping, and early Christian attitudes to astronomy', *Isis*, 81, pp. 8–22.

McCluskey, S. (1998) *Astronomies and Cultures in Early Medieval Europe*. Cambridge: Cambridge University Press.

Moore, R. I. (1987) *The Formation of a Persecuting Society*. Oxford: Blackwell.

Murray, A. (2002) *Reason and Society in the Middle Ages*. Oxford: Oxford University Press.

North, J. D. (1986a) *Horoscopes and History*. London: Warburg Institute.

North, J. D. (1986b) 'Some Norman horoscopes', in J. D. North, *Horoscopes and History*. London: Warburg Institute; revised in C. Burnett (ed.) (1987) *Adelard of Bath, an English Scientist and Arabist of the Early Twelfth Century*. London: Warburg Institute.

North, J. D. (1989) *Stars, Minds, and Fate. Essays in Ancient and Medieval Cosmology*. London: Hambledon Press.

Olsan, L. T. (2003) 'Charms and prayers in medieval medical theory and practice', *Social History of Medicine*, 16, pp. 343–66.

Page, S. (2002) *Astrology in Medieval Manuscripts*. London: British Library.

Page, S. (2004) *Magic in Medieval Manuscripts*. London: British Library.

Page, S. (2013) *Magic in the Cloister, Pious Motives, Illicit Interests, and Occult Approaches to the Medieval Universe*. University Park, Pennsylvania: Pennsylvania State University Press.

Peters, E. (1978) *The Magician, the Witch and the Law*. Hassocks: The Harvester Press.

Pingree, D. (1987) 'The diffusion of Arabic magical texts in Western Europe' in B. Scarcia Amoretti, (ed.) *La diffusione delle scienze islamiche nel Medio Evo europeo. Atti del Convegno Internazionale (Roma, 2–4 ottobre 1984)*. Roma: Accademia Nazionale dei Lincei.

Rider, C. (2006) *Magic and Impotence in the Middle Ages*. Oxford: Oxford University Press.

Rider, C. (2011) 'Medical magic and the church in thirteenth-century England', *Social History of Medicine*, 24, pp. 92–107.

Rider, C. (2012) *Magic and Religion in Medieval England*. London: Reaktion Books.

Rollo, D. (2000) *Glamorous Sorcery. Magic and Literacy in the High Middle Ages*. Minneapolis: University of Minnesota Press.

Rosemann, P. W. (2004) *Peter Lombard*. Oxford: Oxford University Press.

Rosemann, P. W. (2007) *The Story of a Great Medieval Book: Peter Lombard's 'Sentences'*. Toronto: University of Toronto Press.

Russell, J. B. (1972) *Witchcraft in the Middle Ages*. Ithaca, New York: Cornell University Press.

Ryan, M. (2011) *A Kingdom of Stargazers*. Ithaca, New York: Cornell University Press.

Saunders, C. J. (2010) *Magic and the Supernatural in Medieval English Romance*. Cambridge: Brewer.

Singer, D. W. (1932) 'Alchemical writings attributed to Roger Bacon', *Speculum*, 7, pp. 80–6.

Siraisi, N. G. (1990) *Medieval and Early Renaissance Medicine: An Introduction to Knowledge and Practice*. Chicago: University of Chicago Press.

Skemer, D. C. (2006) *Binding Words; Textual Amulets in the Middle Ages*. University Park, Pennsylvania: Pennsylvania State University Press.

Smith, J. A. (2001) *Ordering Women's Lives. Penitentials and Nunnery Rules in the Early Medieval West*. Aldershot: Ashgate.

Sweeney, M. (2000) *Magic in Medieval Romance; from Chretien de Troyes to Geoffrey Chaucer*. Dublin: Four Courts Press.

Tambiah, S. J. (1990) *Magic, Science, Religion and the Scope of Rationality*. Cambridge: Cambridge University Press.

Taylor, F. S. (1976) *The Alchemists*. St Albans: Paladin.

Tester, S. J. (1987) *A History of Western Astrology*. Woodbridge: Boydell.

Thomas, K. (1971) *Religion and the Decline of Magic. Studies in Popular Beliefs in Sixteenth and Seventeenth Century England*. London: Weidenfeld & Nicolson.

Thorndike, L. (1929) *A History of Magic and Experimental Science*, 8 vols. New York: Macmillan.

Tolan, J. V. (1993) *Petrus Alfonsi and his Medieval Readers*. Gainesville: University Press of Florida.

Turning, P. (2010) 'The right to punish: jurisdictional disputes between royal and municipal officials in medieval Toulouse', *French History*, 24, pp. 1–19.

Voigts, L. E. (1986) 'The Latin verse and middle English prose texts on the Sphere of Life and Death in Harley 3719', *Chaucer Review*, 21, pp. 291–305.

Wagner, D. L. (ed.) (1986) *The Seven Liberal Arts in the Middle Ages*. Bloomington, Indiana: Indiana University Press.

Wallis, F. (2010) *Medieval Medicine: A Reader*. Toronto: University of Toronto Press.

Watkins, C. S. (2008) *History and the Supernatural in Medieval England*. Cambridge: Cambridge University Press.

Wedel, T. O. (1920) *The Medieval Attitude Toward Astrology, Particularly in England*. New Haven: Yale University Press.

Whitelock, D. (ed.) (1979) *English Historical Documents Volume 1, c.500–1042*. London: Eyre Methuen.

Weill-Parot, N. (2002) *Les 'Images Astrologiques' au Moyen Âge et à la Renaissance: Speculations Intellectuelles et Pratiques Magiques (XIIe-XVe siècle)*. Paris: Honoré Champion.

Williams, M. (2010) *Fiery Shapes; Celestial Portents and Astrology in Ireland and Wales 650–1650*. Oxford: Oxford University Press.

Ziegler, J. (1998) *Medicine and Religion c.1300: the Case of Arnau de Vilanova*. Oxford: Clarendon Press.

Index

abarquid 114
Abraham Ibn Ezra 72
Abu Ma'shar xiii, 71, 72; *Introductorius major* xiii; *Isagoge minor* xiii, 33
Adelard of Bath xiii, xviii, 10, 30, 33; on the astrolabe 107–8
adjurations xx, 51, 73
Aelfsige 50
Aeneas 6
aeromancy xx, 32, 106
Aethelwold, Bishop of Winchester 50
Age of the Holy Spirit 7
agriculture 14
al-Kindi xiii, 42; *De radiis stellarum* 35
Albertus Magnus xiii, xix, 41, 76; *De mineralibus* 122–23; *Speculum astronomiae* 35, 43, 53, 121
Alcabitius, *Liber introductorius* 34
alchemy xx, 36, 40–41, 111–12
Alexander IV, pope 83
Alexander the Great 18, 77
Alexander the Magnificent 18
Alfonso I of Aragon xviii
Alfonso X 'El Sabio' xvi, 56, 113
Alfred, King 50
Alhandreus 25
almanacs 70, 71
amulets 44
Ancyra, Council of (314 CE) 49, 102
Annals of Forli 10
Antichrist 6, 7, 93, 125
Apocalypse (Book of Revelation) 7, 91
Apocrypha 79
Apostles, the 125
Apuleius Platonicus xiii–xiv, 63, 64–65; *Apologia* xiii; *Golden Ass* xiii; *Herbarius* 57, 116
Aquinas, Thomas xix, 60, 73; on demons 78–80, 125–26; *Summa Theologica* 43, 125–26

Aries 70, 71
Aristotle xiv, xix, 18, 43, 77; *libri naturales* xiv
Arnald of Villanova, *De sigillis* 36
Ars Notoria 37–38, 42–43, 78, 109–11
'*Ars Nova*' 37
Artesius 77
Arthur, King xvii, 5, 8–9
aruspicina 32, 106
astral magic xx, 35–37
astrolabe, the xx, 3, 20, 24, 25; Adelard of Bath on 107–8; and astrology 33–35
astrology xiii, xx, 9–11, 18, 24, 25, 26, 27, 29, 30–31, 32, 36, 40, 53, 55–56, 71, 76, 92–93, 97–98, 106; and the astrolabe 33–35; and medical magic 60, 66–69, 121; monastic 19–21
astronodia 30–31
astronomia 30–31
astronomy xiii, xx, 19–20, 30–31, 110–11
augury xx, 24, 25, 106
Augustine of Hippo, St xiv, 22, 42, 53, 59, 63, 72, 75, 100, 101; *City of God* xiv, 6, 125, 126; *De Doctrina Christiana* 15; *On the Trinity* 126
Augustine, St 85
awenyddion 46, 47
Azareus, King 56; *De lapidibus* 55, 56

Bacon, Roger 12, 41; *Opus maius* xviii, 93; *Opus Tertium* 42–43
Bald's Leechbook 61–63
Baldwin, Archbishop of Canterbury xv, 45
barber-surgeons 71
Bartholomew the Englishman, *On the Properties of Things* 65
basilisk herb 116
Bayeux tapestry 21
Becket, Thomas xvi, 17, 19
ben Moshé, Yehuda xvi, 56

Bernardino of Siena, St, 'Of the Scourges of God' 73–74
bestiaries 28, 57–59, 64, 117–18
Bestiary, the 57–59, 65, 117–18
Bible, the 51, 58, 64, 65, 79
blessings 72
blood-letting 14, 70, 71
Bodleian Bestiary 58
Bolingbroke, Roger 12
Bonatti, Guido xv–xvi, 9, 10; *Liber astronomicae* xvi; *Liber introductorius ad judicia stellarum* 34
Boniface VIII, pope xiv, xvii, xviii, 81–82
Book of Angels, Rings, Characters and Images of Planets 80
'Book of Rings, The' 11
'Books of Fate' 18–19
Books of Hours 69–70
brontologies 14, 98–99

Caladrius 59
calendar, Church 67–69
Camorica 113–14
Canon Episcopi 48–49, 87, 102
canon law 21–23, 48–49, 75–76, 84, 85
Canterbury Cathedral 17
casting of lots *see sortilegia*
Cesarius of Heisterbach xiv, 52; *Dialogus miraculorum* xiv, 23, 102–4
Charlemagne 16, 49
charms xx, 44, 59, 74; and the Church 13–17, 26, 61–63; problem of 61–63
chelonite 55
chiromancy xx, 15
Christ 6, 19, 62, 73, 79, 125
Circe, sorceress 102
Clement V, pope 82
Cobham, Eleanor, Duchess of Gloucester 12, 88
Cockayne, Oswald, *Leechdoms, Wortcunning and Starcraft of Early England* 13
Cocogrecus, 'cursed book on stations to the cult of Venus' 77
comets 21
conception 122
confession 51, 86
confessors' manuals 51–52, 72–74, 86
conjuring tricks 33
Constantine the African xiv; *Pantegni* 67
Corumphiza, astrologer 92–93
Creation 15, 22, 28, 29, 35, 40, 43, 52, 70, 76, 79, 100–1, 124
'critical days,' theory of 67–68

crocote, the 59
Cross, the 73, 102
Crusades, the 6, 28, 45
crystal-gazing 7, 94–95
Curae herbarum 57

Damigeron 54
Daniel, Book of 15
Daniel, prophet 15; *Dream Book* 99
Dante 9
d'Ascoli, Francesco 83
De herbis femininis 57, 115–17
Dee, John 78
Deeds of Hereward 4–5
Democritus 106
demons 56, 60, 64, 71, 72, 75, 85, 102–4, 107; Aquinas on 78–80, 125–26; and deception 33, 38–39, 46, 47, 49, 52, 75–77, 78, 125–26; expelling 55; invoking 128–29; and magical crime 22, 75; as *malefici* 102; and the mandrake 66; manipulate matter 79, 126; names of 73; nature of 79–80, 112, 124; pacts with 24; as pagan deities 50, 51; place in hierarchy of creation 79; power of 24, 25–26, 73–74, 78–79, 100–101; and temptation 27; trafficking with 32, 66; and women 49, 52; worship of 83, 86, 87, 106
Devil/devil(s) 32, 49, 74, 87, 88, 91, 100, 125
devil worship 82
diadocos 55
diamonds 54
Diana, goddess 49
Dioscorides xiv–xv, 54, 64, 65; *De materia medica* xiv–xv, 56, 57
disease horoscope 66–67, 68
diseases, commanding or adjuring 73
divination xx, 7, 14–19, 26, 32, 46, 55, 58–59, 74, 76, 101–2, 106, 107, 128–29
domestic magic 52
Dominican friars 86
dream-interpretation 15, 99
dream-visions 46

Eadwine 17
Eadwine Psalter 17
Easter, date of 19, 20, 67–69
eclipses 19–20
Edward I 81
Egyptian Days xx, 14, 26
elections xxi, 33, 34, 71
elements, natural 32, 55–56, 106

enchanters/enchantresses 9, 73
Enguerrand de Marigny 11
Ergaphalau 30–31, 32

Fall, the 79
fallen angels *see* demons
femina 87
fertility 122
figures and diagrams *see* image magic
forbidden books 3
forbidden magic 27, 30, 46, 73, 85, 124
fortune-telling *see* divination
Franciscan friars 86
Frederick II xvi, 6, 9, 10, 95–97
free will 15, 71–72
friars 73–74, 86

Galen xiv, xv, 54, 67–68
General Admonition (Charlemagne, 789) 16
Generals 37
Genesis, Book of 64, 79
Geoffrey of Monmouth xv, 5; *History of the Kings of Britain* xv, xvii, 17, 18; *Life of Merlin* xv, 18; *Prophetia Merlini* xv
geomancy xxi, 32, 106, 130
geometry 29
Gerald of Wales xv, 45–48; *Description of Wales* 46; *Journey Through Wales* 46–47; *The Topography of Ireland* 47–48, 58
Geraud, Hugues, Bishop of Cahors 11, 83
Gerbert of Aurillac xv, xix, 23–26, 33, 104–5
Gervase of Tilbury xv, 8; *Otia imperialia* xv, 7–8, 53
Gesta Herewardi 4–5
God 62; and creation 15, 22, 28, 29, 35, 40, 43, 52, 70, 76, 79, 100–101, 124; judgement of 124; knowing and serving 127; messages from 15, 19, 46; names of 72–73, 78; and precious stones 53, 54; superiority of 79, 109
Gospels 51, 106
Gratian 30, 75, 87; *Decreti* xv; *Decretum* 22–23, 101–2
Gregory IX, pope, *Vox in Rama* 82–83
guardian angels 80
Gui, Bernard xiv; *Manual for Inquisitors* xiv, 84–85, 128–29
Guibert de Nogent, *Monodies* 122
Guido of Montefeltro 10

Hali Abenragel xvi; *De judiciis astrorum* xvi, 34
Halley's Comet 21

Haroth 32
headaches 62
heliotrope 55, 115–16
Henry I, King 25, 31
Henry II, King xv, 45, 47
Henry the knight 102–4
Henry VI, King 12
herbals 28, 52, 56–57, 60, 64–66, 115–17
herbs 56–57, 78
heresy 2, 14, 22, 26, 27, 68, 71, 72, 80, 82–87, 127–28
Hermann le Boiteux 33
Hermes Trismegistus 77; *The Emerald Table* xvi, 111–12; *Liber lune* 36–37
Hildegard of Bingen 6
Hippocrates xiv, xvi, xxi, 64, 106
'holy drink against the devil's temptations and the power of elves' 63
Holy Office 14
Honorius, son of Euclid 38
horoscopes xxi, 33, 34, 97–98, 106, 117
horoscopia 32
Hugh of Flavigny, *Chronicon Virdunense* 23
Hugh of Fouilloy, *The Avery* 58
Hugh of St Victor, *Didascalicon* xvi, 32, 106–7
hydromancy xxi, 32, 106
hyena 58–59
hyenia 58–59, 117

idolatry 16, 42, 51, 77, 78, 80, 83, 112, 124
illusions 33
image magic 35–38, 43, 54, 55–56, 77–78
incantations 72, 74, 76, 77, 78, 102, 107
incubi 47
Innocent III xxi, 14
Inquisition xxi, 14, 68, 83, 86, 88
interrogations xxi, 33, 34
Ireland 47–48
Isidore of Seville 23, 32, 58, 106; *Etymologies* xvi, 6, 30, 54, 57, 64, 90
Ivo de Taillebois 4–5

Joachim of Fiore xvi, 6–7, 90–92, 95
Joan of Arc 66
Job 126
John, King of England xv, 45, 84
John of Salisbury xvi, 17, 23, 30, 31; *Policraticus* xvi, 7, 23, 25, 93–95
John of Seville 34
John of Worcester 20
John the Evangelist, St 91

John XXII, pope xvii, 11, 83–84, 88; *Super Illius Specula* 84, 127–28
Jourdemayne, Margery 12, 88
judicial astrology xxi, 25, 33, 112
Julius Firmicus Maternus 25

Knights Templar xvii, xviii, 82–83

Lacnunga 61–63
Langton, Walter, Bishop of Coventry 81
lapidaries 28, 52, 53, 54–60, 64, 113–15
Lateran Council (1215) 86
law *see* canon law
lawcodes 48–52
Laws of King Athelstan 50
lay healers 51
'Lay of the Nine Twigs of Woden' 62
laying on of hands 51, 73
Leofric, priest 4, 5
Leonardo da Vinci 11
Liber Raziel 56
Liberal Arts xxi, 29, 30–31, 37, 40, 68
Lincoln, bishops of 18
Llobet de Barcelona 33
Lord's Prayer 102
lot-casting *see sortilegia*
Louis X, King 11
love charms 59, 64
love magic 16, 85
Lovtot, Sir J. 81
Lucifer 79
lunaries xxi, 14–15

magi 77, 106
magic: classifications of 30–33; definition of 1–2, 16, 25, 29–30, 59, 75; demonically inspired crime 22, 75; negative associations 29, 42, 64, 72, 76
magic circles 102–4
magical entertainments 11
magical illusions 107
magical rings 80
magical theory 36
magpies 118
Mahout of Artois 11–12
Maimonides, Moses xvii; *Guide for the Perplexed* xvii, 41–42
'Major Circle, The' 77
male impotence 23, 122
malefici xxi, 16, 50, 77, 102
maleficia 32, 83

Malleus Malleficarum 87
mandrake 64–66
manslaughter 16
mantike see divination
Map, Walter, *De nugis curialium* 25
Marbod of Rennes xvii, 57; *Liber lapidum* 54–55
Maroth 32
marriage 23, 50
Mars 71
Martin IV, Pope 10
Mashallah xvii, 33
mathematics 27
Matthew, Paris, *Prognostica* 19
medical humours xxi, 67
medical magic 3, 14, 36, 40, 50, 60, 85, 107; and astrology 60, 66–69, 121; and natural magic 63–66; and popular magic 70–74
meditation 37, 75
Meilyr, the prophet 46–47
Merlin xv, xvii, 5, 8–9, 17, 53
Militaz 115
mirabilia 53
miracles 48, 52, 77, 78, 125–26
monks 47; astrology 19–21; charms 13–17
Montpellier, University of 68
moon, the 67–68, 69–70, 71, 114–15; eclipses of 19–20; reverence to 102
mugwort 57, 116–17
murder 16, 113

name interpretation *see* onomancy
nativities xxii, 34, 106
natural laws 76
natural magic 52–53, 56, 63–66, 76, 77, 88, 124
natural marvels 47–48, 75–76
natural philosophy xxii, 3, 15, 29, 31, 36, 52, 56, 76, 88
natural world 26
Nebuchadnezzar 15
necromancy xxii, 11, 23–26, 30, 31–32, 77, 81, 84, 102–4, 106, 124
Nectanebus 77
notae 37, 38, 109–11
'notary art' 8

occult properties of nature xx, 52–53, 56–57, 58, 60, 63–64, 67, 76, 85, 88
Odyssey, the 102
On fifteen stars, fifteen stones, fifteen herbs and fifteen images 55, 56
onomancy xxii, 15, 17, 18, 77, 78

optics 29
Orderic Vitalis 5
Otto III, emperor xv
Otto IV, emperor xv, 8

paganism 16, 39, 49–50, 62, 87
palmistry xx, 15, 17–19
Paris, University of 68
Penitential of Theodore 49–50
Penitentials 15–16, 48–50, 51, 85, 113
Peter, Lombard xvii–xviii, 22, 75; *Sententia* xvii–xviii, 22, 100–101
Peter of Abano xviii, 68, 69
Petrus, Alfonsi xviii, xix, 20, 25, 31–32; *Dialogi contra Iudei* 31–32; *Disciplina clericalis* 31; *Epistola ad peripateticos Franciae* 31
Philip IV, King xiv, xviii, 81, 82
Philip V, King 11–12
physiognomy xxii, 28
Physiologus 58, 117–18
Picatrix 56
pilgrimages 72
Pisces 70
plantain 62
Plato xiv
Pliny the Elder xviii, 57, 64; *Natural History* xviii, 54
poison 11, 62
poor, the: healthcare practices 70–71, 72, 74; magic available to 44–45
popular magic 70–74, 85
practical theology 21
praestigia 23
prayer 37–38, 51, 72–73, 75, 110
precious stones 53, 54, 122–23
prognostics xxii, 14, 61, 71, 98–99
'Prophecies of Merlin' 5
prophecy 90
Pseudo John of Seville, *Isagoge in astrologiam* 34
Ptolemy xviii, 25, 55; *Almagest* xviii, xix; *Centiloquium* 33; *Quadripartitum* 33; *Tetrabiblos* xviii
purging 14, 70
pyromancy xxii, 32, 106
Pythagoras 18, 63, 119–20
Pythagoreans 123

Quadripartitum Hermetis 55
quadrivium xv, xxii, 24, 26, 29, 30

Rabanus Maurus 58
Raymond de Marseille 33; *Liber judiciorum* 34
Regino of Prüm 48

Register of Robert of Swaffham 4
Renaissance 27–30
Revelation, Book of 7, 91
revolutions xxii, 34
Rhineland heretics 82–83, 87
Richard I 7, 90–92
Richer de Saint Remy 24
'Ring of Mars' 11
ring of Mars 80
ritual magic xxii, 11–12, 35–37, 38–39, 42, 52, 53, 86, 88, 109–11
Robert, Bishop of Lincoln 18
Robert de Boron 8
Roger II of Sicily 8
Roger of Howden 35; *Chronicle* 7, 90–93; *Deeds of King Richard* 7
Round Table 8
Rule of St Benedict 14, 99

Sahl ibn Bishir, *Liber temporum* 33–34
saints, help from 72
Salerno, University of 68
Salimbene de Parma, *Chronica* 95–97
Santa Maria de Ripoll 24
Satan 79
Saturn 68
Sayf ad-Dawla 34
Scivias (Hildegard of Bingen) 6
Scot, Michael xv, xvii, 9–10, 95–97; *Liber introductorius* xvii
seal of Solomon 78
seals 55
secret killing 50
Sextus Placitus, *Liber medicinae ex animalibus* 118
sexual behaviour 50, 64
show trials, fourteenth century 80–82
Sibylline prophecies 90
sibyls 6, 90
six fixed arts 31
Socrates 18
Solinus 59; *Collectanea rerum memorabilium* xviii; *Polyhistor* 54
Solomon 37, 38, 53, 77, 109; pentagon 78
Song of Solomon 64
sorcery xxii, 11, 49, 50, 68, 72, 77, 78, 81–82, 83, 84, 86–87, 107, 128–29
sortes sanctorum xxii
sortilegia xxii, 32, 101–2, 107
Specials 37
'Sphere of Apuleius' 15, 63, 119–20
'Sphere of Life and Death' 15

stellar rays 35, 42
Stonehenge 5, 53
stones 53, 78; and medical magic 54–55; *see also* lapidaries
Stratton, Adam 81
superstition 13, 32, 42, 43, 51, 63, 72–73, 76, 87, 95, 128–29
Sworn Book of Honorius of Thebes 38–39, 78

talismans 36, 45, 55–56
Tempier, Stephen xviii–xix; *List of Condemned Opinions and Works* (1277) 129–30
Theel: *Liber sigillorum* 55, 56
Theodore of Tarsus 49–50
theology 21–23, 29, 40, 46, 47, 69, 75–76, 88
Theophilus 24
Theophrastus 64
'theory of everything' 43
Thessalonians, second epistle to 125
threats, commanding or adjuring 73
Tiburtine Sibyl 6
Toledo, Council of 102
Tractatus de herbis 57
Trinity 46

Vasari 11
verba ignota 37–38
Vigila of Alveda 113
Vincent of Beauvais, *Speculum historiale* 25
Virgil 6, 8

Visconti, Galeazzo 11, 83–84
Visconti, Matteo 83–84
Viviane the enchantress 9

'Wake, the' 4–5
Walcher of Malvern xviii, xix, 20; *De dracone* xix; Lunar Tables xix
Wales 45–48
wax images 11–12, 77
weather 14, 98–99
William II of Sicily xv, 8
William of Auvergne xix, 38, 42, 53, 80; *De fide et legibus* 53, 112, 124; *De legibus* 76; *De universo* 53, 76
William of Malmesbury xix; *Gesta Regum Anglorum* xix, 24–25, 104–5
William of Rennes 51
William the Conqueror 4–5
witch craze 1, 87–88
witchcraft 50, 84–89
witches 49, 74
Woden 62
wolves 59, 118
women 50, 87; and demons 49, 52; and the Devil 87; as prophets 5–6
wonders 47–48, 75–76, 78

Zahel xix, 71; *Liber introductorium ad astrologiam* xix; *Liber temporum* xix
Zodiac Man 69–70, 120
Zoroaster 106